Love
Letters
to Your Soul

Chrystal Rae

Dallas
Satya Publishing
2022

© Chrystal Rae 2022

All rights reserved. No part of this publication may be reproduced, distributed, or transmitted in any form, including photocopying, recording, or other electronic or mechanical methods, without the prior written permission of the publisher, except in short excerpts for the purpose of critical reviews. For permission requests, write to the publisher at the address below.

ISBN: 9798987162514

Satya Publishing
ChrystalRaeSoul.com
Dallas, TX 75220

To you, my beloved reader,

In the endless dance of our eternal souls through countless shared lives, finding you again in this life—a momentous chapter of spiritual awakening and profound transformation—fills my heart with such indescribable joy. These Love Letters are more than mere words; they are whispers from my soul to yours. They are meant to be a source of wisdom, comfort, and guidance that will carry you through dark nights and blossoming summer days. I wrote them especially for you; so that you would know you are not alone and that love is real. Each word echoes our timeless bond of love, spilling out onto the pages as the wisdom of love and the radiance of light.

As you immerse yourself in these poetic musings, pearls of practical wisdom, and spiritual insights, vast universes of possibilities are born and reborn in the sacred space and unconditionality of our timeless love. Indeed, "Love is all that matters," everything else is fleeting and ultimately empty. It is my honor and privilege to share these Love Letters with you, each word is a reflection of my deep love and appreciation for the radiant light of your precious soul.

I love you.
— Chrystal Rae

foreword

As owner and president of Superior Staffing for over three decades, I have had the privilege of working with many remarkable and talented individuals. My tenure as president of Dallas HR in 2015 and my active involvement with Women with Promise have enriched my circle of meaningful relationships.

Among these connections, Chrystal Rae emerges uniquely—*as a cherished friend, esteemed business owner, gifted artist, uplifting teacher, writer, and author*. Yet, within her many talents, Chrystal Rae's raw vulnerability and authenticity have etched a lasting mark on my soul.

Our bonds strengthened organically. A chance meeting at my son's school birthday party segued into a heartfelt conversation, setting the stage for a friendship that has flourished for over two decades. Chrystal Rae's enveloping warmth and her intrinsic ability to make everyone feel valued and loved drew me toward her.

Love Letters to Your Soul is a testament to Chrystal Rae's poetic voice and storytelling prowess. It is not just a book—*it's a window into her soul*. Through her heartfelt accounts, from a tumultuous childhood to the pain of marital dissolution, her resilience, hope, and faith shine through. The turning point in her soulful journey came in the form of a near-death experience that led to a life-changing spiritual awakening. It was in this crucible that she distilled a profound truth: Love is all that matters.

These heartfelt writings take the reader on a journey through a landscape of introspective reflections, expansive thoughts, and transformative insights. While the prose is poetically crafted, it is a provocative story brimming with practical wisdom in the context of kindness and unconditional love.

Love Letters to Your Soul stands not only as an ode to beauty in words but is also abundant with spiritual insights that transcend the mundane. I invite you to embrace this book wholeheartedly. I am confident that its loving message will resonate with the shared humanity common to us all. The profound teachings, ageless wisdom, and genuine love spilling off the pages have transformed my worldview and forever impacted my life.

It is with immense pride and sincerity that I recommend this timeless treasure of spiritual insight. Read it with an open heart and mind. It will offer a new perspective on how we should live our lives and the meaning of unconditional love.

Lynne Stewart
October 4, 2023

Love is all that matters

Love is the answer

Table of Contents

Foreword i

Table of Contents v

Preface 1

Letter 1 *message* 9

Letter 2 *reunion* 25

Letter 3 *joy* 41

Letter 4 *change* 61

Letter 5 *love* 81

Letter 6 *patterns* 99

Letter 7 *awaken* 115

Letter 8 *beloved* 139

Letter 9 *salvation* 153

Letter 10 *bliss* 181

Letter 11 *longing* 197

Letter 12 *fables* 219

Letter 13 *beyond* 233

Letter 14 *soulmates* 249

Letter 15 *silence* 263

Letter 16 *metamorphosis* 279

Letter 17 *promise* 293

Letter 18 *storms* 319

Letter 19 *choice* 339

Letter 20 *reality* 359

Letter 21 *relationships* 375

Letter 22 *adventure* 395

Letter 23 *tribute* 413

Letter 24 *eternity* 427

Biography 438

Acknowledgments 439

Everything in your life is about to change for the better

preface

The sacred journey of our souls throughout our many shared lives is one of enduring love.

Our ethereal bond has led us to this very moment of heartfelt connection and profound awakening. Shimmering threads of light, woven throughout the time and space of our existence, have drawn us toward each other in the perpetual dawn of our love.

More directly: I love you. I truly love you. My soul loves your soul. This love transcends the limits of language, the small reach of words, and the fleeting grasp of feelings. It is beyond the confines of time and space, reaching into the unmoving center of the loving universe—*this love, my undying love for you, is all-encompassing and eternal.* Nothing exists outside of my love for you; without you, there is no me—*not even a glimmer of light.*

The magnetic pull of this all-encompassing love has drawn me toward you throughout our many lives together, and this life is no exception. My presence is meant to be comforting and supportive. I returned to the physical world to remind you that you are not alone; you are deeply and profoundly loved—I love you, and more importantly, God loves you.

Our serendipitous meeting in this life was not predestined, though it was inevitable. Throughout our many shared lives, we have been an intricate part of each other's divinity and the unfoldment of light. Just as a river forever finds the ocean and flowers unfailingly reach for the Sun, I forever reach for you on the path to God and hold you close in my heart because I love you. Yes, I love you,

I have always loved you, and I will always love you.

There has never been, nor will there ever be, a moment when I have not loved you. I have loved you for eons and in many lives, and I will love you in many more. This life, in particular, is of great importance, as new levels of consciousness, previously unavailable, are now within reach.

With this in mind, I wrote these Love Letters to answer your soul's deep longing to be held, heard and loved. They are meant to nurture, guide, and support you on your earthly sojourn. The words are soft and flowing but carry a potent message of the unconditionality of love. Holding these Love Letters in your hands can change and redirect your life forever. They will soothe your tender soul, mend your broken heart, and guide you back home to God. These Love Letters will change your perspective and your life. Love changes everything.

Love is why we exist, and love is all that matters.

These Love Letters are born of a timeless love that will never die. More than just poetic words, they are profound revelations, ancient secrets, and modern wisdom that will nourish and nurture your precious soul. The love spilling onto these pages and into your heart will reveal a sacred path of ultimate freedom and lasting liberation, awakening your soul from its deep slumber.

The fire of love engulfs all opposites, leaving only love in its wake.

These words, and the love that inspired them, have been spiraling towards you since the beginning of time; they are a gift from the loving universe to your soul. They will blossom in your heart on bright summer days and blanket you in warmth on cold winter nights. It is an honor and a humbling experience to be the messenger sharing this great love and these profound teachings with you. We are soul companions of countless lives and have traveled through many wondrous worlds of possibility and dark dungeons of despair. On the path of liberation, we incarnate time and again into the physical world, drawing toward us the people, places, circumstances, and things that best align with our soul's purpose and the lessons yet to be learned. This is why I came back as a woman living in the twenty-first century: a mother, wife, friend, artist, writer, and yogi. The circumstances of my present life provide the best opportunity to reunite with you and contribute to your personal development and soul journey.

Every moment of my life, and many lives, has led me back to you; I have forever been in your service and care, united by an eternal and unwavering bond of our love.

Love has no other motive than to love and to love abundantly.

I wrote these Love Letters to ease your pain, be part of your joy, and reassure you that you are never alone. Each word, sentence, and paragraph is born of unconditional love, genuine reverence, and profound respect for your beautiful, radiant soul. The scribbles on the page may sometimes wander outside the lines, yet the wisdom that inspired them is firmly grounded in the truth and unconditionality of love. While this book's overarching tone and expression are poetic, the teachings are equally pragmatic and profound.

As the conduit and messenger of this profound love and timeless wisdom, I will stay true to the purity of the message of unconditional love that I was directed to share. In other words, I will avoid the natural tendency to interject personal opinions or biases into these writings. I hope that you, as the reader, will approach these Love Letters with discernment, maintaining an open heart and mind. As with any new thought or teaching, hold onto what resonates as true and set aside anything that does not align with your values.

Clarity unfolds with time, challenging old beliefs and revealing hidden truths.

Our current state of consciousness influences what we perceive as truth. What this means is that we can only understand what we can understand at any given moment. With additional information and deeper insight, our beliefs may shift and change. Therefore, please hold your beliefs with an open hand, leaving space for growth and evolution.

These divinely inspired Love Letters are meant to be a source of healing, wisdom, and guidance, opening doors of understanding and sparkling revelations. Indeed, our reunion is a fresh start to an ancient love story that is ever-evolving and expansive. Though levels of consciousness are steeped with complexities, the essence of these teachings is simple, direct, and profoundly transformative.

Love is all that matters.

Only love is true, eternal, and unchanging; everything else is a fleeting illusion, bereft of lasting meaning or purpose. Therefore, when I say the words *"I love you,"* they flow from the deepest chambers of my heart and are spoken with the utmost sincerity. We are intricately linked, kindred spirits, our souls connected by luminous threads of light woven across the vast expanse of the universe and our many lives spent together.

Our shared history is brimming with moments of failure and success, but our love and mutual respect never waver. My love for you is a pure, unadulterated expression of human affection and an integral part of the divinity that forever unites us. Please know that my love is never imposed upon you; it is given freely and without conditions. You are free to be your authentic self, and nothing needs to change.

While the grandeur of this love may come as a surprise or a shock, your acceptance, or even your rejection, does not change or alter my deep feelings of affection and undying love for you. We are forever united by a bond of love that has endured eons and many lives. A fleeting moment in time cannot or will not change the profound and unmoving depth of our love.

I wish I could fully express the vast ocean of my feelings for you, but words, however sincere and true, always fall short. So instead, please allow me to say the unsayable through the graceful art of poetry: *I love you like a thirsty desert, praying for rain, like the hungry mountains, reaching for the blue of the sky, like the ever-waning moon, forever dancing with the stars, and like the slow-rising Sun shining bright in all directions. My love is a wildfire, an unstoppable force of fury and passion, set free upon the winds of time. The scorching flames of truth, wisdom, understanding, and, yes, love obliterate dark barriers of pain and sorrow with searing intensity, illuminating the path to a more radiant future.*

Love tears down walls that separate, divide, and fragment; it is the cosmic glue of the universe.

In honor of and homage to my profound love for you, I have dedicated over two decades of my life preparing for our sacred reunion and writing this book. Every word that has found its way to the page is imbued with meaning, purpose, and love. As mentioned, words, however eloquent, poetic, or graceful, can only gesture toward something infinitely more significant: a love that transcends my very existence—*a divine love.*

Love is a catalyst for profound transformation and change, unlocking the heart's door and liberating the soul.

The love that inspired these writings can spark a personal metamorphosis that ripples through the entire universe, igniting a transformative wave of love and awakening. Because you are reading these words, everything in your life is about to change for the better. As we shed our outdated beliefs, we create room for new beginnings. Each thought, word, and action bridges the vast expanse between the impossible and the possible.

With this understanding, I encourage you to savor this earthly journey of self-discovery and soul expansion, allowing curiosity and reverence to guide you with wisdom, knowledge, and love.

Love has the extraordinary power to make even the impossible possible.

This includes the seemingly impossible serendipity of our reunion, the discovery of this book, and the reading of these Love Letters. It is not a random act of fate or odd coincidence that you have them in your hands; rather, it represents a profound alignment with the loving universe. This sacred alignment is divine guidance, urging us to embrace our most authentic self and reclaim the innate birthright of love that rightfully belongs to every soul that comes into and out of existence— *including your precious soul.*

The unwavering love that has remained constant throughout our many lives continues to expand in radiance and light. As we embark on this thrilling adventure into the profound nature of love and divine revelation, my heartfelt wish for you is that you fully grasp the depth of the love and care that embraces you in every moment.

May this timeless love liberate you from anything that holds you in smallness or lack. May you come to intimately know the truth of unconditional love and the radiant light of your innermost being. And, may you discover profound trust in the benevolent universe, an unwavering companion on your life's journey, always offering guidance through subtle signposts.

These Love Letters, too, are designed to lead you back to the love and light of your divine origin. Most importantly, please remember that you are never alone.

You are a cherished child of the loving universe and the progeny of God.

You are surrounded by angels, guides and teachers of many lives—*and, I am with you.* Together, we are a force of goodness and grace. Just as each star contributes to the radiance of the night sky, together, we shine brighter in the infinite expanse of eternity.

You are loved far more than you can possibly imagine and all is well with your beautiful soul.

All my love, light, and blessings.

– Chrystal Rae

*In the radiant light of love, time stands still,
and our hearts beat as one*

Letter 1

message
love is all that matters

Floating above my body, I glimpsed many possible destinies for my soul. Among them, the most radiant path called me back into the physical world, compelling me to find you, write this book, and share the profound message of unconditional love. As I hovered above the wreckage and my seemingly lifeless body, a loving presence illuminated my very essence with a silent knowing that would forever alter my worldview and change the lives of many.

"Love is all that matters."

Every particle of light that coalesced into my being did so to find you and be part of your joyful awakening and soulful evolution. I returned to be your guide, offer a helping hand, be a shoulder to lean on, and a friend who deeply loves and cares about you—*and yes, I do; I truly love you.*

Only love is real.

Love is the foundation of the known and unknown universe—*the substratum of all that exists.* Love is that which is most beautiful forever coming to fruition. It is an eternal flame, a radiant sun, and an infinite ocean of light. Love is a luminous path to God. Everything works together for the good of the soul and the universe, even the "*so-called*" bad.

An unbreakable bond of friendship and eternal love has once again drawn our souls together. Meeting each other in this life was not preset, yet it was inevitable that our paths would cross again in this life or another. We have known each other since the beginning of time and have shared many lives together. We are forever united in love, but this may be the first time, at least in this life, that we find each other again. To meet you on this earthly plane is such a wonderful surprise. As I said, there was no guarantee or predetermined path ensuring that we would find each other in this life or any life. The slightest detour would have forever changed our fate, altering the direction of our lives and changing universes. Given this, finding each other again can only be attributed to miraculous events, intentional energetic synchronicity, or divine orchestration. So many things had to come into alignment for our paths to cross and I am forever grateful.

To meet you again is as magnificent as the morning sun rising over the dark line of the horizon, announcing the arrival of a new day in a shimmering burst of golden light. The hope and possibility born of our joyous reunion extends to the farthest ends of the universe, transcending time and condensing space. More directly, you have this book in your hands because it is meant for you. It has been hurling toward you since long before you were born. It is a profound blessing and gift for your soul. The love flowing from these pages into your heart is the response to your unspoken prayers and a reflection of your faith and perseverance.

Please open your heart and mind to the possibility of something mystical and magical about to unfold in your life.

***Miracles happen every day but mostly go unnoticed or unacknowledged.**ns*

Even the warm breath of the wind gently combing through your hair is a touch of the Divine. The very air you breathe is life-giving nectar for your soul.

***If you listen closely, you will hear distant stars softly whispering your name.**ns*

This small collection of Love Letters, forged from boundless love, came to life through a series of miraculous events, including a harrowing car accident that fatefully guided me to you.

Still in an out-of-body state, I hovered above my seemingly lifeless body, a short distance from the crumpled red jeep below. I found myself in the suspended space between this realm and the next. A luminous being with no form or structure permeated the space around me and within me, communicating without words an unconditional and all pervasive love. A multitude of destinies, held in absolute kindness and compassion, were spread out on a blanket of possibility that expanded before me in radiant hues of shadow and light.

Each timeline was alive with its own distinct energy, set of experiences, and subsequent consequences. Every choice echoed with implications not just for my soul but for the entire universe. I understood that whatever path I chose, there was no wrong way to go. With that profound realization, a luminous thread of light pulled me in the direction of my love for you, and I immediately returned to the limited confines of my body. I found myself trapped in the upside-down jeep, its tires spinning wildly in the air, at the base of an icy cliff. I was surprised and grateful to be alive.

Through the grace of our benevolent and loving Creator, I was given another opportunity to fulfill my soul mission, write this book, and find you. Indeed, my presence on the planet and in your life is a manifestation of divine providence.

In a sacred union of Heaven and Earth, each soul is birthed and rebirthed into a world of multiplicity and choice.

We leave our true home behind when we walk into this world of form and structure. To have the human experience, we veil ourselves from the truth of the all-pervasive love of God. This explains the nostalgic feeling of emptiness we may experience, even in good times; it is a deep longing of the soul to go home. Even so, the soul is excited to have the full array of human experiences, including sorrow and pain. Know that amid the inevitable hardships of our earthly journey, there exists a vast well of compassion for our struggles.

Even in our loneliest moments, we are never truly alone. Our guardians, guides, and angels are always by our side, holding us in their loving embrace as we find our way home. In the absence of light or during life's most turbulent storms, these celestial beings are forever by our side, wiping away our tears and illuminating the way.

From our first breath to our last breath, we are embraced with wisdom and held in love.

These guardian angels, insightful mentors, and ethereal companions, *both seen and unseen*, continually shower us with unwavering love and guidance. Their constant presence signifies the interconnectedness of all life and the boundless love of God. Even when we choose a less than radiant path or take the long way home, we are never judged, condemned, or abandoned. Our lives are far more complex than a simple stance *"for"* or *"against"*, there are many gray areas.

Everything has a divine purpose, including blossoming summer days and dark nights of the soul.

In this noble pursuit, together, we have danced through radiant fields of flowers and traveled many dark roads. Indeed, in the human endeavor, weathering life's storms, enduring its heartbreaks, and confronting its betrayals has undeniably tested our resolve. So many times the world just stopped spinning, there was no oxygen, and it was hard to breathe. Loneliness draped over us in a heavy blanket of sorrow, obscuring our souls' radiance and blocking the light. Even in these dark places, angels were always by our side. They slipped in through the broken windows of our disappointment and despair, slid underneath the locked doors of our secret shame and fear, and sliced through the heavy curtains hanging around our broken hearts, bringing with them a glimmer of light and the hope of a new day.

And yes, I am part of your soul family. I left the heavenly realms where everything is made of love and light and purposefully returned to the dark density of the human experience—

because I love you. Nothing can sever our transcendent bond of love. Though you may not remember me as I remember you, I am certain my words and presence will resonate with you as a familiar friend whose name may escape you. Whether you can recall our many lives or our eternal bond of love does not change how I feel about you or my undying love for you. My love and the gift of these teachings do not require reciprocation or acknowledgment.

Love loves for the sake of love and for no other reason.

Love is the unifying force of the universe. It is the thread of light woven into the grand tapestry of divinity that breathes life into existence. In the radiant light of my love for you, even time surrenders to the ageless bond of our eternal connection. Every beat of my heart is a pulse of the Divine. It is an all-encompassing love—*a love so expansive it blurs the boundaries of the known, and willingly dives into the unknown.*

Love draws unto itself that which it is—infinite love.

The magnetic pull of my love for you propelled me to find you again. There is no other alternative for me but to love you; *Love can only love*. Just as the mountain and the sky are forever bound to each other, and the ocean and its depths eternally dance together, we are forever united in unending love. We are not meant to take this soulful journey alone; in fact, nobody would make it through this shadowy world without assistance.

We need each other to learn, grow, and evolve. That's why I have found you again—*we are better together*. Though it may seem that we have just met, we have walked hand in hand through many worlds and countless lives together. It brings me such resplendent joy to be in your divine presence in the physical world and rekindle our sacred bond of love. Each time we find each other, universes collapse, collide, and expand in ecstatic bliss. This very moment marks a pivotal point in our serendipitous reunion across the ages. Indeed, every blossoming flower, drifting cloud, and sparkling star is a quiet celebration of the radiance of your precious soul. Even these Love Letters are an outpouring of Divinity to support, honor, and illuminate your path. Beyond mere poetic verses or eloquent prose, they serve as precise directives to comfort your weary soul, mend your wounded heart, and align you with more radiant possibilities for your life.

The magnitude of this love, God's love, can easily be lost in syntax. We often lose sight of the forest for the trees. The limits of language blunt the truth of love. Words and definitions cannot say the "*unsayable*" or contain the immensity of God's love. Given the impossibility of describing such a love in its fullest expression, these Love Letters point the way toward what really matters, toward the truth of love.

Love is the pure light of undifferentiated consciousness that neither pushes nor pulls, for or against the present moment—embracing all with equanimity.

God is absolute love and radiant light with no opposite or contradiction. It is a love so expansive and all-encompassing that no words, no measure, no idea, nothing can come close to describing such infinite radiance and divine presence. Yet, for many, the concept of God has been misconstrued and misused to justify harm, incite conflicts, and perpetrate injustices. Such a distorted image stands in stark contrast to the all-encompassing love of God. This harsh and punitive portrayal of God is not the truth of God.

God is pure, absolute love.

Any cruel or unkind portrayal of God's love is unfounded. God does not inflict harm or hurt. God is not an abstract concept or an idolized religious figure who looms over us with cruelty, judgment, or condemnation. Nonetheless, if we have been wounded by the manipulation or misrepresentation of God, it may be difficult to perceive the genuine nature of God's infinite love. Embracing the idea of a benevolent Creator is understandably difficult if we have experienced love, or God, through the lens of pain, trauma, or deception.

God's love includes our tears, laughter, joys, and sorrows.

Bearing this in mind, and before we continue, please allow me to address those who have suffered in the name of love or under the guise of God; I am truly sorry for your pain, hurt, and sorrow. Your pain wounds my heart, too. If it were possible, I would ease your suffering and remove your pain, but each of us has to find our own way through the darkness and back to the love and light of God. Though it may be difficult to comprehend or accept that in a loving universe, our every joy or sorrow serves the soul as a lesson or a gift, contributing to our personal transformation and inevitable evolution.

Everything and everyone in the universe is born of God's grace and divine intelligence.

Even our unlikely reunion on the pages of this book and in this life is a necessary movement of the Divine. As a testament to God's boundless grace and infinite wisdom, the very forces of Heaven and Earth have united, so that our paths would cross again, and we would find each other. Our eternal bond of love has once again drawn us toward each other, but it is always our choice to engage or not. In some lives, we choose to walk in opposite directions, passing each other like two ships in the night, while in other lives, as in this life, from our very first breath to our very last breath, we walk toward each other. Either way, there has never been, nor will there ever be a moment when I have not loved you. I have loved you for many lives. I loved you long before you were you. I loved the pure potentiality that manifested as you and the pure light that is you. My soul has loved your soul for eons of time, throughout all of eternity.

Only love is real and lasting, everything else is a fleeting illusion.

Love propels purpose into meaning, movement into matter, silence into sound, nothing into all things, and the temporal into the eternal. Love is beauty unveiled as that which is most beautiful; and yes, that includes you. You are that which is most beauty-filled. You are a stunning expression of the Divine and the necessary unfoldment of God.

As one voice in a chorus of many, I sing this endless love song to you because I can, because I choose to, and because it brings me such joy. You may not know your inherent value, but I do. You are the luminous progeny of God, a beloved child of the loving universe, and my soul companion and cherished friend of many lives. You are a divine expression of love personified and experienced as you. You are a radiant particle of light, God's footstep into the night, and the rising Sun, too.

Each soul, including your precious soul, is a perfectly imperfect reflection of the Divine.

Outside of time, from beyond the boundaries of space, I viewed myself from above the crumpled red jeep and my motionless body below. I was enveloped in a shimmering veil of light and cradled in the warm embrace of the loving universe. My life, from the time of my birth to this very moment, coalesced into one expression of Self—the light that IS me, and that is also part of all that IS, was, or ever will be.

In the quiet aftermath of my crashing descent off an eighty foot ledge to the bottom of the mountain, and just before slamming into an unmoving wall of ice, a radiant presence held me in a loving, evanescent light, comforting me as I viewed a detailed panoramic life review that included every moment since the beginning of time.

I watched myself in my most unkind expressions, falling into the depths of darkness and despair without motive or reprieve. I was also shown rippling moments of kindness, grace, and generosity: stepping over an ant, helping a friend in need, clearing trash from the ocean's edge, offering a kind word to a stranger, planting flowers, and dancing in the rain. Most astoundingly, I was equally loved, regardless of my behavior and irrespective of my good or bad actions. There was no judgment brought upon me. In fact, I was cradled, comforted, and consoled in my guilt, shame, and sorrow. I was compassionately shown that my every thought, word, choice, and action was part of a grander plan meant to empower my soul and add a unique radiance and touch of light to the loving universe.

In an instant of absolute clarity, I understood that there was no need for anything to change. With this understanding, the natural flow of the universe revealed itself—more glorious and radiant than is possible to imagine or describe. There is a perfection to the imperfection of a human life, and nothing needs to change. Nothing, no-thing, is beyond or outside of God's loving embrace.

Every straight path, crooked road, truth declared, unspoken secret, loud scream, quiet whisper, and silent tear is a glorious and necessary expression of the Divine.

Love encompasses, includes, and permeates all that *IS* with more love. I am love; you are love; we are love; a limitless, boundless, endless love. As children of the Divine, we are a necessary part of creation. We are not lonely travelers in a cold and uncaring universe. The whole of Creation exists for us, for our evolution, and for our enjoyment. Every person and everything that comes into being is essential to existence—*including you and me.*

Every pebble on the ground, cloud in the sky, and drop of rain that finds its way to the Earth is an expression of God's unending love.

Nothing is left out of love.

If a single grain of sand were missing from the seashore, there would be no seashore. If a drop of water were missing from the ocean, there would be no ocean, and if your divine soul were missing from existence, there would be no existence at all—*that is how important you are.*

You are a part of something far greater than you believe yourself to be; you are part of Divinity. We are all connected in love and united in the luminous radiance of the Divine. Our very existence proves our divine nature and God's unfathomable love for us.

Love is the silent compass of our soul, guiding us to unforeseen, magical lands of the heart.

Love carries us through tear-filled nights and days filled with joy and laughter. Love is the very pulse of the universe and the ever-present drum of the heart. Love is the map, journey, and the destination, too. Love rearranges the known and points to the unknown. Love takes the form of light and hides in shadows. Love makes all things possible, even the impossible. Love is the collapsing universe and the birth of invisible stars. Love is a happy baby giggling in the safety of her mother's arms and a lonely old man gasping for breath.

Love is a rumbling storm and a cloudless sky. Love is a flower in full bloom and the wilting horizon of time. Love is the vast, velvet sky and the moon's shimmering light. Love is our sweetest dreams and our darkest nightmares. Love is a cat purring and a tail wagging. Love is the moon's circled halo and crickets' clicking wings. Love is the gray silhouette of a winged shadow, softly sailing on the ground below, where earthbound creatures run and hide for cover.

How I wish I could express the expansive radiance of this love, God's love, and my unending love for you, but again, words fail me. Whatever I say is limited by language, the constraints of my consciousness, and my inability to convey the depth and width of this great love.

The immensity of God's love cannot be defined; anything said falls short of the absolute truth.

Even the most eloquent prose or poetic verse pales in comparison to the grand expanse of God's unfathomable love. All words, no matter how beautifully strung, are vague and empty in the vast ocean of God's love. Having said that, as I write these Love Letters, words are my sole instrument. I will do my utmost to weave them together with love and care. I hope to convey the truth of my love and God's love, with its immeasurable magnitude and profound depth, with clarity and hope.

To this end, I will share my love and timeless wisdom with a poetic tone innate to my nature while maintaining a practical and precise approach to ensure clarity. I will honor the creative source that inspired these words by unveiling my soul's hidden secrets with a willingness to be vulnerable and wounded. I will speak directly from my heart to yours. To love you is my greatest strength and my most fragile weakness. In honor of your divine soul, I promise to do everything that I can to ease your pain, support your journey, and be part of your joy. Indeed, if it served your soul, I would walk through the darkest night and gladly embrace the brightest light. I will do all of this and more, much more, simply because I love you.

I loved you before the stars populated the night sky, before darkness gave way to the first ray of light, and before you opened your eyes to this world of limitless possibilities. Wherever you go, I will find you and remind you of our shared bond of love. I will whisper to you in the shifting shadows of a summer's day and sing to you in the hues of light on a starry night. If only you knew your own magnificence, you would never cry another tear or doubt the unconditionality of God's unending love—*or my love for you.*

Your heritage is divine; you are the progeny of God.

God burst into billions upon trillions of particles of light and expressions of life for the pure and absolute joy of it. One joyous particle is you; another is me. Together, we are a magnificent expression of the divine creative God force. Though this definition may sound abstract, the love that created you is closer than your very own breath. God is alive in the very essence of your being, intricately woven into every fiber of your existence, patiently waiting to be recognized and embraced. We are born of love and shall return to love as more love. We are the manifestation of God as more God. While we may perceive ourselves as separate and alone, we are part of a profound Oneness.

If God were an equation, it would be one plus one equals One.

I am you; you are me, and we are eternally One—*infinitely united in love*. This love knows no conditions, chains, locked doors, or barred windows. It is as free as the wind and as boundless and vast as the sky. This is how I love you—*in spacious freedom and unbound grace*. I love the real you, the light within you, and the God that is you. I love the you that you may have forgotten, the spark of light that is you, and the beauty and awe of you. Whatever I say about this love, my unending love for you will never be enough or complete.

Rather than trenching through the opaque limits of language, I will carry you across the barren desert, swim across the ocean of time, gift you the stars, and be the light of your moon. I will crawl on wounded knees to the other side of your pain and willingly dive into the depths of your sorrow. I will do whatever I must so that you will know that you are a cherished child of the loving universe—*you are not alone; I am forever by your side.*

How I wish I could relieve all your pain, mend your every problem, and provide you with all the answers for your life, but that would not serve the great longing of your soul for experience and expansion. All souls long to unveil the truth of love within themselves. It is a joyful journey of inner and outer exploration that may span many lives along myriad paths of shadows and light.

The easy path is not always the best, and the best path is not always easy.

Sometimes we choose the high road; other times, we don't. There is no universal right path for all souls. Whether our journey leads us to the highest mountain of joy and elation or leaves us in the deepest valley of darkness and despair, celestial angels, wise teachers, and trusted guides extend their loving arms, ever ready to catch us should we stumble or fall. The human experience is a magnificent adventure but far from easy. Indeed, based on our choices, life can be quite challenging. Either way, the preferred path of the soul is the one that offers the most opportunities for expansion. Life can be an arduous, lonely journey, but we don't have to walk this path alone.

The moment we call upon our angels, guides, and teachers, they come rushing to our aid.

As a humble servant of the Divine and someone who profoundly loves you, I am forever by your side to assist you. Across many lives, worlds, and beyond, I forever stand guard and offer my support. Undoubtedly, storms will come and rain will fall, yet the joys and sorrows of a human life are not haphazard, arbitrary, or purposefully unkind.

The opposite is true. Everything happens in divine timing for the benefit of your soul and the good of all. Your good or bad circumstances are not the consequence of karmic forces.

Much like the moon reflects the Sun's radiant light, sorrow serves as the backdrop for our joy.

One cannot exist without the other and everything serves the grand purpose of the soul. On another plane, before this particular life, along with your spiritual guides, you lovingly and willingly selected the life circumstances that would best promote your personal development and soul expansion.

The life you are currently living is the most fruitful option for your brave and valiant soul. You came back to this beautiful and sometimes harsh planet to challenge yourself and further your evolution. Indeed, planet Earth can be a stern and rigorous teacher; only the fiercest beings incarnate here. The heavy shadows, dark nights, and consequences of free will make this world seem rather ruthless and barren—*a place of little or no light.*

During the dark night of the soul, it is easy to believe that life is bleak, sad, or tragic. While suffering is undeniable, it is not the entire story or ultimate truth of our lives. All things work together for the good of the individual and the greater good of the whole—including our suffering and pain. Even during our darkest days, we have never been unloved, forsaken, or alone. We are forever surrounded and supported by luminous beings, guardian angels, soul companions, guides, and teachers who love us unconditionally and eternally. These mostly unseen beings have been with us since the beginning of time and are part of our soul family. Though we were mostly unaware of their presence, they held our trembling hands, wiped away our secret tears, and lovingly watched over us while we slept.

No one would survive in this earthly realm without the unseen prompts, gentle guidance, and unconditional love of their spiritual family and loving Creator.

I am part of your spiritual family. You are my beloved of many lives. I love you so very much. My love for you does not waver and has no conditions. I love you in all your beauty and shame. Over the course of our many shared lives, I have beheld your triumphant climbs and somber descents with equal dispassion and love. I have known the depths of your being on your most challenging and glorious days. No matter what, I have always stood faithfully by your side.

Everything is consumed in the fire of love—and then, only love is left.

Through it all, my love for you has been an unyielding, eternal flame. In the service of my profound and undying love for you, I have played the role of both adversary and ally. When it was most beneficial, my presence was a fierce flame; at other times, it was a life-giving rain. Participating in your spiritual journey is my greatest joy and honored privilege. I returned to this world of form and structure to find you and be part of your spiritual awakening because I truly love you. As your spiritual teacher, guide, and friend of many lives, it is such a blessing to once again serve your beautiful soul and contribute to your well-being. For as you blossom and bloom, the garden of my existence is more fragrant and alive. I am forever grateful and in your debt. Our ancient love story began eons ago and extends far into the future, beyond the confines of time and limits of space, shifting timelines and changing universes. I am excited to discover the new worlds and expansive universes yet to be born of our eternal and undying love.

From that ethereal realm beyond my body, between this life and the next, bathed in a luminous embrace of unconditional love, I chose to return to this life and find you. Driven by a purpose greater than myself, I was called to seek you out, write this book, and share the profound message of unconditional love with the world.

"Love is all that matters."

With this profound revelation, in a glorious burst of light, I found myself once again embodying the physical realm, climbing up the icy cliff on a mission to find you and share this profound and transformational message of unconditional love. As we come to the end of this first Love Letter, I hope you sense the depth of my timeless and profound love for you—a love that has spanned ages, endured lifetimes, and explored the hidden realms of the heart.

With profound gratitude and boundless love, I joyfully and wholeheartedly offer my heart, my soul, and the entirety of my being into the eternal fire of my love for you.

I bow at your feet with great reverence,
and I forever love you.
— Chrystal Rae

*We are born of love for the purpose of love,
and we shall return to love as more love*

Letter 2
reunion
we meet again

Trumpets herald, drums roll, choirs sing, and bells toll in a grand celebration of our reunion.

In the expansive journey of our souls, we have walked alongside each other in many lives and explored countless realms and worlds. However, this may be the first time we meet again in this particular life, .

Please allow me the honor, privilege, and pleasure of formally introducing myself. My birth name is Chrystal Rae—*a name that is rich with spiritual significance. "Chrystal"* represents purity, while *"Rae"* is the essence of light. Aligning with these definitions and what they represent is a lifelong journey I willingly embrace, though, admittedly, I often fall short of my own best effort.

I have had my fair share of extraordinary moments graced with inexplicable beauty and awe, yet I am just an ordinary person. I don't have angel wings and I can't fly. I have struggled, failed, and had triumphant moments of great success, but nothing has come easily or without challenge. My life has been punctuated with great joy and deep sorrow.

Nonetheless, I have always tried to do my very best and continue evolving. Even when faced with the great difficulties of a childhood that left me with bruises and bald spots, I never gave up on myself or God. Though my little girl world was covered in darkness and haunted by the monsters that did not disappear when the lights came on, I had great compassion and deep love for my parents. Every night before closing my swollen eyes, I secretly hoped that if God were real, he would help my mother and absent father to stop drinking. Eventually, the walls of my naivete and innocence came tumbling down. Then, there was no escape from the dark shadows of my childhood that would follow me into adulthood. I could not get away from my sadness. During those dark years, there was nothing to hold onto. The very ground beneath my feet was shaky and unstable like my mother.

The torrential rains, hurricanes, and tornadoes that raged through my little girl life came in the form of physical, mental, and emotional abuse. I was betrayed, abused, and neglected by those entrusted to love, protect, and care for me. If not for the grace and goodness of unseen forces and guardian angels I may not have survived my childhood. I certainly would not have made it through those dark nights when the monsters drank too much and I became the beneficiary of their anger, sorrow, and pain.

As a child, I had a unique connection to my personal version of God. In the solitude of my room, like a prima ballerina on an invisible stage, I would dance across the floor, pirouetting, twirling, and leaping into the emptiness of space. I imagined that God was seated upon a golden throne, applauding my efforts. Just as I yearned for the love and approval of my drunken mother and absent father, I also sought the same validation and love from the invisible force I called God. Though my version of God was innocent and naive, the heavenly presence I experienced was real, embracing me with love, kindness, and care.

Our soul family, teachers, guides, and angels are always by our side, watching over us from afar yet as close as our very own breath.

I often felt the comforting presence of heavenly beings watching over me while I slept, accompanying me into my little girl dreams. These luminous beings wrapped their delicate, feathered wings around me, their presence a soothing lullaby to my restless mind. In their loving embrace, I was transported to a serene world where children lived in safety and warmth, untouched by the harshness of reality. It was in these radiant visions and glittering dreams that I found solace, a haven from the lonely challenges of my youth.

These gentle guardians, like radiant stars in the night, guided me through the profound darkness of my formative years, sowing seeds of hope that promised to blossom in a future yet to be born. Through grace and goodness, I weathered my childhood and now stand before you with a message of hope. Whether under sunny skies or amidst stormy days, whatever struggles you encounter, know that you are never alone and will find your way through. You are surrounded by your soul family of angels, teachers, and guides, and I am here too, always with you, offering my unwavering love, guidance, and support.

You are stronger than you know and everything will eventually work out, even if it doesn't.

Everything in our lives serves as either a lesson or a gift, promoting our evolution and connection to the Divine. To this end, the revelations that unfold on these pages are meant to be an anchor of strength, a reason to believe, and a pathway to God. These Love Letters will provide solace for your soul, healing for your body, and empowerment on all levels. I wrote them especially for you.

Everything in our lives had to happen exactly as it did for us to stand on the hallowed ground of the present moment with all its beauty, splendor, and grace.

While you may not remember, we have seen the Sun rise and set, time and again, in our many lives together. We have lost and found each other over and over again. In the vast ocean of time, our bond of love has forever drawn us toward each other, uniting us in eternity. Our reunion in this most important, pivotal, and transformative life is no accident. It is a blessing and gift to our souls that will change the entire universe.

The convergence of our many lives and the unlikely circumstances that drew us together are far from coincidental. They are part of a grander design for the evolution of our souls and the betterment of all. Even our unexpected reunion is a blessing born of our every footstep toward love and away from fear. Every joyous and painful moment had to occur just as it did for our paths to cross again. Even the stars in the night sky orchestrated their alignment in a rare pattern, ensuring the beautiful synchrony of our souls. This glorious occurrence is as spectacular as the clear sky after a heavy rain. It is with great reverence and love that I once again bow to your grace.

It is such a joy to reconnect with you in this wonderful and sometimes challenging, life. Though it may appear that we have only just met, the sudden convergence of our paths and the echoes of our many lives reflects our ageless bond of love. Because I'm sure that my recollection of our past lives and deep soul connection is more vivid than yours, please allow me to share a bit more about my journey and explain why I've written these Love Letters to you.

In this life, rooted in the dynamic city of Dallas, Texas, I wear the hats of a yogi, artist, and poet. As the co-owner of three yoga studios and two teacher training schools, I find fulfillment in creating spaces that are more than just physical locations. They are sacred communities where we share and explore the ancient art of yoga.

Artistically, I express myself through abstract paintings, which are vibrant reflections of my inner landscape. My art adorns corporate spaces and adds color and vitality to my home, a haven I share with my wonderful husband. Our union forms an unexpected but delightful pairing; I am immersed in the world of yoga while he thrives in the music industry.

As an author and poet, writing is my avenue for profound creative expression. This realm, with its blend of succinct phrases and rich prose, offers me another avenue for creative exploration. Indeed, my life, like my writing, balances poetic imagination with pragmatic insight.

Among all my endeavors, the most important mission of my soul is to reconnect with you and renew our sacred bond of love. The unexpected convergence of our paths, not predetermined but divinely inspired, is a testament to our enduring love. I am honored and excited to find you again in this most pivotal life of great opportunity and transformation. Thank you for being you, for allowing me to share my love and wisdom, and for joining me on this exciting adventure through the physical realm, forging a radiant path back to the great love at the center of it all.

Part of my preparation, on the path that led me to you, I had a startling experience that forever changed my life and impacted the lives of many others. On what seemed like an otherwise ordinary day, destiny took a sudden and unexpected turn when a devastating car accident brought me to the brink of death and face-to-face with God. As our small red jeep took a tumultuous descent down an icy mountainside, I saw before me multiple paths of life, each one a different choice I could make.

One path offered the opportunity to depart from my earthly form and this realm altogether. However, I made the conscious choice to return on a mission of love. I recognized that my presence and voice held the power to contribute to the growth and well-being of many. I also understood that I had a divine appointment with you.

Our bond as soul companions throughout our many lives is a testament to the strength of our enduring love. In this out-of-body state, I understood that the hardships of my childhood and personal journey held a purpose beyond mere difficulty. They were not in vain. All my struggles and dark nights prepared me for our eventual meeting and the glorious reunion of our souls.

The car accident marked a subtle yet profound shift in my consciousness. It was as though a secret portal to another dimension suddenly opened, unveiling a realm of pure love and light. Every atom was radiant, alive, and shimmering with ethereal presence.

The journey out of my physical body and into an ethereal realm offered me a myriad of potential realities with the privilege of free will. As I mentioned, the option to depart from this world was open, yet I declined. I came back to find you and share this message of unconditional love with the world:

"Love is all that matters."

The experience of being outside my body, as a conscious observer of my own existence, was serenely spectacular. From this suspended state, untethered from my physical form, I watched as the small red jeep somersaulted and collided with the unyielding ice below.

To my astonishment, a luminous and loving presence enveloped me in a soft cloud of iridescent mist and telepathically communicated that I had many options and that no one path for my life was preset. I was shown and drawn toward the radiant path of continuing in my current life, becoming a conduit of love, finding you, and writing this book.

While being held in the presence of this all-encompassing love and luminous light, many secrets of the loving universe spontaneously unveiled themselves. The benevolent presence radiated a luminous light that enveloped me in grace as a three-dimensional panoramic review of my life unfolded before me.

This life review included my every thought, word, and action, along with their profound ripple effects. Poignantly, it was conveyed, again without words, for me to include in this book that sound and light are the future of medicine.

This miraculous experience was a radiant symphony of light, woven together with threads of beauty, grace, and a profound sense of wonder. Every moment exuded a captivating, luminous light and an overwhelming sense of unconditional love and acceptance. It was so awe-inspiring that it was difficult to grasp the sheer magnitude of the boundless love that enfolded me. Though I was excited to return and complete my soul mission, I could not even imagine or fully comprehend how to share this transformative message of unconditional love.

On another level, I felt too broken and unworthy to serve as a vessel or spokesperson for the Divine. Before I could, with any authority, write a book on love, I had to heal my childhood wounds and make peace with my past. Now, more than twenty years later, the cumulation of my readiness is this collection of Love Letters that you hold in your hands. The accident, years of self-healing, and my dedicated yoga practice have collectively contributed to a profound transformation in my perception of Self, others, and the loving universe. Reflecting on the pivotal lessons that grace, meticulously imparted on that fateful day, a singular truth is self-evident: *Love*.

Only love is real.

The months following the accident were a glorious time of significant change and exponential personal growth, but they were not easy. On the contrary, it was quite a challenging time. I sensed the feelings of others, intuited their thoughts, and knew their greatest joys and deepest sorrows. I was suddenly aware of the glowing hues of iridescent light that shimmer around the physical body, fluctuating with our every thought, feeling, and emotion. I understood on an experiential level that most of us live in fear and are just trying to survive. Rather than living our most radiant life, we hide in the shadows of who we are meant to be.

Despite the intriguing nature of my newly acquired intuitive abilities, clairvoyance and clairaudience were not gifts I actively sought or desired. The involuntary knowledge of the emotions and thoughts of others made me uncomfortable and disconcerted. Being privy to this constant stream of insights overwhelmed me with the weight of fear prevalent in the human condition. I felt completely alienated and alone.

There was no one in my world who understood these intuitive gifts or with whom I could openly share my experiences. The few times I did share, I received blank, vague stares—*as though I had lost my mind*. The few people whom I entrusted with the secret of my newfound abilities would inevitably respond by retracting their energy and filtering their thoughts. Even if they didn't believe me, they were apprehensive that I might be able to glimpse into the depths of their innermost selves and would immediately move away.

I quickly learned to be more selective and discerning with whom I shared these experiences and my energy. It took some time for me to assimilate this new state of heightened knowing and psychic abilities into my life. The accident and everything it entailed, forever impacted my life and transformed who I am. Even those things I previously overlooked or disregarded suddenly took on new significance: *a dog barking, the sound of chimes in the wind, the smell of freshly cut grass, a giggling baby, and a bird on my windowsill were now miraculous and filled with beauty beyond compare.*

What was once ordinary and mundane was now a silent message of grace and love. I transitioned from merely trying to survive and endure pain, to embracing the profound purpose of my life. This shift in my life direction and purpose included finding you, writing this book, and sharing the message of unconditional love.

Nonetheless, during this tumultuous time of transformation and profound spiritual growth, an unanticipated shift in consciousness unfolded within me, leaving a lasting imprint on my soul. I was acutely aware that I was aware. This epiphany reshaped my perspective of myself and others. I understood on a visceral level that my sense of Self transcended the limitations of my corporeal existence and that we are all connected.

With this revelation, it was evident that we all exist as a complex and singular embodiment of love, each a unique and necessary expression of the Divine.

We are born of love for the purpose of love, and we shall return to love as more love.

This abrupt awakening opened a hidden door to a more expansive comprehension of the universe and our loving Creator. It imbued my life with a sense of duty, meaning, and purpose.

However, it was daunting to even think about sharing this profound message of unconditional love. At that time, my life was in disarray. Freshly divorced, with two small children, I was still grappling with the aftermath of my childhood trauma. I was too engulfed in a sense of inadequacy and feelings of unworthiness to shoulder the role of being a messenger of love. How could I guide others when my own life was an enigma and a mess? The weight of my failures pressed heavily on me, amplifying my doubts.

My history lacked Cinderella-esque endings; my relationships invariably crumbled in sorrow and disillusionment. The glass slipper of happiness never fit, and my love stories always concluded on a tragic note. Trust and love, be it from friends or family, consistently led to pain, abandonment, or both. It was a downward cycle in which even my parents partook. Yet, the miraculous events of that pivotal day, when our small red jeep met the icy mountainside, left me with a renewed sense of resilience and purpose.

To describe this life-altering experience and its impact on my life is no easy task; the closest semblance of truth is to say that it was a "*remembrance*." I somehow tapped into knowledge that had always been a part of me but was deliberately set aside to embrace the human experience.

The love that held me in the radiant light as I hovered above my seemingly lifeless body, granted me a profound understanding of the loving universe, our benevolent Creator, and the eternal essence of my very own soul. Integrating the immense love and wisdom shared during these magical moments was a gradual process that extended over many years.

Words, however eloquent, fail to capture the all-encompassing nature of the love I encountered on that icy mountain road. The sheer force of this unending love was so powerful it still reverberates through every cell in my body, transforming and enlivening the very core of my being with purpose and meaning. This transformational experience ignited my desire to do more in the service of love and as an expression of God's radiant light.

From that pivotal moment forward, everything changed, including the trajectory of my life. Every aspect of my being underwent a profound shift accompanied by a heightened sense of awareness, meaning, and purpose. After the car wreck, my consciousness exponentially expanded. I saw everyone, and everything, differently.

Through the lens of unconditional love, the world and everyone in it were a radiant expressions of the Divine.

It was so beautiful that even an ant, a tiny yellow flower, or a soft cloud in the sky would bring salty tears of joy to my eyes. Even those aspects of my past that once seemed too painful or horrific to reconcile with the constraints of human logic, including my childhood experiences, were now seen as an integral part of a divine plan. This one realization instantly softened the wounds that were still bleeding from my past and traumatic childhood.

Over two decades have passed since I emerged from that wintry ordeal—*surviving the accident and the perilous, icy mountain roads*. It has taken me this long to fully embody the profound tenets of unconditional love that I experienced in those transcendent moments when time slowed down, and the world stopped spinning. Returning to this life was a conscious choice, part of my soul's mission. Continuing this human journey wasn't obligatory, but I chose it eagerly, driven by the desire to write this book and find you. It's been a demanding journey, yet now I stand ready to share my soul's light and the profound message of unconditional love with the world.

The absolute euphoria and bliss of my encounter with the luminous presence still lingers in my consciousness, but I have never regretted coming back to find you. It brings me such joy to contribute to the goodness of the world and be part of your happiness.

My love for you knows no bounds and has no limits. I love the smallest speck of your radiant light and the grandest expanse of your glorious sun. I love you exactly as you are right now. Nothing needs to change. You are perfectly imperfect, which makes you absolutely perfect. Even your current state of consciousness, clear or cloudy, bears no weight on my love for you.

Whether you view yourself as virtuous or flawed does not change how I feel about you. Love, in its purest expression, cannot be earned or lost.

True love is unconditional, eternal, and transcendent.

Though the above statement may seem like a conundrum, it's not. True love is not a superficial perception of worthiness or unworthiness. To earn love implies some value assessment or merit, which is not love. That would be a business deal or a contract that could change based on circumstances, and that is not love. Love does not change. Love is always the same.

Love is always love.

My love for you does not fluctuate with the weather or come and go like a storm. It is the space where all storms and sunny days freely come and go. You are free to be you, and I am free to be me, too. Indeed, I am also perfectly imperfect and have made many mistakes in my time. To this point, as previously mentioned, this life has not been an easy life for me. Besides the car accident, I had to survive a failed marriage and a dysfunctional, abusive childhood. The neglect and abuse I received at the hands of my alcoholic mother and absent father left deep emotional wounds that impacted my psychological well-being far into the future. It took many years of intense self-work, inner contemplation, and grace to overcome my sense of inadequacy, abandonment, and unworthiness. Without the intervention of angelic beings and my soul family, I would not have made it through the dark days of my life or the endless nights of my childhood.

These celestial beings played a pivotal role in guiding me through this challenging journey of self-realization. Their loving presence proved instrumental in my ability not only to survive but also to succeed against all odds. The backdrop of my unhappy childhood and failed relationships gave me the grit to carry on, making me stronger and wiser. Having said that, although my parents were my greatest teachers and anti-examples, this does not excuse their behavior nor negate the neglect and abuse I received under their care. To hurt another, in particular, to hurt an innocent child, has profound consequences for the soul.

At some point, in this life or another, we will experience both the joy and sorrow of our thoughts, words, and actions, along with their rippling effects. However, life is neither all black nor white; there are many gray areas. The complexity of human existence becomes evident when we consider that our pre-birth choices encompass a broad spectrum of experiences.

We deliberately select our families and the circumstances of our lives that best serve our soul, and for the benefit of all.

Some lives offer comfort and ease, while others present us with imperfect parents and challenging circumstances an life conditions. This selection process is neither haphazard nor arbitrary; it is deliberate and purposeful. Prior to each life, we are aware of the potential energetic pathways available and the subsequent outcomes. Alongside our spiritual guides, we carefully evaluate our choices, handpicking the circumstances, individuals, and environments that will catalyze our evolution and soul expansion. However, nothing is set in stone. Our lives and the future are fluid and adaptable. Our every thought, word, and action instantly reshapes our lives.

The capacity to influence and mold our future is a testament to the power of our thoughts, intentions, and free will.

There are absolutely no unexpected occurrences in our lives; every potentiality and all possibilities are considered before we accept a particular life path.

We understood the implications of our choices. We were also fully aware of the joy and pain we may cause and endure. This explains the conditions of my tear-filled childhood. The challenges that marked my early years were deliberate soul choices and a conscious strategy of my soul to build character, providing opportunities for forgiveness and grace. The hardships I braved, particularly those countless nights that shook the core of my being, have resolutely etched my love for you onto my soul. This love does not falter or waver, nor is it a fleeting sentiment.

Love recontextualizes everything, including the tragic and dark.

My love is firmly planted in real-life moments and heartfelt experiences. The storms of my childhood, the shattered hopes of my failed marriage, and the battles that life waged against me sparked a fire of change deep within my heart. The echoing pain of my past empowered me to transmute my sorrow and despair into love and compassion. This transformation allowed me to approach your joy and pain with compassion, love, and empathy.

Nothing brings me greater joy than to be part of your healing and happiness. To stand by your side and provide solace, and comfort is an absolute privilege. I'm deeply moved by the profound beauty and limitless light that radiates from the depths of your beautiful soul. You are why I came back into a physical embodiment and this world. Why? Love is why. I came back to the dense temporal world of shadow and light because I love you. Love mends the broken heart. Love soothes the wounded soul. And, love is why we have found each other again. My presence in your life is meant to be a source of solace and strength; I will pick you up if you fall, carry you when needed, and forever love you, no matter what.

A human life is a heroic journey of the soul.

We come to planet Earth each with our individual mission, but always on the path back to our Source, back to love: *God*. It is a magical sojourn ripe with villains, heroes, pain, pleasure, joy, and sorrow. Though suffering is an innate part of life, we are not born to suffer. Life is not a punishment nor the result of bad karma.

The exact opposite is true; life is a wonderful gift and a radiant and rare opportunity to be the perfectly imperfect you. Each soul is here for the absolute bliss of its own existence—*including your beautiful soul*. We did not enter the physical world to just get by or simply survive; there is much more to a human life than mere survival. We are not here to earn our way to Heaven or escape Hell.

We enter the physical world to explore and experience the myriad expressions of shadow and light, from the height of joy to the depth of sorrow, and everything in between.

We came to this world of form and matter for the visceral experience of the smallest particle of dust, suspended in a hazy cloud of sunlight, hovering by an open window. We came to explore the unseen magic of mountains, the vastness of space, and the deep depths of the ocean. We came to stroll down empty hallways and wander through majestic castles made of gold. We came to rise with the morning Sun in all its glory and splendor, and then, at the end of a long, hard day, to peacefully sink back into the restful line of the dark horizon.

We came to experience the brimming abundance of life and its shallow opposite too. We came for the fullness and experience of a human life and to unveil the unchanging richness of our souls in new and novel ways. Life is a doorway to the Divine and a crooked path to truth.

To be human is a beautiful and exciting adventure for the soul. We throw the dice, take our turn, and play the game of life. Whether we win or lose, when the game is over, it's over. We collect all the pieces, return them to the box, and go our merry way. Nothing has changed; after all, it was just a wonderful, or perhaps a horrendous game, but a game all the same. Please remember to have fun and enjoy the blissful experience of being alive—*of being you*.

The bliss of the human experience includes the opaque shadows and illuminated light of our many lives—*past, present, and future*. Through all our shared lives, scattered across the vast expanse of time and space, knowing you exist has been a source of comfort and joy. Each time we find each other again, in the guise of different forms and life circumstances, our reunion strengthens our eternal bond of love. To say "*I love you*" skims the surface of this profound emotion that encompasses every aspect of my being with the warmth and light of the rising Sun, extending to the farthest edge of the darkness in shimmering sheets of golden light.

As each day draws to a close, in the quietude of night, I offer a silent prayer for your safety and happiness. As sleep carries me from one world to the next, our shared past and hopeful future blossom into a fragrant garden of love and light. And on those lonely days when I wake to find myself engulfed in the darkness of your absence, it is our enduring love that illuminates the way back home.

Words cannot convey the raw and intense emotions I feel for you, so let me end this Love Letter by saying welcome home. I have been waiting for you, and I am so glad you have arrived; I love you.

I love you now, I loved you then, and I will love you even more tomorrow.

— Chrystal Rae

Joy is that which enlivens, energizes, and excites the soul

Letter 3
joy
bliss of existence

The flower joyfully blossoms when it is time to blossom, not a moment before.

Imagine the wonderful expression of joy and delight to suddenly find oneself unfolding in the sweet fragrance of a blossoming garden, shimmering with radiant light, alive with the hum and excitement of nature's extraordinary bliss.

Oh, such lovely conversations one could have with the Earth and sky if they were a flower with soft yielding petals, a glorious radiant crown jeweled with droplets of morning dew, and the sweet nectar of the rising sun. And what spectacular amazement to be the wind beneath translucent wings of buzzing bees with delicate limbs bathed in the golden pollen of tomorrow's honey. A dream beyond all dreams and a joy beyond all joy to journey into these faraway places. To venture beyond the vast universes outside the fragrant reach of one's quiet existence and rooted bloom is the most joyful exploration of the soul.

Beyond life's joy and sorrow, only love is real.

All the forces in heaven and on earth unite in support of our shared readiness as we embark on the eternal quest to know ourselves, one another, and the Divine. Yet, no being, not even angels, can fully grasp the absolute joy of being you. In the grand expanse of time and space, you are a never-to-be replicated miracle, and a radiant being of light. As a spiritual being, you are blessed with the liberty to choose your own destiny on the path to the Divine. We will all make our way from bud to blossom, bloom to wilt, back to Mother Earth and the sacred abode of God. In the intricate progression of our soul's liberation, we are freed from the heavy chains and magnetic pull of the material world. Our choices bear deep significance and, at the same time, are essentially empty of meaning.

Within the labyrinth of our fears and the ephemeral nature of illusions, love stands as the unshakable, eternal truth. Though we may encounter monsters lurking in the night, everything originates from love and is woven of light. What we perceive as evil is merely a fleeting manifestation of fragmented, dimmed light, but light nonetheless. It might come as a surprise to discover that even the darkest shadows and blackest night serve a joyful purpose and emerge from divine light.

Nonetheless, when tempests of fire or ice sweep through the barren landscapes of the broken heart, even the most radiant flowers gently close their delicate petals. Their folded blooms, bearing the weight of loss, willingly yield to their imminent end. After the storm, seeds of the past and future awaken with the morning sun, reborn in a flourishing renewal of radiant light.

We are all interconnected; what you do affects me and what I do affects you.

Indeed, a butterfly fanning its wings can change the course of hurricanes, shift ocean currents, and redirect heavy clouds, pregnant with life-giving rain. Within the comforting cradle of unconditional love, every choice is either a gentle rain or a storm brewing. Our decisions not only chart the course of our lives but also impact the trajectory of the loving universe.

One choice leads to joy, another to sorrow.

In this light, our choices have far-reaching implications for our lives, and for those in our circle of influence. When we are joyful, the universe comes alive and celebrates with us. When we are sad, shadows hang low in the sky, and even the sun turns dark with despair. Joy is the most direct path to the Divine.

Our perspective, whether guided by love or overshadowed by fear, steers us along divergent paths. One path deepens our connection to our Creator, while the other veers us away. Either way, joy is never a consequence of external circumstances; it is an alignment with our most elevated, benevolent, and radiant self.

When we consciously choose to see the world with a positive perspective, trusting in something greater than ourselves, even in the midst of life's darkest moments, we cultivate spiritual resilience. This resolve reconnects us to the omnipresent love that permeates the entire universe.

Joy is the foundation upon which the loving universe is built; without joy, there is neither illumination nor the potential for life.

The perceived divide between joy and sorrow dissolves into the truth of love, no longer opposing forces, but different aspects of the same omnipresent force of goodness, grace, and God. When we align with our true selves, an enduring wellspring of joy emerges, untouched by circumstances or passing weather. Drawing from the deep reservoir of God's unending love, we find a joyful haven even within life's inevitable storms. Nonetheless, how we choose to view the world is always a choice. One choice is to see the endless sky with awe and wonder, reveling in its beauty, while another is to gaze with apathy and despair, missing the intrinsic loveliness of life.

The human condition is one of paradox and choice. We assign all meaning to an otherwise meaningless world.

The challenges and gifts of a human life fuel the fire of the soul as radiant opportunities for expansion and personal growth.

Nothing is imposed upon us; we shoulder the responsibility of making the most of our precious time on this beautiful blue planet. Many times we get lost in our own busyness, drowning in the mundane and overlooking the sacred. For the soul to thrive, we must purposefully find a balance between living our lives and honoring the deep longing of the soul for expansion. All too often, we fail to seize the window of opportunity and our life simply passes us by. Though tragic in a relative sense, on the soul level, all is well.

Though we may find ourselves in the same life circumstances, time and again, there will come a day for us all when we will blossom and bloom like fragrant flowers in a garden of light.

The soul is forever called to shine brighter and lighter.

Though unforeseen obstacles may obscure the path of the soul, even in these shadowed realms, joy persists as the silent undercurrent, the unwavering heartbeat, and the animating force of our very existence. Such radiance transcends the smallness of words, even the profound wisdom within these teachings is bound by the limits of language.

In this luminous context, let us continue this conversation with the eloquent and sagacious voice of poetry.

I was sure that I was a seed until I discovered I had roots. In my rooted existence, I believed I would forever dwell in the shadowy comfort of this enigmatic realm of little light. Unexpectedly, I was drawn from my muddy abode and emerged with budding ease into the light of my own transformation. In its fullest glory, life unfolds as fragrant flowers with tender petals that first open and then bow in homage and honor of the rising sun. Even this splendor proves fleeting, for with the arrival of the cold northern breeze the seasons suddenly shift.

As the sun sets, the world turns dark, and pregnant clouds begin to cry. The soon-forgotten petals of a fragrant yesterday, also wilt and fall away. I, too, fade into the afternoon haze where I find myself cold, trembling, and alone—a solitary figure, a mere echo of my former blossoming self.

I am unrecognizable even to my own eyes. My radiant floral crown is now wilted and scattered on the ground. There is nothing left of me, but a fading memory. For a long moment, where I cannot breathe, I am no longer me. Then I tumble down, down, down—down to the unmoving ground, and just as suddenly as it began, everything stops, including my thoughts.

I am free of every ragged remnant of me. I am liberated from everything I once believed myself to be. I am no longer the seed, the root, stem, flower, blossom, the bloom, or the wilting. I am life's longing to live in abundance and adversity. I am the joy of joy, joyously experiencing the joy of existence as me, through me, and for me. I am the tiniest yellow flower, squeezing through the tight cracks of the pressed sidewalk, reaching for the first sliver of light that boldly announces the arrival of a new day.

I am ageless, timeless, and boundless—I am free, pure joy.

I am everything. I am nothing. And, I am so much more. Words cannot describe the serenity of this immaculate divinity manifest as me. The entire universe is a beautiful field of joyful blossoming flowers and so am I. In the empty space of this radiant possibility, you, too, wait patiently for the dormant seeds of what will be—the hope of tomorrow. Everything is new, but somehow the same; there is no judgment, condemnation, or shame. As I unveil the truth of my divinity, your beautiful soul is also liberated and free.

A single heartfelt action is the seed from which countless blossoming universes are born.

However, all too often, our good intentions turn into disappointment, resignation, and unrealized dreams. A perfect example, of which many can relate, is the earnest attempt to keep New Year's resolutions.

Most assuredly, we start out excited and motivated with a firm resolve to *joyfully* honor our promises to ourselves and others, embrace new habits, and change our lives. Over time, familiarity with the known and comfortable can lead us back into the repetitive routines and recurring patterns of the past. This regression isn't necessarily a sign of failure. Most of the time, it serves as a simple reminder that our ambitions demand a sturdy foundation, a compelling reason, and deliberate action. Though all the elements mentioned above are necessary for change to be possible, an essential element is one that many neglect and overlook: *Joy.*

Joy is the most authentic experience of the Divine.

It is a high vibrational field with a potency far above anger, apathy, or resignation. Indeed, for many, change is a slow, painful, and laborious process. It is nearly impossible to succeed when stuck in the grief of letting go, the despair of change, and the comfort of familiar but detrimental ways of being, or long standing habits.

Joy connects us with possibility and opportunity unavailable in lower states of consciousness. The more joyful we are about change, the easier it is to change. When we joyfully celebrate the slightest movement towards change, we align with a higher vibrational energetic field that opens doors that grief and apathy will never pass through.

And yes, change can be laborious, but it doesn't have to be complicated or hard. We can be firm, patient, and forgiving with ourselves. However authentic transformation and purposeful change are usually not a bolt of lightning.

Sustainable change is much like the joyful dawn of a new day, slowly spilling over the distant horizon in a splendid display of iridescent, golden light.

Joy is more than just a fleeting emotion; it is an alignment and sacred communion with the loving universe and God. Indeed, when we are joyful, we are closest to the Divine. However, when we are standing in the pouring rain with a dark cloud looming over our heads, all our choices will seem unacceptable and certainly not joyful.

Even if the sun is shining and skies are clear, when our inner world is dark, joy may seem to be a distant dream where God is as nebulous as clouds. The opposite can also be perplexing; when life is in full bloom and everything is sparkling with happiness and hope, all our choices may seem equally wonderful. In either case, knowing which option is best can be a challenge.

Whether we are overwhelmed by abundance or sink into darkness and doom, discerning our next step can be daunting. We are all at different stages and everyone is on a unique journey.

Each soul's path is distinct, marked by its unique life lessons and heavenly gifts.

Recognizing and honoring where we are in our evolutionary process can be a source of comfort and empowerment. Our current life circumstances are but fleeting moments in the grand narrative of our eternal soul. Beyond the ever-changing landscape of our lives, joy turns obstacles into stepping stones, bridging our earthly challenges with spiritual serenity. When we are joyful, life is more fulfilling. Regardless of our inner or outer circumstances, joy is the stable foundation that grounds us in love.

Joy enlivens, energizes, and excites the soul.

Though we may not always experience life as joyful, joy is the heartbeat of God, and the very pulse of the loving universe. Even when our journey into the physical world is heavy with burdens, joy is the very spark that makes it all possible and the light that makes it delightful.

Nonetheless, it may be challenging to comprehend how in a loving universe, darkness and despair can even exist, let alone be an expression of joy. Please allow me to explain. At the heart of existence, everything resonates with divine energy. What we perceive to be solid is actually luminous light at a particular frequency with a unique vibration. The denser the mass, the slower the frequency; the lighter the mass, the faster the frequency.

What determines this ethereal weight? Spiritually speaking, it is our proximity to Source. Aligning our thoughts, words, and actions with the high vibrational field of unconditional love not only instills a heightened sense of joy, but also nurtures a profound inner peace. When we align with the divine, our very presence radiates benevolence, goodness, and grace.

In the loving universe, guided by the law of attraction, our inner state of being and current level of consciousness attracts similar energetic qualities that are vibrating on the same frequency: *Like indeed attracts like.*

We each hold a unique vibrational frequency, our soul's distinctive signature.

Our current energetic state, be it elevated or subdued, mirrors the highest joy attainable at our present level of consciousness. Within this dynamic spectrum, it's important to acknowledge that "*energy*" itself is neutral; it is our intention, perception, and interpretation that infuse it with meaning and significance.

Our every thought, word, and action, whether positive or negative, endlessly ripple out, not only shaping our lives, but also leaving an indelible mark on the entire universe.

To illustrate this point, envision a sunny day where you feel wonderful, and everything seems to perfectly align. Tune into the energy of this scenario, paying close attention to the body's sensations without categorizing them as good or bad. Observe the flow and intensity of this energy in the body from a neutral standpoint, without emotional attachment or commentary.

From this perspective, it becomes evident that energy itself is neither inherently positive nor negative. The energy that fuels our emotions, whether they are positive or negative, remains constant. To further explain, recall a dark day when you felt unwell, agitated, or alarmed. In a similar manner, tune into the energy of this experience, paying close attention to the sensations in your body, again, without attaching any labels of good or bad. Simply observe the flow and intensity of this energy. As you do, become aware that the weight and intensity are much the same as in the previous joyful example.

The key difference is that now it is experienced in the opposite direction, with a negative polarization. Again, it is our intention, perception, and interpretation that give these emotions their specific qualities and directions. Through this simple observation, we realize that when we add emotional weight to the movement of energy, positive expressions invigorate and enliven, while negative expressions deplete and deaden.

The following poignant story vividly illustrates how context shapes content. A young man, deeply in love, surprised his girlfriend with a ring and a marriage proposal. Overwhelmed, she gasped and said, "*Oh no, I'm not ready for such a huge commitment,*" and ran away. The following week was the darkest period this young man had ever experienced. Unshaven and in despair, he sat alone in the darkness of his room, unable to eat or sleep.

Unexpectedly, there came a knock at the door, and he shouted, "*Go away!*" The voice on the other side of the door replied, *"It's me, please open the door. I am so sorry for my reaction to your marriage proposal."* Happy to hear her voice but still broken hearten, he hesitantly opened the door. She continued by saying *"I was taken by surprise and overwhelmed, but I never meant to hurt you. I've had a week to reflect on everything, and I've realized how much I miss you. The answer is yes, I will marry you, I love you."* In that instant, the heavy clouds of despair lifted, and the young man embraced his bride to be, now filled with joy and excitement.

This story highlights the profound influence of circumstances and emotional context on our perceptions, reactions, and the overall course of our lives. It's evident that the young man's emotions, both happy and sad, emanated from the same source. What differentiated it was the contrast between his unfulfilled and fulfilled desires. Regardless of the context, and the resulting emotional expression, the underlying energy that fueled both experiences remained fundamentally neutral—*pure energy*.

This example emphasizes how our perspective can significantly shape our emotional responses. With the understanding of how energy works, we can consciously choose how to utilize our precious life force. Rather than being swayed by external circumstances and the ever-changing nature of life, we can decide beforehand that no matter what happens, we will choose love and joy. This is an important decision for, as demonstrated in the previous example, our perspective influences the nature of our life experiences.

We must be vigilant in what we choose to energetically entertain or we will get pulled into a downward spiral. In the case of the young man, while it was not an ideal situation, there were alternative choices beyond succumbing to depression and disheartenment. He could have chosen to view his girlfriend's hesitation to marry as an opportunity to prioritize her happiness over his desire to put a ring on her finger. Expressing, *"I am sad that you are not ready to get married, but I love you and want your happiness above all,"* could have transformed his perspective.

Although the outcome might have remained the same, the journey would unquestionably have been more enjoyable. The lesson learned from this simple example is relative to the whole of our existence. To maintain inner peace and joy, we must consciously transition from a fear-based existence to a more loving perspective that honors both ourselves and others. By actively nurturing a positive mindset, we can confront life's challenges with heightened emotional intelligence, resilience, and, yes, joy.

When it comes to the question of how to be truly joyful, especially in the face of life's adversities, the most direct answer is to cultivate gratitude. Like the morning sun spilling over the dark line of the horizon, ushering in the dawn of a new day, gratitude floods our life with love, warmth, and light. In addition, when we are grateful and acknowledge the goodness and grace inherent in life, we harmonize with the higher frequencies of our soul and strengthen our eternal connection with the Divine.

Much like the industrious bees with translucent wings, journeying to distant realms, we, too, can joyfully harvest the honey of the future. When we gratefully gaze at the clear skies and dark clouds with the innocence, joy and awe of a child, we plant seeds of the future that will one day blossom into a fragrant garden of love. Just as flowers dutifully follow their natural cycle of blossoming, blooming, wilting, and returning to the earth, we find ourselves humbled, falling to our knees in awe and wonder at the exquisite beauty of our own cyclical existence—*its privileges and its inevitable end.*

By shifting our gaze from the mundane to the profound, everything becomes more radiant, vibrant, and stunningly alive.

Of course, when skies are clear and everything goes our way, it is easier to see the good and be grateful. On the other hand, when shrouded in darkness, drowning in despair, or overcome by the seeming futility of life, it is just as easy to become bitter, angry, or hopeless. Though it may be difficult to understand, even these darker times are part of the joyous experience of being human. Indeed, everyone, without exception, will pass through their own version of the dark night.

Having said that, please know that we are not feeble, helpless beings, forever lost in the darkness; the opposite is true. We are radiant children of the loving universe, the progeny of God. In truth, we are powerful spiritual beings, born of love and made of light. The very instant we call out into the black abyss, all the angelic forces of Heaven and Earth come rushing to our side. When we surrender to the will of God, we align ourselves with elevated energetic possibilities far beyond the confines of our limited consciousness. The slightest shift in our thoughts changes everything; one genuinely positive thought or movement of love can redirect our life forever.

In our surrender of smallness, we are granted greatness.

Though it sounds simple, it can be challenging for many to let go of their belief in separateness and smallness. It takes a certain amount of spiritual development and wisdom to even consider surrendering our will to a higher power. Nonetheless, this conscious decision to be joyful and see the good from a place of gratitude, shifts our energy, aligning us with completely different possibilities and opening doors for previously unavailable potentialities and subsequent realities.

Apart from gratitude and joy, another path to soul expansion, equanimity, inner peace and contentment is found in the Buddhist teaching of non-attachment: *True inner peace is found in being peaceful even in the absence of peace.* Often it is our resistance to discomfort that amplifies our suffering. Accepting and even embracing our uneasiness is the first step in transcending it.

We find peace and serenity through the art and practice of non-attachment. As a result, we are able to transcend the confines of our pain, opening the door to an unmoving state of equanimity. When we do not demand that life shows up in any other way than it is right now, we stop needlessly suffering. Then rather than wasting our precious life force by fighting against the wind, we conserve our energy, make the best of any situation, and become a force of good. Another way to find peace, joy and tranquility is to accept life on life's terms, embracing our ability to feel deeply, even when it is painful and hurts.

To be truly alive is to cry all our tears and to laugh all our laughter.

To feel all of our emotions and feelings without judging them as good or bad provides space and depth to an otherwise hollow and narrow existence. Our every thought, emotion, and intention emit an invisible energy field. Though not visible to the naked eye, this field of energy is palpable and real. Over time, our consistent energetic state manifests as emotionally driven thoughts and feelings that attract more of the same.

To better understand this concept, think about tuning into a particular radio station, in the same way that with the click of a knob, we can change stations; a small shift in our thoughts can change our reality. As soon as we change our thoughts, feelings, and emotions, we attract different realities and subsequent outcomes.

This is important, for when we alter our internal emotional state, we inevitably alter the energy we project, thus affecting the conditions of our lives, and the circumstances we attract.

By embracing our emotions, from the depths of sorrow to the heights of joy, we deepen our connection to the Divine.

To maintain an inner state of tranquility amidst life's storms is not something natural for most of us; it is a skill nurtured through intention and practice. When we are able to bring divinity into life's simplest and most complex moments, inner peace and joy are the result. With continued devotion, even life's greatest challenges cannot move us from our center or dampen our joy. Every experience, from a warm cup of coffee to the rhythm of bustling traffic, becomes a testament to life's profound beauty and intricacies.

In the cultivation of inner peace, our world transforms into a realm of harmony and joy.

The journey towards inner peace is much like the unpredictable flow of a river, sometimes the river is wild and unruly, while at other times, it is as calm as a warm summer day. Even great luminaries of the past were not strangers to life's ever-changing weather. The universe, in its benevolent wisdom, may test our resolve, reminding us that growth is a continuous and ongoing process.

In the calm and chaos of life, our breath can recenter and ground us. Each breath is an opportunity to release emotions, recalibrate, and realign with our divine nature. When life is frightening and dark, our breath can serve as a mantra and a silent affirmation of our resilience, anchoring us back to our joyful connection with the Divine.

Another powerful tool of inner peace is the practice of grounding. In the modern, technological world of emails, text, computer screens, high-speed Internet, and smartphones, many have lost their connection with the healing quality of the natural world.

Deep diaphragmatic breath calms the body, heals the mind, and soothes the soul.

Walking barefoot or even just visualizing roots extending from the bottom of our feet to the earth's core can help anchor our energy and make us feel more centered and connected. The simple act of grounding our energy has far-reaching benefits for the body, mind, and spirit. As we reconnect with Mother Earth, we get out of our heads and back into our breath and bodies, calming the central nervous system. The calming effect of the breath opens a joyful path to the Divine.

In every breath, we have the freedom to move toward or away from love.

Though we cannot control external events such as other people, places, and things, we have complete dominion over our reactions. The breath calms the central nervous system and facilitates staying in our center. When we consciously choose to be peaceful about not being peaceful, we reclaim our decisive power. Then, rather than fighting the darkness, we become a light, a candle in the night, and a blessing to all.

The decision to not wage war, be it with another or within oneself, conserves the energy typically drained by such confrontations. Though staying peaceful amid life's highs and lows sounds wonderful, it is not necessarily easy. Unfortunately, most of us are emotionally driven, enslaved by our habitual ways, and at the mercy of the good or bad behavior of others. With the slightest gust of wind in one direction or the other, emotions flood our bodies with a sudden storm of joy or a deluge of sorrow.

Like clouds, feelings come and go, best not to get attached. Some feelings are soft and fluffy, while others are dark and heavy. Just as clouds drift across the sky, our feelings ebb and flow within us. But clouds are just clouds, and feelings are just feelings; they come and go like the wind.

No emotion, no matter how intense, lasts forever.

Often, we become attached or repelled by our feelings, making us emotionally reactive to life's internal or external climate. This reactiveness is usually rooted in intense feelings of victimism and entitlement. And again, according to the Buddha, the best solution to our natural inclination to be swept away by life's storms is to follow the middle way of equanimity.

The art of non-attachment frees us from the bondage of pleasure and pain.

Rather than reaching for life's heights or resisting its depths, we maintain our inner peace and tranquility by holding a neutral space of acceptance and faith. We reclaim our power when we approach life with discernment, conscious awareness, and love. By allowing the dark clouds and sunny days to drift by without a push or pull towards or away, we are no longer a slave to the ever-changing weather of life.

In addition, when we recognize our own impermanence, every moment becomes full with meaning and heightened with purpose. Everything, including our emotions and experiences, has a beginning, a middle, and an end. Therefore, letting go of our attachments and preferences allows life to show up as it does, and we stop suffering. We are no longer ensnared by the emotional intensity of feelings or the gravitational pull of emotions. With practice, instead of clinging to nebulous feelings or orchestrating a good or bad story about life, we can observe our thoughts, feelings, and circumstances from a place of serenity and peace. As we cultivate the ability to observe our thoughts and emotions, without being entangled in them, we free ourselves from the dark allure of desire.

Over time, through the utilization of breath and mindfulness, we learn to respond to life's challenges with joy, peace, and equanimity. Then rather than reacting out of fear, habit, or impulse, we can make more conscious choices rooted in the high vibrational frequency of unconditional love.

Just as the vastness of the sky remains unaffected by passing clouds, our essential nature is unaffected by the transient emotions and experiences of life.

In a world of constant change, these teachings guide us to find stability without unnecessary resistance. Balancing presence with non-attachment brings freedom from life's ever-changing weather, grounding us in tranquility, equanimity, and yes, the innate joy of the universe.

Peace is not the absence of storms but the capacity to remain calm amid them.

From the serene vantage point of non-attachment, we recognize the difference between the restless mind and the silent observer. The mind is tumultuous, laden with emotions, swinging toward or away from the present moment, often causing fear and distress. Conversely, the silent observer is at the helm of our consciousness, anchored in tranquility and undisturbed by the ebb and flow of life. As the silent observer, through the practice of non-attachment, we reclaim our power and are no longer enslaved by life's inner or outer noise. Then it is possible to be more conscious and discerning on an ongoing basis.

As conscious observers of our own existence, we meet each moment, tragic or beautiful, with acceptance, non-attachment, and most importantly, with an underlying sense of joy. In the cultivation of this joyful state of balance and equanimity, we are no longer dragged around by the whims of our emotions or the fleeting nature of our feelings. Instead of being whipped around by the winds of change, we stand firm and hold our ground through life's ever changing seasons.

Our inner tranquility is rooted in our ability to embrace whatever life offers, free from attachment to any specific outcome.

We cultivate a space where joy, tranquility, and peace can grow and flourish by witnessing emotions and understanding their transient nature. This awareness is not detachment. Rather, it is a profound and insightful connection to the unchanging nature of the divine, permeating all of existence.

Indeed, the unalterable joy of the divine reminds us that we are more than our momentary feelings or challenges; we are the unmoving witness of our own existence and the silent observer of our lives. When we adopt this witness consciousness and observer perspective, rather than reacting impulsively, we respond to life with greater joy, love, and intentionality.

The practice of non-attachment and acceptance is a journey of patience and commitment—*standing firm, even when everything comes tumbling down*. With time, the chaos becomes less daunting, replaced by a knowing that everything works together for the good of the individual and the benefit of all. Through this profound understanding, and by purposefully choosing to live a more conscious life, we become a force of grace and goodness.

To see the good and to be the good brings more goodness.

The path paved with conscious intent is a luminous stairway to heaven, guiding us towards the Divine. Each step we take with loving intent bridges the distance between Heaven and Earth. And yes, in the dark shadow of yesterday, another flower is joyously born today, and on and on it goes.

As we come to the close of this Love Letter, please know that these words were meant solely for you. In a joyous celebration of our unending bond of love, I wrote them for you. Our joyful reunion is the most blissful possibility of the loving universe.

Our meeting again in this life was as inevitable and joyful as the wind carrying busy bees with gossamer wings to far-off places while fragrant flowers blossom and bloom in the radiant light of the summer sun.

It is my greatest joy in this life, and all lives, to find you again.

Love without limits.
Eternally yours.
— Chrystal Rae

In our surrender of smallness, we are granted greatness

If nothing changes, nothing changes

letter 4
change
do something different

This is a pivotal moment in your life and lives; boundless potential stretches before you, offering profound opportunities for personal growth, evolution, and transformative change.

It is time for you to become a more joyous version of yourself. Time to liberate yourself from recurrent cycles of pain and suffering. It's time to be free and truly happy. You have been preparing for many lives, and now you are ready for an exponential change in consciousness. You are ready to shine brighter and to live a more abundant, joyful life. While there is not a one-size-fits-all approach to a more joyful and abundant life, achieving it is more attainable than it might initially seem. Einstein's wisdom rings true. We cannot solve a problem with the same mindset that gave rise to it. If we want something different, we have to do something different.

If nothing changes, nothing changes.

Most of the time, the process of change pulls us out of the familiar and leaves us in a state of uncertainty.

For lasting change, we must summon the courage to venture beyond the confines of the known and comfortable, challenging what we believe to be true and possible.

Nonetheless, change can be unsettling and sometimes, even painful, testing our resolve. While we may genuinely desire to change our circumstances, the people in our lives, or the places we inhabit, embarking on this journey and keeping our commitment can prove to be monumental.

When confronted by life's formidable challenges, many people surrender without even attempting to take the first step. In the midst of looming storms and darkened skies, it's only natural to feel paralyzed by fear and engulfed by uncertainty.

In our journey toward profound personal change and lasting transformation, it's essential to nurture our inner wellspring of strength and firmly maintain our resolve when confronting life's formidable challenges. We embark on this journey with the understanding that, at times, our deepest fears may cast long shadows. Yet, it is precisely in these moments of fear's looming presence that we find the crucible in which we forge our transformation, persevering with unwavering determination.

For true transformation and enduring change, we must be bold and unwavering in our resolve.

Personal transformation is a unique and individual journey, and it typically requires time, effort, and commitment. There are no instant solutions or shortcuts when it comes to real and lasting personal growth. While we might long for a miraculous intervention or a rescuing hand, life requires that we take proactive steps towards our own salvation. On the rare occasions that a hero arrives and miraculously fixes all our problems, challenges inevitably resurface, reminding us of the indispensable power of choice we possess as sentient beings. We did not come into this world of form and structure to be passive spectators or to let another dictate our soul's journey.

Personal autonomy and self-reliance are the foundation upon which true transformation is built.

While we all draw strength from the love, support, and guidance of others, excessive dependency, neglecting our innate desires, or surrendering to indecision can erode our personal autonomy. In this state, we become susceptible, subject to the ebb and flow of external forces. Disregarding our inner wisdom and the authentic yearnings of our soul for autonomy and self-expression inadvertently stifles our innate potential and personal evolution.

Genuine authenticity and empowerment arise from embracing our desires, making purposeful choices, and wholeheartedly shouldering responsibility for our actions and their profound implications. When we align with truth, take full ownership of our choices, and fully embrace the responsibility for our lives, we not only reclaim our inherent power but also reshape our destiny and redirect the course of our future.

Even in the midst of uncertainty, the gift of choice and personal autonomy remains our most cherished possession. As previously mentioned, if all our problems were miraculously solved, we would inevitably create new ones. Our soul thrives on deciphering challenges, discovering its unique life purpose, and forging its own path—*this is a journey only we can undertake; no one can do it for us.*

We alone direct the path of our soul; not even our angels, teachers, guides, nor God, will intervene.

Nonetheless, without the grace of a loving universe, no one would make it through a single day of existence, much less the dark night of the soul. Our earthly journey often leads us into uncharted territories of the soul and unexplored realms of the heart, demanding not just courage but also unwavering resolve and determination. Facing the unknown can be daunting, yet it is precisely within these untapped realms that our true potential unfolds, urging us to rise and meet our higher selves. The winds of change are ceaseless, and the world does not stop spinning for our convenience. Regardless of our readiness or reservations, life's onward procession continues.

In its infinite wisdom, the loving universe does not allow for a vacuum or void.

When we become passive or indecisive, the loving universe takes charge, *sometimes with a subtle hint and at other times with an undeniable push, challenging us to explore, adapt, and evolve.* These purposeful proddings from the loving universe frequently manifest as unexpected events, crises, tragedies, or losses, compelling us to confront rapid and perhaps unforeseen changes.

While we may not have control over every aspect of life, our response to its challenges remains firmly within our grasp. Inner peace and true contentment are not tied to life's unpredictable weather or ever-changing seasons. To embrace the present moment without attachment or the need for change requires continual practice.

Life presents us with two fundamental choices: love or fear.

We can seek out the goodness and grace inherent to life, and purposefully choose to be the light. Or, we can sink into the shadows, get lost in the darkness, and live in doubt. *Everything is available and allowed in the loving universe—and we get to choose.* With that in mind, a true transformation is a deliberate act of progressively making more enlightened choices, marked by renewed clarity and vigor. Most of the time, sustainable change is not an impulsive dive into the unknown; rapid shifts may be too taxing on the soul. Instead, it's preferable to move at the pace of grace with conscious intention.

Just as one foot follows the other in a steady progression, authentic transformation unfolds through mindful, gradual shifts of consciousness.

Personal development and spiritual growth demand more than mere wishful thinking; conscious transformation and change call for active participation. Recognizing our impulsive or restless behavior isn't enough. *As mentioned, we must do something different if we want something different.* Merely hoping for different outcomes while repeating the same actions is futile. The comfort of familiarity can bind us, making it hard to shed old habits. However, grace is forever within our reach and the entire universe is always there to support us. Grounding ourselves in spiritual truths, tapping into our innate wisdom, and advancing with deliberate intent set the stage for personal and collective transformation. While the allure of rapid or drastic change can be tempting, wisdom teaches the value of patience, discernment, and pacing.

Venturing into the depths of truth and wisdom not only open the door to boundless potential within our soul but also unveils hidden realms of possibility that transcend imagination.

With the exception of miraculous occurrences, our unfoldment doesn't usually happen overnight. Just like a seed requires time, care, and a nurturing environment to blossom, we also require time, space, and love for our spiritual unfoldment. Though we might wish for instant enlightenment or sudden transformation, the most profound shifts often happen quietly, gradually, in small moments of clarity and realization.

Every step toward a more loving existence reaffirms our connection with the Divine, opening the door for genuine and lasting change. The universe showers us with serendipitous signs and undeniable synchronicities, assuring us that we're not alone. Staying open, watchful, and thankful for these gentle prompts is crucial: the more awareness we bring, the more miracles abound.

Our personal transformation is a delicate dance between free will and divine guidance.

Staying anchored in spiritual truths makes our earthly journey deeply fulfilling. Spiritual growth requires consistent, measured steps, as sudden leaps in consciousness may not endure. Rather than plunging recklessly into the unpredictable currents of change, when possible, it is prudent to begin gradually to avoid becoming overwhelmed. Even with a cautious approach, change can test our resolve, challenge our confidence, and may even make us question our faith. Indeed, embracing change takes courage, resolve and determination. This is especially true and relative when facing the unknown or uncertain.

The paradox of change is that it can trigger both excitement and apprehension; it can energize us and, at the same time, immobilize us. Sustainable change and true transformation are the step-by-step progressive journey. Though our small victories may seem insignificant, collectively, they define our journey upward. Cultivating a more positive outlook instead of dwelling on problems is the first step to change: shifting our consciousness and aligning us with more radiant possibilities. Again, because the universe will not allow for a void, when we change our habits and upgrade our energy, less radiant expressions will be replaced with more luminous choices.

Change pulls us from the past into an undiscovered future always alive within the present moment. In the ongoing turbulence of life, personal transformation enriches our spiritual insight, crystallizes our purpose, and brings clarity to our decisions. Indeed, in a magnetic universe, we attract what we are, not necessarily what we want.

Under the law of attraction, our inner thoughts and feelings act as magnets, pulling in similar energies and experiences.

While our energetic alignments influence our life lessons and earthly experiences, they do not alter the inherent purity of our souls. By cultivating a positive inner state, we magnetize opportunities and draw insights within our current capacity to comprehend. Think of this selective alignment with specific outcomes and the absence of others as a complex math problem. While many solutions to an equation may exist, we may not be able to solve the problem with our current level of comprehension. Similarly, in the soul's journey, out of the vast array of choices, only those that harmonize with our current energetic alignments are available.

Life mirrors the intricate design of the universe.

When we are children, we gaze at the stars in the night sky with awe and wonder, oblivious to the vast complexities of the cosmos. As our knowledge grows, so does our comprehension of these celestial bodies. In the same way, our soul's journey toward enlightenment becomes more lucid with increased insight, wisdom, and experience. Nonetheless, just as an astronomer might stand before the night sky, feeling its infinity and his limited grasp of it, we, too, can feel overwhelmed by the magnitude of life's mysteries. This feeling of inadequacy and overwhelm does not mean that our efforts to understand are in vain; instead, it underscores the idea that our soul's capacity to learn and grow is infinite. In every moment, we are both the teacher and student of life, constantly learning from our environment, experiences, and the good and bad examples of others.

Our past, present, and future merge into the kaleidoscope of the Eternal Now.

Much like a radio set to a specific station, we will only receive signals that match our current bandwidth. At this moment, we may not be ready or equipped to comprehend the profundity of a particular lesson; however, tomorrow, next year, or a decade from now, as our inner landscapes shift and mature, answers will naturally rise to the surface of our consciousness.

Our understanding of life is a delicate dance between the known and the unknown. We often stand at the edge of our knowledge, hesitant and afraid, gazing into the dark abyss of the unknown. With time, patience, and the unfoldment of wisdom, we inch closer to the profound truths that await us. Our infinite souls remains pure and unchanged regardless of our earthly experiences or ability to comprehend the universe, God, or love. Our consciousness mirrors our personal choices, default decisions and energetic constitutions but doesn't diminish our inherent worth.

The pace of our evolution is directly related to our current stage of spiritual development.

Some of us are younger souls, while others carry the wisdom of ages. Wherever we currently find ourselves along the evolutionary path, each soul brings a unique perspective and light to the world. Every step in our spiritual evolution is a bridge to the next. Life unfolds sequentially, as does our evolution. Skipping any step or stage of the evolutionary process is not possible, as it would hinder the soul's growth and development.

Just as infants must first be cradled, then crawl, and eventually walk; our souls have their unique growth cycle. Younger souls, like babies, are often swayed by impulses and external conditions, lacking full autonomy. They react instinctively, need constant guidance, and lean on others. Recognizing and nurturing this inherent vulnerability with empathy for oneself and others is essential in our spiritual ascent. We will all pass through each evolutionary stage; only the pace may vary. We may sprint ahead or take a leisurely stroll. This variance is inherent in the evolutionary journey, but does not categorize us as either good or bad. Even if we momentarily lose our way or get lost in the darkness, it is all part of the divinity of our lives, inevitably leading back to the loving arms of God.

Our soul remains eternally pure and untouched by the experiences of a short human life.

The shadows and light gathered and discarded during the brief journey into and out of the transient world of form and matter pave the way for our ultimate transformation and realization. Immersing ourselves in the physical realm provides a unique perspective from distinctly different settings and lives, allowing us to deepen our understanding of ourselves, the universe, and our loving Creator. The distinctive experiences of each life, in conjunction with the cumulative impact of all our lives across time, cultivate self-awareness, personal evolution, and divine connection. Evolution is a *"remembrance"* of the innate and unchanging perfection of the soul. The soul is whole and immutable by nature; *it is timeless, boundless, and forever pure*. Nothing we experience in this world, or any other, alters the fundamental radiance of our being.

The foundation of the universe is love and more love.

Our short foray into the tangible world of form and structure is an act of sheer delight for the absolute wonder of seeing ourselves and the Divine anew with a rejuvenated perspective. The soul IS forever pure, perfect, and complete. Everything that IS, already IS. This all-encompassing love is expressed and experienced in infinite variations of shadow and light. As unique expressions of the creative God source, we exist for the pure and absolute joy of our experience. Together, through our gathered experiences, God is born and reborn in every possible expression of shadow and light. That which is most beautiful and necessary endlessly and joyfully comes into fruition, including your beautiful soul.

The source determines the seed.

God, as the pure embodiment of love, is the source of all existence. Everything that was, IS, or ever will be is a divine expression of God's love. Though shrouded in forgetfulness, our human sojourn is a quest to remember the innate and unchanging purity of the soul. New and novel experiences enhance and enrich our understanding of self, others, and the universe. Every intention, fleeting thought, and movement through time and space is a glorious expression of love and more love.

The signature of each soul is distinct and essential to the unfoldment of God.

Contrary to many spiritual beliefs and religious teachings, there is no urgency to evolve, expand, or complete a particular life cycle. We are free to evolve and express at our own rhythm; it is perfectly okay to float along and enjoy the ride of being human for as long as it brings us joy. Our evolution does not follow a strict timeline; it unfolds as a serene exploration of love. Whatever brings the soul the most joy will manifest.

Even in the darkest of nights, there's a divine light serving the soul's longing for evolution and radiance. The universe is an endless realm where every potential patiently awaits our unique alignment and exploration. In time, we will all naturally and inevitably move toward our next most radiant version of self. All possibilities have already come to completion and every desire is already fulfilled in the *"Eternal Now"*. There is nothing new in the universe.

Within the vast expanse of time and space, every expression of love and light is poised to manifest, patiently waiting for us to arrive. Our current circumstances reflect our choices and decisions, echoing their lessons, gifts, and consequences. Yet, as our awareness deepens, once-closed doors suddenly open to reveal untapped possibilities. As previously mentioned, evolution is the sacred process of *"remembrance,"* and the rediscovery of our inherent and unchanging divinity. The natural unfoldment of consciousness is inevitable: only the path and timeline vary. Bearing this in mind, while evolution is a part of our journey, it is not our ultimate purpose: Love is our purpose.

Love is the meaning of life. Love is why we exist. And, love is why we are here.

However, love is never imposed upon us, dangled as a threat, or leveraged against us. We have the liberty and choice to stand still, retreat, move sideways, or advance along our individual and collective spiritual path. Our chosen path may be shadowed or bathed in light; either way, love does not change. We get to choose the roads we will travel; some will be muddy and dark, while others will be illuminated with light.

There is no wrong way to go; all roads lead home.

One road to God is no better than another; they are just different. A particular path that serves me may not serve you, and vice-versa. Ultimately, we are all drawn back into the loving embrace of the Divine; there is no rush or need to hurry. Everything unfolds in divine timing, orchestrated for the betterment of our soul and the greater good of all.

We began this chapter with the premise that *"if nothing changes, nothing changes."* Throughout our exploration, we've come to understand that the path of change and personal transformation isn't defined by grand gestures but rather by the consistent, intentional choices we make each day. With the more expansive view of the soul, one fundamental truth becomes abundantly clear:

Change requires our active participation in sustainable ways, guided by the benevolent universe. Shifting to brighter, more loving possibilities becomes less daunting when we consistently choose love in small and big ways. Want friendship? Extend it. Seek integrity? Live your truth.

True transformation begins from within.

These patterns repeat across countless scenarios, underscoring the simple yet profound principle that for genuine, enduring change, with love as our guiding light, we must take the first step and follow through with our good intentions. In the simplest gestures of love and kindness, vast universes of unprecedented opportunity are born and realized. A single act of love and kindness creates a ripple effect that reverberates throughout the entire universe, changing paradigms and shifting timelines.

Love is a universal language.

Indeed, when we receive love and kindness, we are more likely to pay it forward. This chain reaction can reach far beyond the initial gesture. An act of love and kindness, especially during challenging times, can shift our perspective, give us hope, and forever change our lives; it also fosters a sense of community and belonging, breaking down barriers and building trust.

Though the saying that *"Hurt people, hurt people"* is a valid statement, the opposite is also true: *"Healed people heal people"*. Another often-overlooked gift of personal healing is the transformative impact it has beyond our own lives. As we travel along the path of self-healing, we inadvertently become a beacon of hope for others. Our very presence will be a potent force for healing, positively influencing those around us. In addition, when we are treated with love and kindness, we are more likely to do the same. Love serves as a bridge that transcends all boundaries, connecting us and deepening our understanding of one another, God, and the universe.

Love's vibrational power is so potent that merely witnessing acts of love and compassion inspires us to embody them. Every small stride taken toward more love, compassion, and service contributes to meaningful change in the world. This truth is a testament to the fact that each individual holds the power to make a difference. No matter how seemingly insignificant our actions may seem, every step, whether toward or away from love, sends ripples throughout the vast universe, leaving a lasting impact on our souls, creation, and even the Divine.

If we truly understood the magnificence of a single breath of life, we would never waste another valuable moment or opportunity to choose love or be kind.

Nonetheless, many of us are trapped by the daily grind, prioritizing success over soul and wealth over depth. In this race, we often miss life's deeper purpose, finding only emptiness in our accumulation. Material rewards always fall short; only love can fulfill us. Unfortunately, the fleeting nature of life often escapes our awareness until we stand at the precipice of our own mortality.

Death comes as night follows day; no one escapes it.

In the grand tapestry of time, even a century is a mere stitch. In a heartbeat, we come into existence, and in another we prepare for our journey back to the loving arms of God. We blink, and we are born; we blink again, and it's time for us to go home. It is time to reassess, rest, and recover. Following the recalibration of our soul, we embark on yet another life, where we encounter diverse scenarios with similar life lessons.

These repetitive lessons are not punitive measures or karmic retribution but pathways for our soul's ultimate enlightenment. To be reborn and provided with another opportunity to continue our soul's evolution is a profound gift. It allows us not only to live and relive experiences previously understood only through inference but also to transcend them.

It is a grand privilege to experience the *"Self"* within the context of a human life. We are not victims of our circumstances; we direct the course of our lives, consciously or not. Even in surrendering decisions to others, the choice remains ours. We are the authors of our own story; at any moment, we can rewrite the script, change the plot, rework the storyline, reselect the characters, and re-imagine the narrative and story of our lives.

We can change our lives right now by simply making different choices, more loving choices. We have been doing this all along, often without realizing the weight and consequences of our choices. Once awakened to our ability to impact reality, change the world and re-frame our personal stories, we can make more meaningful and loving choices.

We have boundless, untapped potential to change ourselves and the world.

The conscious choice of love over fear reshapes our history, redefines our present, and re-imagines our future. Our personal autonomy is vital for our souls' growth. The stories we tell ourselves become true, *even if they are false*. Bearing this in mind, we are far more powerful than most of us realize. With conscious intent, we can shift our narrative, pivot our journey, fast-track our growth, and redefine ourselves. This mindful recalibration nurtures our spirit and sends reverberations of healing and light throughout the loving universe.

When we heal ourselves, we heal the world; our personal empowerment empowers all.

Our presence alone becomes a healing force. By healing our wounds and reclaiming our personal autonomy, we empower all those who have been in similar life circumstances, or who have suffered the same trauma that once bound us. Nevertheless, on our journey of enlightenment, we may take two steps forward and one back; that's how the soul's finds balance. Just as nature has its seasons, we go through cycles of growth, rest, and renewal.

The pace of our progress is less important than the tidbits of wisdom and shards of light we collect and share along the way. The intricate and vast human experience serves as an ideal space for the soul to mature and flourish. Each breath is an exploration of our unchanging Divinity within the context of love and in the space of personal autonomy and choice. Our spiritual sojourn is an eternal dance from twilight's mystery to dawn's clarity.

The interplay of joy and sorrow is a catalyst for our spiritual development.

Transformational fires burn with intensity in moments of expansion, driving rapid evolution. In simpler terms, during difficult times of significant adversity, hidden opportunities for remarkable growth emerge. Indeed, there are lives where burdens become so overwhelming that they hinder our personal growth. On the other extreme, in some of our more joyful and abundant lives, we may become complacent or stagnant.

Though seemingly idle, these very different life experiences provide a space for self-reflection and serve as essential groundwork for the forthcoming, more demanding chapters of our future destiny.

Life is not a test we can pass or fail; our mere existence is a testament to triumph.

Please allow me to elaborate. Sometimes, following a more challenging life, our soul craves the peace of a gentler existence. On the other hand, after a long, peaceful life, we may intentionally seek out a life of more intensity with deeper lessons. Throughout each phase of our spiritual journey, we are infinitely cherished, eternally embraced, and unconditionally loved. Our soul family, celestial guardians, spiritual guides, and revered teachers are always present, silently supporting us and illuminating our path. Regardless of where we find ourselves on our spiritual journey, we are always precisely where we are meant to be.

Whether we realize our soul's aspirations in this particular life or not is of no great consequence in the grand scheme of our evolutionary journey. The success of the soul is not contingent on achieving a specific goal within a single lifetime; it serves as the baseline and starting point for our soul's ongoing evolutionary process. More directly, you, my dear, are a radiant manifestation of the universe's grandeur and the boundless love of God. You emerged from the depths of nothingness as a natural progression of that which is most beautiful and cherished. You are a divine realization of God's boundless grace and limitless love. Having said that, please know, please know that although the soul is forever pure and unchanged, within the scope of a brief human existence, our personal agency carries profound significance. Even a subtle shift in the compass of our consciousness ushers us into entirely new territories, intersections, and opportunities for soulful growth.

Embodying greater love, compassion, and kindness catalyzes profound transformation.

As we reconfigure our thoughts, we reshape our minds, transform our lives, and bathe our souls in radiant illumination. Like the unpredictable course of a river, the human experience presents us with many unexpected and divergent opportunities. However, within this unpredictability rests our ultimate power: *the power of perception and response*. Similar to a river that may transition between moments of serenity and turbulence, we also harbor the capacity for unpredictability and radical transformation.

We cannot control the course of the ever widening river of life, yet our dance upon its waters is of our own creation.

Every ripple and wave within the current of life extends an invitation for us to either gracefully flow with their rhythm or resist their inexorable pull. The choice, as always, remains ours to make. Our lives mirror the unpredictable nature of existence, where everything is in constant flux, and nothing is set. Each moment offers us a choice *to engage, retreat, embrace, or resist*. In the whirling waves and rough currents of a human life, we find our strength, learning that true mastery is not in controlling the waters but in steering our vessel with grace.

One of the most significant lessons of the human experience is the realization that there is beauty in both the depths and the shallows of our temporal existence and fleeting lives.

Evolution is a question of "when" and not "if".

Each choice directs our spiritual sojourn back to the divine embrace of God's love. Taking responsibility and stewardship of our lives hastens our journey of enlightenment. Yet, such luminescence doesn't absolve us from life's inherent pain.

Many times, profound suffering is the crucible for our soulful metamorphosis. Bearing this in mind, as you immerse yourself in the wisdom of these Love Letters, know that you stand on the precipice of great change and soul expansion. While deeper insight does not grant us immunity from life's trials and tribulations, it serves as a cushion, offering a helping hand to lift us from the ashes of our pain. In the fire of our own discomfort, we uncover the resilience of the human spirit, learning to embrace both the joys and sorrows of existence.

Every time we choose love over fear, we make the world a better place.

In the vast expanse of our being, suffering is but a small fragment within our soul's evolutionary journey of *"remembrance."* As we progress along our spiritual path, pain and suffering gradually relinquish their roles as our primary instructors. Much like a single candle that instantly dispels the darkness, the growing luminosity of the soul ushers in a brighter and more radiant experience. Although life may repeatedly confront us with similar painful circumstances, choosing to act from a place of love instead of fear elevates our consciousness.

This transformation in our worldview empowers us to navigate even the most daunting situations with increased grace and resilience. By embracing love as our guiding principle, we not only alter our personal experiences but also contribute to a more harmonious world.

Furthermore, even as we encounter similar challenging circumstances, we can consciously choose to avoid additional suffering and the temptation to dwell in negativity that impedes our personal evolution. Rather than defaulting to reactions of aggression or defensiveness, we will naturally incline towards a more loving, compassionate, and peaceful way of being. This shift in our approach not only alleviates our own struggles but also fosters a more understanding and harmonious environment around us

Thoughts, words, and actions born of love and compassion ripple out as positivity, shaping the future and impacting many lives.

This Love Letter concludes with a powerful affirmation: our ability to shape our lives is a testament to our potential to create a more beautiful, harmonious world. I will leave you with the following treasury of energetic tools, a sacred cache of wisdom to light your earthly journey. Each element, a pearl of insight, guides your soul homeward, revealing profound truths and your soul's intrinsic worth. Indeed, in each pearl of wisdom lies a universe of understanding, waiting to be discovered. These tools, though simple, unlock deep insights through reflection, rippling through creation and forging transformative waves. May these pearls of wisdom illuminate your path as you embark on your soul's majestic journey in and beyond the physical realm. Embrace this journey with an open heart, knowing each step taken is a part of a larger, intricate tapestry of existence, woven with the threads of your experiences, dreams, and aspirations.

This collection is not just a guide; it's a reflection of the limitless possibilities within you, a reminder of the light you carry within, ready to brighten the world.

The Radiant Self

1. Practice Gratitude: Embrace life's beauty with reverence.

2. Listen to Your Inner Knowing: Tune in to your soul's whispers.

3. Realize Your Self-Worth: You are a beloved child of the universe.

4. You Matter: Your light is essential to creation.

5. Trust the Love that Created You: Your existence is a testament to divine love.

6. No one Will Be Left Behind: Love ensures no one is abandoned.

7. Make Small Changes: Quantum shifts begin with tiny steps.

8. Choose Joy: It's not just an emotion; it's your essence.

9. Be Patient with the Process: Evolution follows divine timing.

10. Know that God Loves You: There is great love here for you, and all is well.

May these loving words and this inspirational list guide you toward greater love and radiance, unlocking the boundless potential of your radiant soul.

I love you.
– Chrystal Rae

One loving choice changes everything

*You are loved more than you could possibly imagine,
and all is well with your beautiful soul*

Letter 5
love
let me count the ways

Let's talk about love.

Have I told you today that I love you? Well, I do. My soul profoundly loves your soul. Throughout all of eternity, I have always loved you, and I always will. I love you with all my heart, my soul, and everything I am. I love you in the pure, unfiltered way of a child, to the farthest reaches of the night sky and beyond. I love you with the gentleness of butterfly kisses, a radiance that rivals the Sun, and the brightness of a thousand stars.

My love for you goes beyond mere words: *it is an all-encompassing embrace, a love born of the deepest parts of my soul.* Words fall short; whatever I say will never be enough. The magnitude of my love is beyond measure; it is a force, a light, a boundless energy that will forever find you. The loud and clear voice of this love echoes from the highest mountains to the deepest valleys; it is an arrow aiming straight for your heart.

Though repetition might dull the sentiment of my words, I will keep professing my love for you, reminding you of our profound connection, eternal bond, and undying love.

Every time I say I love you, I love you even more.

Please allow my words to seep into the depths of your being as if you were hearing them for the very first time: *I love you.* I love you without conditions or reservation. I love the real you. I love the you beneath the earthly disguise, the you beyond pretense or facade. I love every facet of you—

the light and dark, the beautiful and flawed, the truth and lies. There is nothing about you that is not embraced by my love. My love is greater than any words that I could speak. It is beyond description, transcending the limits of language.

My declaration of love may still surprise you. How I or anyone, in this earthly realm could love you so profoundly may be perplexing. The answer is simple, though perhaps not obvious. I love you because you are you. I love everything about you: your beautiful soul, the divine spark that created you, and the love that is you. There is no need of context for this love, and there is no grand reason either—*I simply love you*. There is no one like you in the entire universe, nor will there ever be. In my heart you are irreplaceable and singular. You are a bright star in the black of my night, a courageous warrior of the soul, a radiant being of light, and a cherished child of the loving universe.

You are loved far more than you could possibly imagine, and all is well.

These words and this all-encompassing love have found you again because you needed to know that a love like this exists, that I love you, and more importantly, that God loves you. The love that sourced these words is beyond comprehension: it is a vast, timeless and eternal love. You are not forgotten, forsaken, or alone. God is with you. I am with you, and your spiritual family of angels, guides, and teachers are also with you. They stand by your side, forever watching over you with great care, love, and compassion.

God does, indeed, move in mysterious ways. My presence in your life attests to the wondrous and unpredictable movement of the Divine.

God is alive and love is real.

Love is often misunderstood in the context of the modern world. We view love as conditional, transactional, and fleeting. However, the opposite is true: love is unchanging, free, and eternal.

Love can't be bought, borrowed or stolen. Love is ubiquitous in the universe, and it is our very essence. Love simply loves for the sake of loving and for no other purpose. Love gives of itself freely and asks for nothing in return. Regardless of the ever-changing circumstances of our lives, and irrespective of the good or bad behavior of others, love is an unwavering constant,

Love is o sturdy anchor of safety in the stormy seas of life, tethering us to the Divine.

This collection of Love Letters will remind you of what your soul already knows to be true. Love is a manifestation of God, pure and untainted, and it is your birthright. Nonetheless, in this world of dark shadows and flickering lights, we will all face moments where love seems absent, the night seems endless, and hope seems empty. It is in these very moments of desperation and despair that love is of the greatest comfort and support.

When we awaken to the love within, we discover the strength to embrace life's challenges with peace, wisdom, and grace.

In a loving universe, everything happens for our well-being and the benefit of all. Even the quiet rustle of leaves, the radiant light of stars, and the gentle hum of galaxies are whispers of the Divine and a gift to our souls.

Love is encoded into our very DNA and is the animating force of all life. Love fills the otherwise empty space of existence with purpose and meaning. Indeed, on the path of love, the temporal world is a wonderful and challenging backdrop for the soul's sacred journey. Nevertheless, in the cacophony of our daily lives with its societal pressures, the weight of mass consciousness, and the tumult of our very own thoughts, it is easy to lose sight of what really matters: *Love*.

Even in the depths of confusion and despair, the loving universe softly whispers to our soul, reminding us that we are never truly alone. In this light, the love pouring off these pages into your heart is meant to be a source of comfort, and to assure you that you are forever held in God's loving embrace. Bearing this in mind, these Love Letters transcend mere poetic verses or practical spiritual guidance; they serve as a magnetic compass, leading you toward the profound truth and love within your own soul. Along with our many shared past lives and those yet to be born in the future, this life is yet another step we will take together on our unending pilgrimage back to the sacred realm of the Divine.

The human endeavor, marked by both straight and crooked paths, ultimately guides us back to God's loving arms. Though we may stumble upon the unhealed wounds of bygone days, and yesterday's sorrows may unexpectedly emerge as unwelcome apparitions of the past, it is all part of a divine plan for our souls. Together, on the pages of this book, we will embark on this transformational healing journey, courageously trudging through the muddied yesterdays and more hopeful tomorrows with unwavering resolve.

The dynamic stillness of the Divine calms the turbulent waves of the temporal world, leaving only love and more love in its wake.

God's love is so radiant and alive that universes are born and divided in endless waves of undifferentiated light that we call life. Indeed, love is the simplest and most complex of human experiences; it is deeply personal and universally shared. Some say love is the glue that binds us, while others believe it is the very space that separates us. Either way, love reminds us of our eternal connection to each other, the vast universe, and our loving Creator.

Love is the journey, the destination, and the path back to God.

Love is the very essence of who we are. It is an infinite force stretching beyond the horizon of the known into the nebulous realm of the unknown. Love is so intimate to our being it pulses with every beat of our heart. Many have sought to capture love's fragrant bloom in poetry, music, and art. While these endeavors bring us closer to love's unsolvable mysteries, they can only offer a glimpse.

To truly know love, we must embody it.

Love is not an intellectual experience or a creation of the mind. Love is a joyful movement of radiant energy lived and expressed through thoughts, words and actions. Love is a gentle kindness that enlivens and enriches all our relationships—*including, and most importantly, our relationship with ourselves*.

Love transcends the fleeting nature of thoughts, feelings, and emotions. Love is an unmoving, profound connection to the Divine. Love is mirrored in both the ordinary and the extraordinary. Love stands alone without an opposite or definition. Love is the primal source of all that exists. Love is the foundation of the entire universe and everything in it, including you and me.

Nonetheless, in the veiled human condition of forgetfulness, it is common to confuse love with infatuation, which can bring intense emotional highs and lows. What is often perceived as heartbreak or the loss of a connection is in reality an attachment to an illusion and not love. Neither the highs nor lows of attraction or repulsion are the truth of the all-encompassing embrace of true love.

Both the brightest stars and the darkest nights are consumed in the transformative fire of love.

Love always loves, *no matter what*. There is no other possibility for love than to love. At times, love uplifts the wounded soul in a radiant celebration of exquisite joy and happiness, while, at other times, love forces us to grow and find resilience through the lack of light or the black intensity of night. These shadows are not merely dark spots to be feared or avoided; they are opportunities for profound growth and understanding that otherwise may not be available.

The challenges of a physical embodiment deepen our understanding of the truth of the loving universe and our role in it.

As we embrace the depth and width of love, our heart opens to the beauty and complexity of human emotions in all their nuanced glory.

In our earthly sojourn, we often contend with what appears to be the dual nature of love. This is particularly prevalent in romantic relationships that can quickly shift from moments of ecstasy to the depths of despair. Beyond these temporal experiences lies the unconditional, unchanging, and eternal love of God. The ultimate truth of God's love transcends all seeming dualities.

Love is the container that contains everything, including itself.

This love, God's love, calls us home, back to our most authentic selves. It is a love that does not demand, judge, or expect; it simply IS. In the presence of God's radiant love, all barriers dissolve, all wounds heal, and all souls find peace.

As we ponder the vast profundity of love, let's remember that love is not something to be dissected or understood but to be felt, celebrated, experienced, and revered. Our existence is a testament to the boundless love of the universe. Our very breath is an echo of God's all-encompassing love. Each moment, from the first ray of light to the darkest point of night, is an expression of love. In times of doubt, fear, or loneliness, we can find solace and strength in the unending and unchanging love of the Divine. Indeed, we are born of love for the purpose of love, and we shall return to love as more love: what happens in between is the shared experience of our lives.

For clarity's sake, please allow me to speak directly to your beautiful soul. You are a beloved child of the loving universe, *a glorious manifestation of God's unending love.* You are the essence of goodness, the softness of grace, and the perfection of imperfection. You are meant to be you; there is no other possibility for your beautiful soul. Just as the ocean can only be the ocean, the mountain can only be the mountain, and the desert can only be the desert: you, my dearest, can only be you. Do you realize your vital role in the grand unfoldment of creation? You are so essential that nothing would exist without you. Can you grasp the boundless nature of God's love, a love beyond definition, measure, or words? How can you know the unknowable? Indeed you are so very loved that all the forces of Heaven and Earth brought these words and this love to your beautiful heart and soul.

Love shines forth from the farthest reaches of the vast universe as a radiant all-encompassing light, leaving no star untouched and no soul forever lost in the darkness.

Indeed every fallen cherry blossom holds within it the power of a thousand storms. As our stories unfold, we discover the depth of our own existence, the interconnectedness of our souls, and the grandeur of God's eternal love. Alone we are but a drop, yet together, we are the vast ocean. Our individual growth is a soft breeze that brushes through the entire forest. Our healing is a single note that harmonizes with all of creation. Unconditional love heals and empowers both the giver and the receiver.

Everything affects everything, and everyone affects everyone. What you do affects me, and vice versa. Much like cascading dominoes, our actions have far-reaching effects that continue beyond the known and obvious.

We are all connected in love: one thing inevitably leads to another, rippling out ad infinitum.

Our every thought, word, and action is an energetic wave that creates and destroys universes in an instant. The collective human experience is an expression of God's infinite love. Bearing this in mind, you can be sure that our paths have crossed again as a result of our shared resonance and similar energetic frequencies. Within the endless dance of cause and effect, our meeting was not only probable, it was inevitable—*of this, I am sure because you are reading these words.*

These Love Letters transcend mere words on the page; they are whispers of the loving universe, and a love song from my soul to yours. They stand as the fulfillment of a sacred promise to eternally find each other. Every word, sentence, and paragraph within these writings is an exploration of the profound depths of our eternal bond of love. Throughout eternity, I have always been by your side. Even as our paths took different turns or our roads were divergent, our souls continued their whispered conversations.

Tethered by a luminous thread of iridescent light, we are inseparably united in love, a testament to an unbreakable bond that defies distance, time and space.

Even in your darkest moments, you were never truly alone; angels were always with you, their presence a gentle, loving constant. Alongside your soul family, teachers, and guides, I, too, was a shoulder to lean on and a comforting hand to hold. Time and again, I dried your salty tears, lit candles in the night, and gently lulled you into a peaceful sleep. Like the eternal dance of dawn and dusk, we are forever drawn towards each other in a loving embrace of surrender and allowance.

Our bond of love has been the silent constant throughout every heartfelt challenge, within every salty tear, and beyond every fleeting moment of joy. In a constantly changing world where nothing is fixed, our unbreakable bond of love is an unwavering force that forever draws us toward each other. Time and again, in the guise of different lives, we are forever reunited by our deep, unyielding love. The lack of certainty, the gamble against astronomical odds, gives our story an added richness and depth. Each decision, every coincidence, and every seemingly inconsequential moment played a part in orchestrating our meeting again in this life.

In the "oneness of love," we transcend individuality, merging into a timeless unity.

The eternal bond we share is a testament to the power of intent, the resilience of love, and the grand mystery of life. Our narrative is a rare gem in a universe filled with countless stories, an ode to serendipity, and love's enduring presence.

When you hear the words *"I love you"* fall from my lips, a long-lost lover has found you again. Our reunion is joyous and much celebrated in the heavens. When my thoughts and words extend to touch your soul, I embrace not just you but also the essence of my own self. In your eyes, I discover my reflection; your words carry the melody of my voice, and even your absence holds a visceral expression of your presence.

You are me, I am you, and we are one: One in love.

In a world of seeming opposites and separation, it is easy to see everyone and everything as "*the other*," distinct and apart. Without deeper contemplation, this makes sense, but it is not the ultimate truth. Every time we find each other, there is an unspoken recognition, a knowing that transcends the limitations of word and the movement of time.

Centuries of shared memories and lifetimes of laughter, tears, and dreams echo loudly in the depths of our souls. We are not just a chapter; we are an unending love story, a testament to the true timelessness of love. Though, at times, the world can feel empty and alien, our reunion collapses all fear and sorrow into the intimate space of love, and then even this dark world shines brighter. When you are near, the weight of solitude lifts, and I remember the truth of who I really am—*a beloved child of an omnipresent Creator*. No words are necessary in our shared silences. Every time our souls cross, I am reminded of a promise made eons ago: *to find each other again and again amidst the chaos of existence.*

You are the long-lost companion of my soul, the missing verse in the sacred song of my life, and you are the perpetual blossom of my love in bloom. In the fullness of existence, your presence is the very pulse of my heart. In a universe of endless possibilities, you are my chosen certainty, and my only reason to be. Indeed, in the ever-changing ocean of life, you are the unmoving ground beneath my feet. There has never been, nor will there ever be a moment when you were separate from me. Our every shared glance and whispered word deepens our endless bond of love.

Just as the Sun and its light are inseparable, so too are our hearts.

We are eternally united in the warmth and radiance of God's love. Our souls, distinct yet intertwined, sing an eternal song of love and connection. This love is an endless dance of divinity that is untethered, boundless and free. It is a profound unity expressed as you and me. Often the most riveting revelations of life emerge from the ordinary and mundane.

Every moment of existence is crucial, every encounter carries a profound purpose, and every soul, including your precious soul, is a divine expression of God's infinite love.

Even our soulful reunion is the orchestration of divinity and divine providence. Our reunion in this particular life is more than a simple chance or happenstance; it is living proof of our timeless bond of love. The love reaching out to you, in this very moment, is not an obscure sentiment or a mere philosophical notion. It is tangible, immediate, and deeply persona*l: I love you*. Please allow these three seemingly insignificant words to truly touch your soul and sink into the core of your being. Know that this love, *my enduring love for you*, is unconditional, boundless, and forever free. I love you when you are radiant and expansive, the most evolved expression of Self. I also love you when you judge yourself as guilty or fall short of your own best effort. In the transient world of form and matter, we all have our unique challenges and special gifts. Yet, through it all, love remains an ever-present constant.

Love asks for nothing, welcoming all with an open heart and a warm embrace, expecting nothing in return.

In this light, my greatest gift to you is my love. Yes, I love you—*no matter what*. My love for you does not falter or fade like the ever-changing seasons, it is eternal and deeply personal. Please do not gloss over these words or the loving sentiment they hold. Receive this love directly from my soul to yours; let it fill you with the healing light of unconditional love. Keep in mind that our purpose is not to attain perfection in this life; rather, we are here to consistently become the finest rendition of ourselves possible in every moment, *constantly learning, evolving, and expanding our consciousness*.

Give yourself and others the latitude to be human: fragile, strong, broken, beautiful, enlightened, and lost, all at the same time.

Life on Earth is a kaleidoscope of magical moments of joy and dark periods of adversity. At times, life can be an uphill battle where every step is harder than the one before. Even this is part of the divine plan for your soul, challenging you to persevere and expand in consciousness. On a more personal note, please allow me to speak directly to your soul. I know how hard it has been to keep your head above water, and I am so proud of all the work you have done. To meet you again in this life was a miracle in and of itself, but you made it, as did I. As previously noted, this is a pivotal and important life for you.

The sacred reunion of our souls is yet another footstep toward the Divine. So many things had to happen for us to meet again. Our reunion is the result of a heightened energetic resonance and the conscious movement of love. You are further along the evolutionary path than you may realize. However, this does not mean that you will never have a rainy day or that storms will never darken your skies.

A common misconception is that the more enlightened are shielded from hardship. Many envision those further along the spiritual path as constantly immersed in joy and untouched by pain or sorrow. The truth is more intricate and complex; growth frequently sprouts from adversity. Indeed, our challenges are seeds of growth and opportunities for self-reflection. Regardless of where we find ourselves on the evolutionary path, we all stand on equal ground and are equally loved. We are doing our best in every moment; the proof is that we didn't do any better or worse.

The human experience is framed by love, benevolence, and grace, yet it is not without trials and tribulations. Our paths are riddled with success and setbacks, but these are merely stepping stones leading us back to the Divine: *God's infinite grace and love cushions every misstep.* We are so loved that when we cry the space around us is dampened with the tears of the Divine, and when we are joyful the whole of creation celebrates with us. We are never alone, abandoned, or discarded.

In every moment, we are tenderly held by the unconditional love of the Divine.

Though we may not see them or recognize their divine presence, our soul family of angels, teachers and guides have always stood by our side with love and support, helping us to help ourselves. In this light, as one of your most significant soul companions of many lives, my presence is proof of my devotion and love for you. Though we may only meet on the pages of this book, my love is real and our bond is eternal.

With this in mind, please allow me to address those whom I may not encounter in this earthly existence. You can be assured that my affection for you is not contingent on physical proximity. Your soul and my soul are eternally interwoven in an unbreakable bond of enduring love.

We are multi-dimensional beings of light, connected in ways that science has yet to discover.

This concept might seem vast and overwhelming, so let's simplify it. Think about someone you deeply love or are intimately connected with—*a parent, mate, lover, dear friend, or child*. Even in their absence, the mere thought of them fills you with warmth, comfort, and joy. The essence of this love and connection is precisely how your soul family feels about you but on an even grander scale. They have loved and cherished you since time immemorial. With your spiritual guides, teachers, and soulmates there is no need for pretense.

Our soulmates, having known us through countless ages, have witnessed our every facet, both shadow and light, in vast variety of forms and manifestations, which only intensifies their love. We are not lonely travelers on a meaningless journey; we are all in this together, forever united and connected in love.

Each soul, including your beautiful soul, is the eternal unfoldment of love as more love.

While the material world offers a fraction of our identity, our true nature is vast, interconnected, and transcendent. As science delves deeper, it only begins to scratch the surface of the profound interconnectivity that binds us all. The boundaries we perceive are mere illusions, for in the grand tapestry of existence, every thread is interwoven, making us all an inseparable part of the whole.

What you are seeking is seeking you. ~ Rumi

In all we seek, love remains a constant and unchanging truth. Every act of love, whether marred by imperfections or resplendent with beauty is a reflection of the Divine. This revelation is the dawning of a new day and the cause for much celebration. For as we recognize our own divinity, our soul awakens. Then, even as life's storms rage, we are able to stand strong in the truth of God's unending love.

Love is both the question and the answer, guiding us through every uncertainty. Though this love may seem unwarranted or overwhelming; the opposite is true. You are worthy and ready to step into the next most radiant version of yourself. In fact, your beautiful soul is more radiant than all the stars in the sky. In you, the universe has unveiled a masterpiece, a symphony of light and love, the epitome of divine beauty. You are the perfection of all perfection, beauty beyond compare; pure light expressed in the most spectacular expression of God manifest.

You are living proof of love's infinite depths, an embodiment of the loving universe in its purest form—as you, through you, and for you.

Describing the radiance of your soul is beyond the limits of language and the smallness of words, so let this simple truth suffice: I, infinitely and boundlessly, love you. To share the life-giving water of love with you quenches my soul's thirst, too. I will forever be in your debt and I am grateful for the light of your soul.

You are God manifest as more God, and a divine expression of love as more love.

To complete this Love Letters in a way that honors you, I am proud to share the following Letter that I wrote for you in the not-so-distant past of another life. Though I penned it on another day, under a different Sun, and in another world, the love it speaks of is the same love that has found you on these pages. It is timeless, ageless, transcendent, and meant for you.

My Dearest,

With the summer stretching long, hot, and laden, I find myself reminiscing of bygone days. Your lovely skin now feels fragile and cold, like the delicate breath of winter; I know your departure from this world is at hand. But you are mine, at least, for now, in the perennial summer of our love, as I have always been yours. The dance of our fingers forever seeking each other reminds me of two children holding hands on their way to school. There is a knowing that, soon, one will have to let go. When that dreaded bell tolls, it will be me left behind.

The thought of your suffering or loneliness torments my heart. I find solace knowing that it will be me who remains while you ascend with angel wings, greeted by celestial melodies and heavenly songs. Every day I still have with you, I hold you close, cherishing each moment.

The memories flood in, of the times when our roles were reversed, when I glimpsed you through the half-open door, cradling our child, your silhouette swaying gently like the trees in the lullaby of the wind. That sight—a testament of pure love, grace, and beauty—is forever etched in my heart. And now, my dearest, with my arms wrapped around you, I hum softly to you, cradling your tender soul.

This morning, as the Sun came through the wilted curtains of your dark room, there was a spark of recognition in your eyes. That fleeting moment when you might have remembered who I was snatched away by the cruel progression of time. Yet, in my heart's gallery, you remain unchanged. The radiant youth with flowing hair, sparkling eyes, and contagious laughter that could make the stars dance. I still reside in that sacred space where only your presence is permitted, where your laughter is my life's song.

In rare moments of clarity and light, you still reach for me with outstretched arms and open hands, calling my name with the glory of a songbird's song, while in the next breath, the veil of forgetfulness falls, and tears stain your cheeks again. Born of a knowing that reaches beyond the fading light of your memory, even when your eyes are closed, you softly utter my name and draw me close. And, amidst this sorrow, the afternoon sun shines brighter when you smile at the white roses by your bedside: your favorite, my dearest.

In my memory of you, I return to that glorious day when our souls first intertwined; in that instant, everything changed, including me. I did not know that life could be so beautiful until I found you. We built a life filled with love, joys, challenges, and memories. It was a timeless connection, a recognition of souls, and an eternal bond of unwavering and unending love. Now, as I watch you fade like the warm Sun sinking into the dark line of the distant horizon, the sudden arrival of this starless night brings tears to my eyes. Yet, love transcends all, and our souls will find each other in every life. Even in death, we shall not be parted. I will forever be by your side in every way possible. If you falter, I will catch you. If you cry, I will wipe your tears. If you are afraid, I will pull you close, wrap my arms around you and comfort you.

You once whispered that only love is eternal, and as the shadows grow longer and our time draws near its end, I realize the profound truth of those words. My heart echoes with love, a love that will endure beyond the constraints of this mortal realm. Until we find each other again in the vast dance of the universe, I hold close the memories that paint our endless love story—the joys, the tears, and all the little moments that deepened our love.

Your love remains the only star in the black of my night. The thought of you lightens every corner of my life, seeping even into my dreams. Every second with you has been a priceless gift. Even these threaded moments of absent recognition are treasured bits and pieces of light that I will forever carry close to my heart.

When you leave this world with all its joys and sorrows, the stars will dim and the Sun will no longer shine. The looming shadow of your absence will opaque my soul and dampen my world with unending tears. My only solace is the badge of love I will forever carry in my heart—for you, my dearest. Until our paths cross again, I will seek you out in the morning Sun, find you in the fragrance of flowers, and feel your soft embrace in the gentleness of rain. I will dance with you in the darkness of my dreams and discover you anew in the light of each new day.

Though I never found the courage to tell you my deepest feelings and hidden secrets, I want to share them with you now: I am eternally grateful for the mountains we climbed, the deserts we crossed, and the oceans of love that carried us through it all. Life with you has been unlike any other, a dream beyond dreams, and joy beyond joy. I will miss you more with each passing moment and grieve your absence with each dark day haunted by your loss.

Even now, while I still hold you in my arms, I miss you. I am grateful to feel such pain and sorrow; I pray that it never fades. My sorrow and my tears are the last threads of light that connect me to you, and even this I cherish. I would say I love you, but that would not be enough; words are too hollow and empty of meaning to hold the truth of my undying love and affection for you.

So instead, my dearest, I will simply say farewell, until we meet again; I am forever yours.

Our love will never die.
— Chrystael Rae

*Nature's most essential lesson
is consistency within change*

Letter 6

patterns
nature of Self

Let's take an imaginary walk together.

In your mind's eye, take my hand and walk with me along the ocean's edge. Let your footsteps and your breath find the rhythm of the waves. Enjoy the foamy bubbles washing over your feet and sink into the soft, slippery sand between your toes. Feel the warm Sun on your skin and taste the salty ocean on your tongue. Hear the children laughing, playing, splashing, and building sandcastles that are soon washed away. Become part of their joy and innocence. Listen to the hushed hum of empty seashells and the thunderous sound of rolling waves as they crash into the rocky seashore. Take flight with the seagulls that soar high above the soft, cotton clouds, magically suspended in the sapphire blue of the sky. Melt into the vast expanse of space around you and within you. Take a deep breath and remember you are alive. This is your life, your lovely, lovely life.

Nature heals the wounded heart, quiets the busy mind, and soothes the tired soul.

In her gentle embrace, we find solace, serenity, and rejuvenation. Nature transports us to simpler times of innocence and joy. If we listen, she whispers secrets of the universe that can awaken and enliven our very being. The empty clouds tell of distant storms, rustling leaves recall bygone days, and singing birds announce the arrival of dawn. In her timeless wisdom, Nature gently guides us along the path of the soul, leading us back to our true origin, the very essence of our being—*back to love*. Wrapped in her unyielding beauty, Nature reconnects us with the divinity all around us and within us. She is the *"inhale"* of life and the *"exhale"* of existence.

One of Nature's most essential lessons is consistency within change.

The seasons cycle with reliable precision, yet each turn brings its unique array of colors, scents, and sensations. Tides surrender with the setting Sun and the icy solitude of barren beaches. Trees lose their autumn leaves, standing bare against the northern chill, only to burgeon anew with the touch of spring. In this eternal dance of constancy and transformation, Nature teaches us resilience and adaptation, promising a new beginning is alive within every ending.

A wave is born; a baby takes its first breath. The ocean crashes into the seashore; an adolescent discovers his limits and pushes them. The tide rises, crests, falls, and dissolves back into the ocean. The boy becomes a man; the wave becomes a storm. A strong undercurrent pulls the tides from the safety of the seashore. The timeless journey begins again in every wave, and every man.

Patterns repeat themselves until the gift is received or the lesson is learned.

We, too, ride the waves of the ever-changing currents of our lives. The tides of personal will and choice lead us to distant seashores of bliss, or pull us into the raging storms of change. Our conscious and unconscious choices direct the course of our lives. We are both the participant and the observer of our own existence, witnessing ourselves from a calm center—*even in the midst of a storm.*

Nature has her own cycle of growth, decay, and rebirth. Observing this cycle can offer hope, teach resilience, and be a quiet reminder that even in difficult times, there is always the possibility of renewal and growth. Within Nature's tranquil embrace, we find a sacred sanctuary for our soul.

Waves come and go, live and die, and return to the sky. Nature moves us toward our next life-giving breath, our next footstep in the sand, and our next most radiant version of Self. We exist for the joy of our own existence, and for the benefit of all.

The sea, the sand, the boy, the man, the waves, and the tides all rise and fall in the ocean of bliss and sadness. The eternal dance of transcendence and existence continues on, long after we are gone. In the human experience we surf the waves of personal transformation while exploring the unchanging depths of the Divine. The shadows and light of human life reveal the inherent goodness and grace of the loving universe, and benevolent God.

Innocence is the unchanging locus of love.

For the sheer joy of the experience, we walk together along a luminous path of love and radiant light, leaving our footprints in the sands of time. The soul's greatest joy is selfless service. My greatest joy is to serve you. I will always do my best to be a light in the dark of night, but please do not put me on a pedestal or make these teachings into a doctrine.

The insights shared in these pages are dynamic and infused with love, yet they are not rigid truths. They're here to offer comfort, guide you homeward, and reconnect you with your divine roots, but not to provide all the answers. Each reader will perceive these unfolding truths differently, filtered through the lens of their unique journey.

Our understanding is shaped by where we stand in life.

As our consciousness evolves and expands, so too will our grasp of these layers of love and levels of light, revealing themselves in harmony with our personal growth. Perfection and imperfection are inherent aspects of our shared human experience. Bearing this in mind, the words on these pages are offered with love and should be received in the same spirit, yet also with thoughtful discernment.

Like you, I embody the beauty of being perfectly imperfect. I am human with deep feelings and raw emotions. I, too, experience moments of doubt, flaws, and missteps. Life's turbulent waves can jostle me, and at times, I find myself plunging into the depths of my own inner darkness. I have failed and succeeded many times throughout the span of my existence, yet the love that IS me, and speaks through me, remains ever pure and untainted.

Being human, with its challenges, is an evolutionary path that we willingly embrace for the expansive experience and the unfoldment of love.

Indeed, a human life is defined by personal will, stark contrasts, constant change, and profound inner growth. It is a glorious endeavor of the soul that fosters the expansion of consciousness, offering a distinct experience of awareness, but it is not easy for any of us.

Nonetheless, many envision those further along the spiritual path to be angels with feathered wings, living a perfect, pious life. While such exalted states of radiance do occur, (*Bodhisattva*) they are rare. For most of us, the spiritual journey is extremely nuanced and life is a bit muddier. The human condition is designed in such a way that weakness and flaws are part of our radiance. Indeed, we will all fumble and fall on the path to enlightenment.

The spiritual path is seldom straight or narrow; for most, it is a winding road with many detours.

Regardless of the roads we travel or the directions we take, we are all inevitably destined to reunite in the comforting and eternal embrace of the Divine. While our hearts may reach for celestial heights, the true splendor of life often unfolds in the shared experiences of our struggles. It is in these poignant moments, filled with both trials and triumphs, that the profound beauty of our human journey is revealed, enriching our collective narrative with purpose and meaning.

Waves tumble and fall many times over before finally finding their way to the soft sand of the distant seashore. The soul follows a similar beauty-filled and turbulent path, treading through the mud and reaching for the stars in a never-ending cycle of stagnation, growth, and expansion.

The trials and challenges of a human life, though often difficult, are profound lessons in disguise, offering invaluable gifts to the soul. Though at times uncomfortable, life's challenges serve as catalysts for growth, urging us to evolve, expand, and exceed our limits. They test our resolve and fortify our character, expanding our awareness and leading us toward a more enlightened future.

Life's hardships unlock our potential to explore and learn, deepening our understanding of how to love ourselves and others. In addition, each of us have distinct strengths and gifts, counterbalanced by our own unique lessons to be learned and burdens to bear. Indeed, human life is more intricate than a one-size-fits-all definition, rich with layers of meaning and varying levels of understanding.

To this point, an enlightened being might consciously choose a life filled with heavy burdens in the service of the soul, and for the benefit of others. A good example is the drunken old man, standing on the street corner with a brown paper bag and a sign that says, "*God Bless*." Most look at him with pity, repulsion, or apathy. On rare occasion, we see him through the eyes of care and compassion. Whatever our perception, most assuredly, we do not see the illuminated being who stands before us. Often what goes unnoticed is the deeper truth that these valiant hearts, while shouldering their hefty burdens, also bring invaluable lessons for everyone. Their battles, whether with addiction or other adversities, are not just personal, but communal. These valiant souls prompt introspection of our personal values and challenge society to examine its collective ethos, moving us into compassion, and enhancing our capacity for empathy and care.

Nothing is left out of love.

Behind every challenge lies a story, a journey, and a purpose. Yet, often blinded by arrogance and ignorance, we fail to recognize the courageous individuals who intentionally embrace a human life marked by a strong inclination toward alcohol, addictions, and other challenges. They take on these struggles as a deliberate choice, challenging both themselves and those around them to seek change and growth.

A life burdened by addiction or similar hardships is a daunting journey, often undertaken by souls that are either young in spirit, strong in resolve, or seasoned with experience.

Whether we see the drunken old man through the eyes of disgust, pity, or compassion is of little consequence. Our judgments do not affect the eternal, unchanging love that created all things, including the drunken old man. In all our interactions, we have a choice to acknowledge the inherent divinity in every being or to pass judgment based on appearances. In a broader context, our judgments are more indicative of our own spiritual growth and understanding than of the qualities we attribute to others. Our perception of the world is filtered through our own personal understanding, not its actual reality.

Every person we meet acts as a mirror, reflecting aspects of our own soul's evolution, nudging us towards growth, and encouraging us to embrace love and compassion.

Responsibility resides not only with those bearing the burden but also with those observing from a distance. The ultimate goal is to recognize the sacred in everyone, transcending superficial judgments with empathy, compassion, and unconditional love.

Every footstep in the sand and every wave on the ocean is a necessary, never-to-be-replicated unfolding expression of the loving universe. Just as shimmering light ripples on the surface of dark waters, revealing an ongoing narrative between the Sun and Moon, the shadows and light of our lives contribute to a larger story and a greater truth.

Even the drunken old man's life, though seemingly tragic, when seen through the eyes of love and compassion is a heroic journey of great service to many. His sad, silent, and, perhaps, unspoken message reminds us that our choices matter. Like a river carving a path through mountains, our choices sculpt the landscape of our lives. In the struggles and strife of the staggering old man, we recognize the frailty of the human condition and the thin line that separates joy from despair, purpose from nihilism, and truth from lies.

With a more expansive perspective, the old man symbolizes the value of choice, reflection, and transformation. The very sight of him, soiled, dirty, and drunk on the street may inspire us to put our own bottle down. It may be precisely what is needed to halt the inertia of our own missteps and bad choices. His powerful anti-example may be the very reason that we find the strength and resolve to change. It may stop us from destroying ourselves before we, too, hit a tipping point, making it nearly impossible to escape the dark current of our own personal hell. That said, saving grace is a real phenomenon and available to all

__Hidden in the darkest corners of the soul, lies the dormant potential for transformation.__

No soul is ever truly lost; each carries the unborn seed of redemption. Recognizing the divinity in all, even those mired in the depths of despair, is a testament to God's boundless love and grace. Nothing is impossible in a loving universe. Miracles happen every day, yet they are often dismissed, ignored, or go entirely unnoticed. Even this book and the love it contains is the unfoldment of a miracle. So many things had to happen for you to have it in your hands, including the absolute miracle of your existence and being born.

__Every grain of sand, cloud in the sky, and wave on the ocean is a miraculous gift, inviting us to embrace the vast, intricate beauty of our lives and the world we live in.__

Whether we recognize the seemingly inconsequential as miraculous or mundane, miracles are real. The old man begging on the street corner can move us deeply into compassion and be a powerful catalyst for change. His drunken presence, failure, and raw addiction may repel and remind us of our own weakness and fragility. In his struggles, we see a reflection of our shared humanity, our vulnerabilities, and our strengths. The contrasts and contradictions of life deepen our understanding of love and our true selves.

In the peripheral vision of the soul, we are blessed by the drunken old man's sacrifice and tragic life. Nonetheless, the dissonance between what we would rather not see and what stands before us is often difficult to reconcile. To see someone suffering can pain us on a deep level of our own humanity. Our innate connection to everyone and everything forces us to confront uncomfortable truths about the world around us and our inner landscape.

We are inherently empathetic beings; when we see others in pain, we are wounded too.

This tug-of-war is a testament to our capacity for compassion and the desire for a world without suffering. Yet, the presence of pain is a stark reminder of life's imperfections and the inherent duality of existence. Confronting this duality pushes us towards introspection. Why does suffering unsettle us so? Because it echoes our fears, vulnerabilities, and past traumas. In the face of another's pain, we are reminded of our own helplessness and potential to suffer.

The presence of joy or pain does not define us, rather, our response to life's ever-changing currents shape our world.

Just as a seed must breakthrough its hard shell to plant roots and find its way through the muddy earth into the light of the radiant Sun of tomorrow, our internal struggle also offers us a pathway to growth.

By leaning into our discomfort, acknowledging and addressing our reactions to suffering, we foster a deeper understanding of ourselves, the world we live in, and the love that created us. Do we turn away, shielding ourselves from discomfort? Or do we approach with empathy, understanding, and a desire to make a difference? This choice, along with the transformative power of love, resides within us. Through loving reflection and heartfelt compassion, we acknowledge that a quick turn of fate could also plunge us into darkness and despair.

When the shadow of disappointment, betrayal, loss, or uncertainty darkens our world, it can be quite daunting, but it's in these moments that our resilience is forged and our empathy deepens.

Love remains the ever-present answer.

No one will be left behind, abandoned, forsaken, or forgotten. The universe is kind, benevolent, and loving; *as is our loving Creator*. The plight of the old man with soiled clothes, stumbling over his own feet, is a living cautionary tale. His sad life, though tragic, serves as a stark warning and anti-example, and on another level may save many from a similar fate. His sacrificial life is a great offering of compassion, service, and love. Beyond the threshold of mortality, this same man emerges in a new light, free from pain, regret, and judgment. He stands resplendent, bathed in a golden aura, a testament to the sacrifices born in the shadows and pain of his earthly existence.

Indeed, this world of form and structure is forever in flux. We do not have dominion over every facet of our lives, including the people we encounter, the places we go, or the events that shape us. However, we choose our response to life's unending tides.

To push against the weather of life or battle against the winds of change is a fruitless fight that leaves us defeated and exhausted.

Even the smallest acts of love and kindness, toward ourselves and others, have transformative effects, rippling out and impacting the entire universe and the whole of Creation. Rather than resisting the forces of Nature, God, and the universe, we can ride the waves of change with grace, patience, and peace. It is worth repeating that regardless of the twists and turns of fate, we alone choose the path of the soul. Bearing this in mind, irrespective of the circumstances of our lives, we are ultimately and solely responsible for our response to life's ever-changing currents.

The old man on the street may be a signpost of things yet to come, but it is always a choice. In every moment, with each thought, and every action, we create our own destiny. We are far more powerful than most of us realize. Our view of the world changes our experience of it. We can lift our gaze and see the splendor of life or lower our eyes and see the muddy ground; everything is available.

Perspective determines if the glass is half empty or half full.

Our focus, and the energy we invest, shapes the contours of our lives, impacting the evolution of the soul. This realization empowers us to rise above our circumstances and consciously direct the course of our lives. Rather than being victims of circumstance, or being led by the unruly hand of fate, our choices actively shape the world we live in. However, even if our choices are radiant and pure, we are not guaranteed a life free from adversity or struggle. In addition, there are many forces that direct and alter the course of our lives.

Our journey is significantly influenced by our choices, actions, preexisting conditions, the alignment of the stars, random circumstance, chance, and the whims of fate.

In pursuit of comfort and pleasure, and to avoid pain and suffering, we often resort to escape mechanisms like drugs, alcohol, sex, work, exercise, or food. To avoid uncertainty and discomfort, we frequently overlook the splendor of life and fail to recognize its innate beauty.

Though tragic in a relative sense, even these darker roads inevitably lead us back to God, albeit the long way home. There are no random events in our lives and we are never given more than we can handle. Everything that happens, good and bad, is meant to empower us to make more conscientious choices on the path of self-realization. If we listen, every grain of sand, wave on the ocean, and breath of life has something to teach us. Indeed, to be fully realized, free beings, we must listen to the waves, to the quiet whispering of the soul, to the deep longing, and strong pull toward something greater than ourselves—*towards love, service, grace, and God*. When we are attentive, the whole of life is our teacher.

My favorite time to experience the ocean is in the early morning when the waves gently lap onto the seashore, welcoming the dawn of a new day and the golden arrival of the morning light. The waves come without fail, regardless of the weather; they come in service to all. They come to find you, to find me, to find the drunken old man, to find the children playing and the sandcastles they left behind. The waves come in many disguises, some gentle and playful, others dark and angry. Large or small, the waves ride the breath of the wind, collapse back unto the seashore, and are born again on another day.

Nature teaches many lessons, including the inevitability of change.

Life is perpetually in flux. Even the frothy waves that tickle our toes exist only for a fleeting moment before sinking back into the rocky seashore. You, the eternal you, and I, the eternal I, do the same; we joyfully embody a particular form for a specific evolutionary end. Then, we transform into the next most radiant possibility and version of self. Like the waves, we rise and fall together in the ocean of existence. The wave believes it is just a wave, though it is the entirety of the ocean, expressed and experienced in singularity.

We, too, experience ourselves as separate, alone, and disconnected from our Source; however, our every particle of light is God manifest. We are the cherished children of the loving universe; love expressed as more love. To put it more poetically, we are the waves, the ocean, and everything in it. We are God bursting forth into particles of light for the absolute bliss of the experience. One particle is me, and the other is you; together we are God manifest, divinity unveiled, and the perfection of love.

As the outpouring of the loving universe, the unfoldment of love, and the radiant expressions of God, we carry the weight of existence within our very breath. Divinity permeates all things, including the turbulent waves that rush to the seashore of their own demise. You and I, much like the waves, take a similar, difficult and joyful journey from love back to love, as more love.

Joy is why we exist.

And, joy is why we have taken this walk together. We have taken this walk on the ocean's edge in many lives, and we will take it in many more. In some lives, we follow in the footsteps of others, while, in our bravest lives, we paved our own way, anchoring ourselves in the love and grace of God. In our most challenging lives, when our beaches were barren and our spirit broken, the strong undertow, raging current of change, and unexpected jolt of tragedy pulled us down, drowning our hopes and dreams in the whirling wake of pain and sorrow.

Though tragic in the moment, when the tides receded and the skies cleared, the Sun again found its way through the heavy carpet of clouds, lighter and brighter. There is a divinity to our lives, and all is well, even when it's not.

In unending cycles, recurrent rhythms, and unfolding patterns, Nature, our perennial teacher, shares her timeless wisdom.

From the relentless waves, forever crashing into the seashore, we learn resilience. The deeply rooted trees, swaying gently in the wind, teach the art of non-resistance. In the perennial flowers, patiently awaiting the warmth of the summer's bloom and winter's wilt, we see reflections of our own cycles of growth, blossoming, and letting go. Even the rhythmic cycle of tides, rising from the ocean's depths and faithfully journeying back to the seashore, echoes our own passage from the depths of night to the hope and radiance of morning light.

Again, if we listen closely, the waves will whisper their timeless truths, and the distant horizon will remind us of the endless possibilities for our lives.

Each moment of existence is a reflection of the soul's resilience and its unyielding capacity to heal, evolve, and love.

Just as the sand briefly holds the imprint of our feet, only to be whisked away by the ceaseless tides, so too, our troubles shall pass, leaving behind the everlasting resonance of love and grace. The inevitable storms and unfolding patterns of life reshape the landscape of our existence, challenging us to change, stimulating growth, and sweeping away the old to make way for the new.

Though winter storms and summer harvests may uproot trees, they also serve to nourish the soil. In the same way, sunny days and stormy nights guide us closer to understanding ourselves, the purpose of life, and the meaning of love. The blue sky is an ocean of hope that eternally blossoms into limitless possibilities. While, in a crashing moment, the most devastating storms wash away *"what was,"* to make room for *"what will be."*

Each step into and out of the physical realm enhances our understanding of Self, Nature, Grace, and the Divine.

The myriad of life experiences transform us in ways that otherwise would be impossible. Because the soul longs to know itself from all perspectives, even the darkness is part of our light. Indeed, we have walked on water with the saints and dived into the darkest of nights to know ourselves more fully. New and unfathomable universes are born out of the ashes of our fiery transformation. In the timeless rhythm of Nature, we find our place, gracefully attuning to its perpetual ebb and flow.

Just as waves forever return to kiss the sandy seashore, and the howling winds whisper tales of distant lands, we, too, will forever find our way back to each other. Each glorious sunrise bathes the ocean in golden light, and each wave that returns to the rippled seashore is a silent reminder of our timeless love.

Everything unfolds exactly as it should for the benefit of our soul and the good of all. Every wave, storm, sunlit day and cloudy sky is a vital footstep on the path to God. Even this short walk through Nature, along the seashore of time is a path to the Divine. If only we could grasp the depth of love and adoration that forever embraces and surrounds us, we would know that our lives are a treasured path of illumination.

For those who listen with an open heart and attentive mind, Nature reveals the hidden secrets of the loving universe and the truth of God's unconditional love. Our very existence echoes through the depths of the oceans and soars to the mountain tops, spanning the boundless expanse of time and space into the infinite.

Our soulful journey is a boundless trek of self-discovery and personal empowerment.

With the gift of autonomy and choice comes the responsibility of our own transformation. We are destined to walk, hand in hand, through our many shared lives on the path back to God, *only to discover that we never left.*

We have never been separate from our Source, nor will we ever be. We are veiled from this truth for the privilege and expansive experience of being human. And yes, each life is yet another footstep toward the Divine.

As we find ourselves once again at the edge of the ocean, I invite you to dip your toes into the frothy waves of your existence with reverence and joy. How glorious to be alive and know the truth of love. We are indeed the fortunate ones who are aware that we are aware.

With the gift of this awareness, a vital question of great significance to the soul arises: "*What will we do with our precious life?*" There only two choices: to embrace love or succumb to fear. I hope you choose the luminous path of love.

The path of love is a hallowed journey to our innermost self, a quiet awakening of the radiant heart, and a sacred communion with the Divine.

As our time together at the ocean's edge draws to its inevitable end, I invite you to gaze upon the vast horizon of potential and radiant possibilities for your life, born and reborn in the unfolding patterns of love and light. Every footstep carries us to new and exciting lands of exploration and discovery, where we meet ourselves and the Divine in endless waves of love and luminous light.

Choose wisely, dear one, for each decision shapes your journey, carves your path, and etches your legacy into the eternal sands of time.

With every wave and every breath,
I love you more and more.
— Chrystal Rae

*We are never given more than we can handle
and we can handle a lot*

Letter 7
awaken
practices for life

Thoughts become things; what we think about, we bring about.

In the previous Love Letters, we explored the significance of taking charge of our own destiny. Now, let's further unpack what that entails in real time and how we can practically embody this notion. At the heart of our conversation is the idea that everything, even our thoughts, is made up of energy. Most of us underestimate the power of our thoughts. While the physical world seems solid, it's actually pure energy. Our thoughts, whether we're aware of them or not, are energetic forces, each with its unique outcome. They align with correlating realities and energetic possibilities, shaping our experiences. Put simply, the circumstances and events and in our daily lives reflect our conscious or unconscious choices. One thought is a rose in a vase on the table, another is a broom in hand sweeping the floor, and yet another is an imaginary lion in the sea of clouds that hover outside the bedroom window.

Wherever thought goes, energy flows.

The experiences that unfold before us reflect our current energetic alignments and chosen life path. Within the vast expanse of the *Eternal Now*, every conceivable reality exists and has reached its culmination. This non-linear approach and understanding of time is the seed and source of my unconditional love for you. Our timeless bond and eternal connection are unbreakable in our current timeline. In other words, our epic love story has unveiled itself in every imaginable iteration within the timelessness of the *Eternal Now*.

Despite life's unpredictability, the melody of our eternal connection always finds its way back to the same beautiful note: a love that deepens with time. While there is much more to explore about the concept of the Eternal Now, that discussion belongs to another book. For now, it's essential to grasp that our present reality perfectly aligns with our current energetic state. This realization isn't just enlightening; it's truly empowering. It places the reins in our hands, enabling us to steer our lives with intention and purpose.

When we change our minds, we change our lives.

The formula for change is clear: to achieve a different outcome, we must make different choices and evolve our consciousness. To evolve our consciousness, we must transform our thoughts. Transforming our thoughts necessitates daring to think differently. Embracing a new perspective demands the courage to step out of our comfort zone. To achieve true liberation and freedom, we must be prepared to leave behind the familiar and find the courage to part ways with people and things that no longer align with our higher good.

To truly be alive, we must confront our fears and be ready to let go of everything, even our very existence.

To live fearlessly, we must embrace uncertainty and trust in a compassionate Creator and a benevolent universe. This courage arises from recognizing the Divine presence in all beings. Acknowledging the Divine means embracing our imperfections, addressing mistakes, and moving forward, even in uncertainty. Interestingly, it's through acts of courage that we discover courage itself. The human experience, a blend of shadows and light, vividly embodies the Divine. This introspective life journey is part of a profound cycle of personal growth and soul expansion, ultimately leading us back to our source—*Love.*

Thus, since the universe and everything within it are manifestations of God's boundless love, there is *"nothing to fear except fear itself."* Conscious transformation necessitates a deliberate shift in how we perceive the universe, transitioning from a mindset of scarcity to one of abundance. This enlightened perspective redirects our energy, anchoring us in the present moment with an amplified sense of love, radiance, and connection to the Divine.

Personal transformation is a journey defined by courage, determination, and faith in something greater than ourselves.

To nurture and fortify these virtues, practicing mindfulness and intention in our thoughts, words, and actions is crucial. Opting for love over fear and aligning with our loftiest aspirations, especially in challenging moments, serves as the driving force propelling us towards transformation.

Personal responsibility and an integrous life go hand in hand.

In our ongoing spiritual journey, setbacks are not only natural but also inevitable, especially when acquiring new skills. The notion of *"getting back on the horse"* after a fall holds great significance, as it builds resilience and strengthens our resolve to confront fears. Nonetheless, as the adage reminds us, *"Rome wasn't built in a day."* Let's remember to be kinder and gentler with our beautiful souls. There's no benefit in belittling or criticizing ourselves for not achieving more. We should keep in mind that we're all doing our best in every moment, and there's always room for improvement. In the human experience, we may stumble and fall repeatedly. Yet, with time, dedication, persistent effort, and the grace of God, we will all find our way and witness the transformative journey of our souls.

The natural evolution of a human life is an exhilarating journey, touching multiple dimensions of our existence, *both physical and spiritual*. As we align with higher energetic possibilities, our life circumstances also shift positively, leading us through a profound transformation. Breaking free from ingrained habits requires time, tenacity, and persistence. In this context, our choices carry significant weight. Their importance cannot be overstated. Even a deferred decision or the choice not to choose is a decision.

It is solely through the choices we make that we shape our life experiences; no one else can make them on our behalf.

If others were to dictate our choices, it would be an affront to the soul's yearning for sovereignty and freedom. Even so, amidst the chaos of daily life, it's easy to lose touch with our inner wisdom and higher truths. To reignite this connection, we must take proactive, self-reliant steps, listening to the subtle whispers of our soul and heeding the wisdom and guidance of those who care for us. Accepting assistance is not a sign of weakness; the love and support of others are invaluable. Although guidance and advice can be beneficial, as mentioned earlier, it remains our personal responsibility to shape our lives.

Self-reliance is a prerequisite for spiritual growth.

External factors are not the true determinant of our inner serenity or turmoil. It is always our conscious or unconscious choices that shape our experiences. And again, everything begins with a thought; when we change our thoughts, we change our lives. The power to embody goodness, grace, and love is always a personal choice. Although breaking free from familiar and deeply rooted habits can be a formidable challenge, it is indeed possible. The burdens we carry are never greater than our capacity to bear them; the benevolent universe unfailingly supports us.

Self-reliance doesn't mean isolation or being lone wolves. Instead, it reflects our dedication to giving our best while entrusting the rest to the grace of God. It also means being open to accepting help from others when necessary. Along our journey, we may experience both successes and challenges, but when we give our best, even failure can be a victory in its own way. Whether basking in the radiant light of the sun or shivering under dark clouds, we create the atmosphere of our inner world, consciously or not. Regardless of life's circumstances, the power to choose happiness forever remains within our grasp. Our life experiences stem from choices rooted in love or fear. We cannot ascribe our current state or life's journey to external factors such as family, partners, circumstances, health, institutions, nature, or even the Divine.

We are the architect of our own destiny.

Life unfolds in diverse ways, colored by either love or fear. Through both our conscious and unconscious thoughts and beliefs, we mold our inner world, experiencing it as either joy or sorrow. Yet, the notion that happiness is a choice, always accessible to us, can be elusive, especially during difficult times or profound loss. Emotions and uncertainties may burden us, but even in the midst of life's darkest storms, our greatest strength is our ability to choose love over fear. With this realization, the question of how arises. How do we summon the inner strength, resolve, and determination to opt for love over fear? How do we embrace happiness, regardless of our inner or outer circumstances? How do we find joy in a world often marred by pain and sorrow? How do we intentionally shift our consciousness? These questions are profound, and although there is no one universal answer, love is always the right answer.

We each find the truth of love in our own time, and when that moment comes, the entire universe undergoes a remarkable transformation.

A particular path that resonates with one person might not resonate with another. My solution may not necessarily work for you and vice versa, but again the universal answer is always love. Yet, as we explore the spiritual terrains of the soul, experimenting with what aligns with our truth and what does not, we discover our strengths and vulnerabilities. We may learn more through our failures than our successes. Through it all, self-reliance fosters resilience, cultivates character, and instills faith in a loving universe and the providence of God.

While we attract the circumstances of our lives through our choices and energetic alignments, we are never burdened beyond our current capacity.

The loving universe always has our back; we are not meant to face life's challenges alone.

This is precisely why our paths have crossed again in this life. I came back to be of assistance, to share my wisdom, and to love you as only I can. You might wonder why I am so dedicated to you and why I love you so deeply, especially if we have yet to meet in this life. The answer is simple, I have loved you for eons of time, and I will love you more and more with each passing day. Indeed, my return to this earthly realm is a testament to my love for you. I am here to facilitate change, promote your well-being, and be a caring friend you can lean on.

Nevertheless, this short foray into the human experience is not always easy; in fact, it can be quite challenging. I know this to be true from my own personal experience. There have been times in this life when I've felt utterly overwhelmed, completely isolated, and profoundly alone. However, the truth of the loving universe is the exact opposite of these transient states and fleeting emotions, we are never judged, abandoned, or disregarded.

Even in our darkest hours, we are not forsaken.

Regardless of our deeds, whether good or bad, we are forever held with unconditional love and care. Our soul family of angels, teachers, and guides are forever by our side, watching over us with deep affection, love, and care. Indeed, these divine beings have been by your side for eons, and they know you better than you know yourself. And yes, I am one of them. This is precisely why we have met again. I returned to this life to comfort and support you. In a heartfelt gesture of my unending love for you, I have meticulously crafted this unique compilation of easy-to-implement spiritual practices to facilitate change and accelerate your spiritual transformation.

These transformative practices can effortlessly integrate into your daily routine, enriching and enhancing your life experience. They serve as a guide through uncertain times, offering solace on days when heavy clouds loom and skies darken. Their purpose is to empower you, enabling a shift in energy towards a brighter, more radiant version of yourself. Please take a moment to read through the entire list and choose the practice that most resonates with you. Then practice it with diligence and deliberate intent. Allow yourself the time and space to explore the potential of each subsequent practice. If you happen upon a particular practice that deeply resonates with you then purposefully find ways to integrate and incorporate it into your life. On the other hand, if a practice feels misaligned or loses its allure over time, remain open to exploring the next one.

We all have unique learning styles and preferences, which dictate the most effective approach for utilizing these profound transformational practices. You may find that combining several of these practices is most effective, while others might prefer cycling through practices one at a time. Finding the correct practice and the right rhythm for your learning style ensures a refreshing and continuous journey of growth. The ultimate goal is to pinpoint what enhances your understanding and empowerment, facilitating change and allowing you to take full ownership of your life.

Remember to spark change, we must first be willing to change ourselves.

Continuing to follow familiar patterns will lead to predictable outcomes. Achieving lasting change requires us to become agents of transformation, putting in consistent effort to actively contribute to our own transformational process and spiritual expansion.

The conscious choice of love over fear exponentially accelerates our spiritual growth.

This simple yet transformative shift in consciousness not only transforms our lives but also creates a positive ripple that extends to those around us. The spiritual work we undertake not only profoundly transforms our lives but also has the potential to create and destroy universes, thereby fostering a deep connection with the Divine.

To begin this journey, once you discover the spiritual practice that resonates most with you, make it your private ritual. I emphasize *"private"* because there's no need to share it with others. Widely sharing our spiritual practices can inadvertently dilute their effectiveness and diminish their impact.

Spiritual work is the quiet, inner work of the soul.

We should only share our spiritual journey with those we trust, individuals who have proven to be worthy of our confidence. Embarking on a spiritual journey is like diving into the inner sanctums of the Self, away from the external noise and chaos. This introspection, though deeply personal, also profoundly affects our outer world. Like shedding layers of an onion, it involves peeling away beliefs, relationships, and behaviors that no longer serve our higher purpose.

Furthermore, as we undergo this profound shift in consciousness, it's advisable to steer clear of self-sabotage and negative influences, including naysayers who may prefer our stagnation. Spiritual growth cultivates discernment, guiding us towards relationships that resonate with our true selves. This does not mean the relationships we leave behind are inherently bad or that those individuals are lesser. It simply points to a divergence in paths.

While this process can be emotionally challenging, it opens doors to deeper connections rooted in genuine understanding, shared growth, and mutual respect. Personal growth profoundly impacts all our relationships by enriching those aligned with a higher good or naturally dissolving connections that no longer serve our souls. This metamorphosis is like outgrowing a cocoon that once served and protected us but is now limiting our potential to spread our wings and fly.

Life is dynamic, constantly changing, and ever-evolving. As we elevate our consciousness and energy, it is only natural that our outer circumstances will reflect this inner transformation. Our choices and subsequent energetic alignments attract or repel certain situations and individuals into or out of our lives.

Fundamentally, relationships are energetic exchanges.

Some relationships nourish and elevate us, while others can drain or even stunt our growth. It is essential to recognize that every relationship serves a purpose, and when that purpose is fulfilled, we must be willing to let go with grace, love, and gratitude.

While parting ways with relationships that no longer nurture our souls can evoke feelings of loss and mourning, this process can also be profoundly liberating. Even amidst pain, releasing what no longer serves us opens up space for healthier relationships—*with both ourselves and others*. Much like someone who chooses sobriety and, in doing so, discovers a supportive tribe that understands their journey, we, too, will encounter connections that resonate with our evolving selves.

Part of life's exquisite beauty lies in its impermanence and continual transformation.

Like an ever-changing kaleidoscope, life unveils many captivating realities through the ever-shifting patterns of impermanence. With an understanding of life's fluctuating nature, we can approach our relationships with an open heart, recognizing their value and pivotal role in our life's narrative, yet without attachment. To do this, we must embrace the new, cherish the old, and move forward with love.

The journey of self-transformation and growth is both intricate and profound. The profound practices outlined below pave the path to a brighter future by reshaping our perspectives, breaking old habits, and dispelling limiting beliefs. But they are not a magic wand that instantly transforms our reality. They are tools, and their effectiveness lies in our commitment to using them and integrating their wisdom into our daily lives.

While spiritual growth can and does occasionally unfold spontaneously as a gift of grace, more often, it necessitates our active participation while maintaining trust in the divine nature of the loving universe.

Personal growth is an ongoing journey of self discovery and spiritual transformation.

This transformative journey includes acknowledging our darkest shadows, facing our deepest fears, and actively progressing toward a more radiant version of self. This more conscious evolutionary path can lead to profound transformation and a deeper understanding of ourselves and others. Our personal evolution is a journey where the process is as important, if not more so, than the destination or how we get there.

Though the path of enlightenment may be long and winding, each step toward love will reveal the truth of our existence and unveil the boundless nature of the Divine.

In a world that often seeks instant gratification, the allure of shortcuts may be strong. However, when it comes to our soul work and personal development, shortcuts can deprive us of the richness of experience, the wisdom gained through struggle, and the deep satisfaction of earned progress.

The following spiritual practices won't bypass life's challenges; instead, they empower us to face them head-on with love and compassion. Every step of our earthly journey is meticulously orchestrated within a divine plan, designed to enrich our souls and contribute to the collective well-being. Our challenges, doubts, and triumphant moments are integral to our soul's growth. These spiritual practices are designed to illuminate the path of personal development and spiritual evolution. Nevertheless, it falls upon us to tread that path, with trust that every step, stumble, and leap forward shapes our destiny in profound ways. In essence, the profound journey into and out of the temporal world is a sacred pathway to the Divine.

It is within the crucible of our struggles, pain, and sorrow that our true self undergoes refinement and revelation.

With the following powerful practices as allies, we can move forward confidently, knowing that we are equipped to embrace whatever our journey brings and emerge stronger, wiser, and more aligned with our highest version of self.

The soul longs for the growth and expansion that is only attainable through deliberate intent, purposeful effort, and conscious choices.

Similar to any tool or practice for self-development, the purpose of these spiritual practices is functional. They are intended to facilitate growth, transformation, and alignment with our truest selves. However, the moment these tools are seen as the end rather than the means, their essence and utility can become obscured. In this regard, these practices contribute to our spiritual and emotional well-being, much like how brushing our teeth is a routine for oral health and physical well-being. They are not meant to be elevated or placed on a pedestal but rather integrated into our daily lives, making our journey smoother and more insightful.

When we elevate any spiritual practice, self-development tool, or individual to the status of an idol or deity, we run the risk of losing sight of their true purpose. These tools are not the transformation itself; they serve as facilitators in the process. The real power and divinity lie within us, in our innate ability to change, grow, and evolve. These spiritual practices are simply aids in that process. As we evolve, so will our spiritual practices. In this light, what serves us at one stage of our journey may be less relevant or practical at another. With this understanding, please use the following spiritual practices as stepping stones on your path to connect with the Divine.

Seven Spiritual Practices

1. Prayer: Supplication and surrender to the grace of a higher power.

2. Meditation: Quieting the mind to find inner peace and clarity.

3. Self-Inquiry: Philosophical exploration to discover one's true essence.

4. Devotion: Emotional bond with the Divine, emphasizing love and service.

5. Mantra: Repeating powerful phrases or words to align with positive energies.

6. Discipline: Staying committed to spiritual practices over time and amid distractions.

7. Affirmations: Positive statements to rewire the mind and foster empowering beliefs.

Prayer

Prayer is a communication or petition to a higher power or deity, often seeking guidance, support, or an expression of gratitude.

Prayer resonates deeply with those who have a firm belief in a higher power, regardless of the specific name or form given. Praying is not about the label we use to represent the divine nature of the universe but it is about connecting, surrendering, and aligning ourselves with the Divine. It is this genuine act of reaching out, trusting, and seeking guidance that holds transformative power.

As we acknowledge there are forces greater than ourselves, surrender dissolves the ego. It also aligns us with a higher vibrational field and opens greater possibilities for our lives.

Prayer is the spiritual fire of a light warrior, conquering the darkness through supplication, grace, and surrender to an omnipresent creative source: God.

Meditation

Meditation is a specific term for a broad spectrum of techniques used to quiet the mind so that we can listen to the inner voice of intuition and connect with divine intelligence.

Meditation is an inward listening, whereas prayer involves reaching out to a higher power. Meditation targets the core of disruptive thoughts, calming and reshaping the subconscious mind. This transformative tool adjusts our emotional, mental, and spiritual perspectives.

Unlike the external reach of prayer, meditation is an introspective tuning into our inner wisdom. Techniques like breath control aid in calming the mind and fostering focus. Although meditation stands apart from religious practices and is not strictly tied to the concept of God, it amplifies one's spiritual journey.

For those who lean toward a systematic and thoughtful approach to self-growth, discipline, and spirituality, maintaining stillness in meditation is most beneficial. While opinions vary on the best meditation techniques, choosing a method that resonates with you is essential for a sustainable and enjoyable practice. Commit to practice periods for at least ten to thirty minutes, once to three times daily.

Meditation is a potent tool, effectively breaking patterns of stagnation and habituation. We cultivate inner strength, clarity, and self-awareness through meditation, unlocking our true potential.

Self-Inquiry

The practice of self-inquiry seeks to uncover the essence of our existence through the exploration of the profound question: "Who am I?" beyond the fleeting and material world.

Self-inquiry propels us beyond the superficialities and impermanence of our daily lives, guiding us into the realm of the timeless, ageless, and unchanging. It challenges the frameworks and identities we often attach ourselves to, such as names, careers, relationships, roles, and physical forms. Instead, self-inquiry directs us toward an enduring essence amidst the ever-changing flux of existence.

Through the continuous questioning of *"Who am I?"*, we gradually strip away the accumulated layers of conditioned beliefs, societal norms, and identities driven by ego. Embracing self-inquiry does not negate the experiences of the material world; rather, it offers a more profound perspective where one is not lost or wholly defined by them. It allows one to participate in the world while remaining anchored in a deep understanding of one's true nature, which is interconnected, eternal, and beyond the confines of the physical world.

When delving into the concept of self-inquiry, we often allude to the higher Self, emphasized with a capital "S." Among its most distinguished advocates was the Indian sage Ramana Maharshi. In his youth, a profound near-death experience left him seemingly lifeless for a considerable duration. Yet, from this experience, the great saint recognized an unyielding, eternal essence that existed independently of the physical body.

This revelation sparked a relentless pursuit to unravel the enigma, *"Who am I?"* beyond the fleeting confines of a material existence. Through this journey, he realized his identity transcended mere temporal existence.

Through self-inquiry, we transcend the ordinary and materialistic understanding of self, rising to recognize our true nature: a timeless, immutable, and radiant being of light.

Devotion

Devotion, in its purest form, is the most joy-filled pathway to the Divine

Devotion is not just a practice but a state of being. It is where the self melts away, leaving only the pure essence of divine love. This love is not bound by rituals, temples, or scriptures; rather, it is experienced in the simple, everyday moments that remind us of the omnipresent Divine.

Whether in the rustling of leaves, the laughter of children, or the stillness of meditation, the devoted find God everywhere. The beauty of devotion lies in its simplicity.

While other spiritual paths might demand rigorous practices, devotion only requires an open heart.

This openness allows divine grace to flow freely, nourishing the soul and elevating the spirit. Bhakti yoga, *the yoga of devotion*, emphasizes the heart over the intellect, and feeling over reasoning. It holds true that love is the greatest purifier and healer. As devotees immerse themselves in a loving existence, the barriers of ego and self-doubt dissolve, revealing the luminous soul within.

The tools of prayer, meditation, self-inquiry, and discipline are not seen as separate practices on a devotional path but as interconnected facets of a holistic spiritual journey.

Each complements the other, ensuring that the devotee remains grounded and connected, no matter the external circumstances. In the end, devotion is about surrendering to the Divine, not out of fear, but out of love. On the devotional path, and for those who are enamored with God, every word is a prayer, every breath a meditation, every thought is an opportunity for self-inquiry, and every act is a deliberate dedication of love to the Divine.

As one progresses along the devotional path, everything is surrendered in the fire of devotion and love, including the self. Then there is only love, and more love.

Devotion is the most direct path to the absolute union with God.

Traditionally, Bhakti yogis, who immerse themselves in the path of devotional love, often resided in ashrams and monasteries, taking on roles such as priests, monks, nuns, or ascetic yogis. Yet, in today's age, the essence of devotion is not restricted to these spiritual havens. Instead, it blossoms in the hearts of everyday people, allowing them to lead an ordinary life steeped in sacredness and devotion, recognizing the Divine in all aspects of existence.

Those who embrace this devotional path radiate qualities of benevolence, kindness, tolerance, and compassion. Their every action, no matter how seemingly mundane, becomes a dedicated service, a tribute to the Divine.

Mantra

A mantra is the recitation of a meaningful phrase that promotes spiritual growth and evolution, either bestowed by an enlightened guide or self-discovered.

In certain instances, mantras develop spontaneously as repeated inner contemplations. Such was my case, emerging after a transformative near-death experience. Long before grasping the depth and meaning of a "*Mantra,*" a life changing phrase surfaced within me: *"I am love, I am loving, and I am loved."* This mantra has since rooted itself in my daily practice, serving as a beacon of serenity, grounding me in love and truth, and maintaining a heightened energetic resonance.

Historically, mantras were reserved for the truly devoted, conferred by a master teacher. Today, with the rise of commercialized spirituality, discernment becomes essential. While genuine, enlightened teachers still exist, they are rare. It is wise to initially seek wisdom from within before looking elsewhere. In an energetic universe where "*like attracts like*," there is a high probability that because you are reading these words, you already know your personal mantra. You may even have a few mantras you consciously or unconsciously whisper to yourself, as I do.

Irrespective of how we come upon our mantra, we will recognize it as truth when we hear it. It will be profound, meaningful, and uplifting to our souls. It may be a temporary mantra *(for a particular time of our life)* or a lifelong mantra that anchors all other mantras.

The potency of a mantra is not just in its audible recitation, but in the depth of one's connection and intention behind it. As one delves deeper into the practice of mantra, moving from spoken to whispered to silent repetition, the mantra's resonance shifts from the external realm to the internal heart space. This internalization signifies a more profound connection, making the silent mantra the most potent. It becomes an ever-present vibration, aligning one's energy, thoughts, and actions with the mantra's essence.

The more inward the mantra, the more profound its effects.

The journey with a mantra is profoundly personal and evolving. Initially, its audible repetition helps in embedding it into one's consciousness. As familiarity grows, it transitions into a whispered echo, resonating from within. In its silent form, it becomes a constant undercurrent, harmonizing the rhythms of daily life.

The frequency of recitation is an individual choice. For some, utilizing a mantra may effortlessly weave into their thoughts, while for others, it may take intentional practice. Regardless of the pace, the consistent engagement with the mantra deepens its impact, making it a comforting companion, even during the stillness of sleep.

The more we recite our mantra, the more powerful it becomes.

When repeatedly invoked, mantras are charged with personal intent and the depth of one's spirit. As they mature within us, they transform into pillars of resilience, bolstering us amidst life's adversities and tumultuous times. The inherent strength of a mantra lies in its ability to align our focus swiftly, bridging the gap between the earthly and the ethereal, offering a connection to the broader universe and a grander intent. Additionally, mantras function as guiding compasses, aiding us in realigning our understanding of self and the Divine, sifting through the transient to embrace the eternal.

The legend of Gandhi's final moments exemplifies the profound potency of mantras. Meeting his fate at the hands of an assassin's bullet, as he confronted the ultimate transition, the repetition of *"Rama"* exemplified the transcendental power of a word imbued with profound spiritual conviction. This act was not just a reflex but a testament to a lifetime of discipline, where the mantra *"Rama"* became an intrinsic part of his being. Such stories mark the timeless wisdom of mantras. When genuinely internalized, a mantra can provide unshakable inner peace and sustain our spirit, even in the face of life's gravest challenges.

We can stay anchored in a high vibrational state through mantras even unto death.

Discipline

Discipline, often perceived as a rigorous commitment to a set of rules or practices, is essential for spiritual advancement.

Traditionally, ascetics utilized austerities to control and conquer their primal urges. Discipline provides a structure that keeps one focused on the path, enabling the transcendence of the mundane distractions that can lead one astray. There are still some modern-day ascetics, mainly in

India, who roam the Himalayas with little food or clothing, practicing extreme acts of austerity to conquer primal urges and as a devotional gift to their expression of a higher power or God (*usually a Deity*). While extreme asceticism is a choice few make today, the underlying principle of self-control remains relevant.

While discipline greatly assists in freeing oneself from the bondage of desire, attachments, and ego, when taken to an extreme, it can be detrimental to our spiritual advancement. The path of the *Middle Way*, proposed by the Buddha, suggests balance. Instead of extreme deprivation or indulgence, a moderate approach that cultivates wisdom, ethical conduct, and mental discipline is advised. This perspective underscores that it is not the severity of discipline that matters but its consistency, intention, and purpose. In our modern context, discipline can manifest in many forms: consistent meditation, regular study of spiritual texts, or dedicated acts of service. The key to finding the right balance in any form of discipline is to temper its fire with kindness and love.

In the realm of spiritual growth, discipline is comparable to the training of a marathon runner: it is consistent, methodically structured, and focused on achieving a higher state of potential. While discipline provides a framework, the principle of Ahimsa (non-harming) ensures this structure does not become a cage. By adhering to non-harming, the spiritual seeker ensures their rigorous practices uplift rather than suppress. A disciplined approach to spirituality can intensify the effects of other practices. When one combines discipline with prayer, the result is a consistent connection with the Divine. When combined with meditation, discipline brings more profound insights and prolonged inner peace.

Discipline in self-inquiry involves the persistent questioning and search for one's true self.

When combined with devotion, discipline ensures that one's love for the divine is not just a fleeting emotion but a sustained commitment. In essence, while discipline sets the rhythm, the dance can vary. It may be a heartfelt prayer, a silent meditation, a profound question, or a song of devotion. Regardless of the path, each step, taken with unwavering intention and commitment, leads one closer to the ultimate truth of love. Nonetheless, the transformation that emerges from discipline demands considerable time, effort, and unwavering consistency. Just as a river patiently carves its meandering course through formidable mountains over time, so does the path of discipline.

Affirmations

Affirmations are statements that can change our energetic patterns.

When embarking on the spiritual journey of utilizing affirmations, it is essential to understand their intricacies. Affirmations are about manifesting what we desire and altering our deep-seated beliefs, perceptions, or internal narratives. The utilization of an affirmation is about aligning our subconscious desires with our conscious aspirations. In addition, affirmations operate on the principle of neuroplasticity, the brain's ability to reorganize and form new neural connections throughout our lives. We can effectively rewire our brains to develop more beneficial thought patterns and habits by repeatedly instilling positive and empowering messages into our subconscious minds. As with any practice, intentionality and awareness are key.

The power of an affirmation lies in its emotional resonance.

When spoken with sincere conviction, deep emotion, and vivid visualization, an affirmation transcends mere repetition of words. It goes beyond stating something like *"I am healthy"* to genuinely feeling and believing in that state of health, visualizing it, and taking actions aligned with our desired state of being.

The one caveat is in the emotional undercurrent beneath the affirmation. If one says, *"I am healthy"* while feeling unwell or fearful about their health, the emotional charge of fear may override the positive intent. In such cases, crafting affirmations that acknowledge one's current state while leaning toward the desired outcome is more beneficial. For instance, instead of affirming something that may not yet be true, we can opt for a more open-ended statement like this: *"Every day, I make choices that bring me closer to vibrant health."*

In addition, integrating affirmations with other spiritual practices can amplify their potency. Coupling affirmations with visualization exercises, where one not only repeats the desired state but also visualizes it in vivid detail, can significantly boost their efficacy. While affirmations might seem superficial or counterintuitive, when approached with understanding, intentionality, and consistency, they can be valuable in one's spiritual development. To this point, in the receptive state of sleep, we can more easily integrate new thoughts and ideas directly into the subconscious, where true transformation and change always begin.

The moments just before sleep are considered sacred in many traditions. As we drift into slumber, the conscious barriers we erect during waking hours dissolve, making our subconscious more permeable to influence. This transitional phase between wakefulness and sleep, known as the hypnagogic state, is a time when our brain waves slow down, and we become susceptible to suggestions. The same is true for the hypnopompic state, transitioning from sleep to wakefulness. These periods are akin to natural forms of trance, during which our subconscious mind can readily absorb and assimilate information. There is wisdom in ancient practices where bedtime rituals involve reading scriptures, chanting mantras, praying, or engaging in meditative activities. These actions help center the mind, infuse positive energies, and affirm spiritual or life values.

Affirmations serve as gentle reminders of our innate power to shape our reality and our narratives about ourselves and the world.

In summary, still considering that *"thoughts become things,"* the aforementioned spiritual practices, along with many others not listed, serve as catalysts to enhance our energetic homeostasis, pushing our energy toward its pinnacle and amplifying our soul's brilliance. They are tools of empowerment that promote a more fulfilling and joyful experience of life, connecting us with our loving Creator, and advancing our spiritual evolution.

To conclude this chapter on everyday spiritual practices to awaken the soul, let's revisit the beginning and reflect on the notion that life is a gift we have the privilege to unwrap in our own unique way. Remember that these practices are potent tools for personal transformation and require a certain level of consciousness to use effectively. I encourage you to explore the practices that resonate best with your unique personality. There is no right or wrong way to use them. The greatest benefit may come from dedicating yourself to a specific practice, exploring a combination of several, or even engaging in all of them simultaneously. Nonetheless, it's crucial to remember that these spiritual practices are tools meant to support your spiritual journey. Avoid idolizing them or attaching undue importance. Think of them as training wheels, designed to be discarded as you evolve into your authentic, empowered self.

May the flame of my love and the transformative power of these spiritual practices rekindle the fire within your soul as you embark on a journey of self-discovery, growth, and ultimate liberation into a world of abundance and expansion.

Forever and a day,
eternally yours,
— Chrystal Rae

The conscious choice of love over fear exponentially accelerates our spiritual growth

*You are God in the making,
God manifest, and God realized*

Letter 8
beloved
ode to you

This Love Letter is in reverence to you, my beloved of many lives.

It is an outpouring of my soul to yours and a joyous celebration of our many shared lives. It is such a wonderful surprise to find you again. Herein begins a new chapter in our never-ending love story. To meet you again in the physical world is as radiant as the morning Sun breaking through a heavy blanket of clouds after a long, cold winter night.

These Love Letters are meant to remind you of my deep love and appreciation for your beautiful soul. I came back to this life and the temporal world for you. Every step I take toward you, toward love, and toward God is more joyful than the one before. The great fortune of finding you again has breathed new life into me.

I have been searching for you in the empty space and hollow void of your absence for lifetimes. It has taken some time to find you as we were not always aligned or on the same path. I had to first conquer the dark of my night before I could recognize your radiance and light. It was a necessary preparation.

Just as a mother prepares to meet her unborn child, I prepared a room in my heart for you. I put your picture beside my bed to find you in my dreams and recognize you in my waking. I see your true beauty, cherish your innocence, trust your wisdom, and bow to your grace. I know you in all your sadness and glory, though you may not acknowledge this for yourself.

I am in awe of your impenetrable spirit and tender soul. I know the truth of you: your fierce resolve and wounded heart. You have been my beloved throughout many lives, yet not all our shared journeys were ripe for our hearts to reunite. Even when the fickle whims of fate drew us along divergent paths, my love for you was an ever-present fire; nothing can extinguish our love. There has never been a day when I did not seek you out in the guise of shadows or the beauty of light. You are as familiar to me as my own reflection. I know you in the slightest of movements, thoughts, and actions: a passing glance, a sigh of recognition, and a felt connection.

Throughout time, when life or death pulled us apart, the unending echo of your presence has always comforted me, even in your absence. In every life, including this life, a silent, spiritual knowing forever draws me toward you. The glorious reunion of our souls is a raging, unstoppable bonfire. It is the manifestation of pure love and radiant light. For you, my beloved, I am humbled, exalted, and more alive.

The lover and the beloved forever find each other in the warm embrace of their shared bond of love. You are my beloved of many lives: my every thought, word, and action is a silent prayer for you. The union of our souls is an infinite and unstoppable fire. It is an eternal flame forged from the ashes of yesterday, burning with the fire of today, and simmering with the hope of tomorrow. Our rapture is imprinted upon the Heavens and quakes through the Earth, birthing new universes and ushering them forth from the darkness into the light of a new day.

Only love is eternal and unchanging.

Love is the very essence of our existence, the driving force that compels us to embrace life and face our own mortality. Our bond of love is an eternal flame dancing with graceful precision in the ever-changing winds of our lives. Our love is wild and free, a mesmerizing and uncontainable energy that heals and empowers all blessed to be touched by its grace.

A gift bestowed upon both the giver and the receiver, love is a potent and transformative force that transcends the earthly realm. Love is the pure manifestation of beauty and grace; it is nothing short of ethereal. Love is the gentle heartbeat of existence and the pulse of a benevolent universe. Love is a radiant light that bestows meaning and purpose on an otherwise dark and empty world. Love is the reason we have undertaken this wonderful and challenging sojourn together, venturing into and out of the physical realm.

Love is the answer to our silent prayers.

We could continue this profound exploration into the true meaning of love, noting every nuance, every victory, and every splendor, but first, a pause to address an underlying sentiment that may echo in the hearts of some. For many, the words *"I love you"* resound with memories of hurt, betrayal, or sorrow. If this is the sentiment you hold, know from my heart, I am truly sorry for your tears. My heart aches for the pain you have endured and the wounds inflicted under the guise of love. The pain you have suffered and the wounds you still carry weigh heavily on my soul. Having said that, please know that regardless of what has happened or how deeply we have been wounded or betrayed, we can break the chains of our past and reinvent ourselves. Rather than being held hostage by another's fear, hurt, or cruelty, we can reclaim our autonomy and personal power, consciously choosing not to let our past dictate our future.

In the raging bonfire of unconditional love, even the lingering pain of yesterday fuels the fire of a more radiant tomorrow.

In the spirit of Gandhi's wisdom, amidst the most trying and desolate moments of our lives, we can make the conscious choice to *"be the change we want to see in the world."* We make the world a better place by simply being better people. This choice should emanate from the innate goodness within our souls rather than from the fear of punishment or the specter of a vengeful, angry God.

In addition, being a better person is not synonymous with the attainment of perfection; pursuing such an ideal is a futile endeavor. If not for the omnipresent love and care of our Creator, the world, as we know it, would stop spinning, *and everything would fall apart*. Though we are mostly veiled from this truth, it is true all the same.

Truth does not change based on our ability to perceive it, or the capacity to understand it.

There are moments when the circumstances of our lives seem inexplicable, illogical, or unfair. During these challenging times, when our problems lack obvious answers or explanations, we are compelled to place our faith in the loving providence of the universe. Just as we hold the enduring truth that the Sun continues its radiant vigil behind dark clouds, there is a profound wisdom in acknowledging a force greater than ourselves. We are meant to be both broken and beautiful, human and divine.

Through our imperfections, cracks, and fissures, the light seeps in.

Our soul discovers balance in the truth, experiences peace through devotion, and gains strength in the surrender to something greater than ourselves. Indeed, with love as our unmoving foundation, we can meet life's challenges with serenity and grace. While others hide or attempt to escape, we keep the faith and stand our ground. In the grand cacophony of life, our silence is a loud and clear message. Though some may grasp and hold tightly, with love as our anchor, we release with grace and ease. Even in moments of anger and fear, we respond with gentle words, compassion, and kindness. When others panic and run, we move at a measured, deliberate pace. While some may leave, abandon or forsake, we still choose love time and again.

That said, the radiant path of love is neither straightforward nor without challenges. To truly love, we must be willing to walk away and lose everything. This is a journey of self-reliance and autonomy that is often marked by trials and introspection, along with profound personal growth. Nonetheless, standing resolute during life's storms is not natural for most of us. This ability is cultivated through perseverance, patience, and a deeper understanding of oneself, God, and the loving universe. Each experience, challenge, and encounter in our earthly sojourn serves as a stepping stone and a pathway to God. Our soulful journey unfolds through lessons disguised as obstacles, insights born from heartbreaks, and truths hidden within life's quiet mysteries.

The true essence of love stretches far beyond the idyllic and comforting.

Love nudges us to explore the complexities of our psyche, beckons us to wrestle with our inner demons, and invites us to acknowledge and honor the many expressions of life. By exploring the profundity of our own mind, we unearth, illuminate, and confront the hidden aspects of our being. In the pursuit of understanding these veiled dimensions of self, we don't just uncover hidden truths; we reveal our true nature as children of a loving universe.

In the acknowledgment of our sacred origin, as beings of light and the progeny of God, we consciously call forth the purest expression of love. As we learn to love and accept our brightest light and darkest shadows, once-locked doors of the heart are opened, fostering a true connection with ourselves and others. With the progressive and inevitable evolution of our soul, from dark to light, all pretense and fear fall away in the radiance of love. In this unveiling, it is clear that the true sanctuary and sacred abode of the Divine is found in the very depths of our own hearts. Every ragged remnant of yesterday is consumed in the fire of love.

Allow your heart to be broken a thousand times every day so you can love more fully.

Out of the smoldering ashes, the phoenix with its burgeoning wings, arises anew and takes flight. In this way, we too are transformed and find our angel wings.

To truly love, we must be strong enough to be vulnerable and vulnerable enough to be strong.

For love, if it finds us worthy, will shake us to the very bone, testing our resolve and deepening our connection to the Divine. Our strengths and weaknesses not only teach us about love, they teach us about ourselves and others. For when we dare to lay our hearts bare, allowing them to break, shatter, and courageously begin anew, we reconstruct the luminous bridge that connects us to our shared humanity and the loving universe.

Life is an eternal dance of shadow and light, tears and laughter, glory and shame. It may be tempting to shield ourselves from suffering, but in our darkest moments of vulnerability and pain, we uncover profound truths about ourselves and the meaning of life. Indeed, in the divine light of God's love, uniquely expressed in each of us, we undergo a profound healing and transformation. Every fissure of the broken heart is a testament to our resilience, every scar is a badge of our perseverance, and every loving connection we forge brings us closer to the Divine.

Inevitably, in the human condition, we will all stumble and fall. However, our very imperfections are part of our divinity. Extending grace and kindness to ourselves and others, even in our less-than-radiant moments, is essential if we are ever to truly love.

We are not meant to be perfect; every crack, missing piece, and imperfect edge adds to our radiance and the glory of God.

Being broken and beautiful, radiant and dark, perfect and imperfect is what makes us human. Our raw authenticity is both a gift and a burden. In the vast universe, our struggles—though at times seemingly insurmountable—are, in reality, radiant opportunities for growth. The challenges of a human life serve as catalysts for our spiritual evolution, propelling us toward our next most radiant self and the glory of God.

When pain comes knocking, open your door and welcome it, not as an unwelcome guest but as a teacher guiding you toward a more radiant and resilient version of yourself. Through it all, remember that the flame of love, however faint or dim, dispels the darkest of nights, guiding, healing, and restoring our souls.

The tears of the lover are joyful tears, drenched with pain and sorrow; they wash away the fear that bolts the heart shut. When the heart breaks open, like a baby bird that suddenly finds its wings, the soul takes flight. Love awakens us from the deep slumber of our everyday existence and the dark dream of separation.

Love empowers us to trust in something greater than ourselves—God.

Even in the face of life's greatest tragedies, most calloused cruelties, and darkest disappointments, love carries us to the other side of our pain. Though a human life may push us to our limits and beyond, it is within these challenges that we discover the depths of our resilience and potential for growth.

The moon may eclipse the sun, plunging us into darkness and despair, but we are never abandoned, forgotten, forsaken, or alone. We are forever held in the loving embrace of the Divine.

Love is why we exist. Love is the answer. Love is all that matters.

There is a profound purpose for our lives beyond the mundane and superficial; each of us exists to experience love in a way that is uniquely our own. In every shared moment of humanity, through its joys and sorrows, the unyielding love of the Divine prevails. Every success and failure strengthens our collective bond. Though we may wander into the darkness or get lost on divergent paths, heavenly forces invariably guide us back home.

A human life offers an unencumbered and unique opportunity for the soul to deepen its understanding of itself, others, and God. We all play a vital role in the vast unfoldment of the loving universe and the collective consciousness of humankind. The bond that links us to each other is profound, eternal, and true. Our shared experiences reinforce our interconnectedness and the unending love that unites us all. On this shared journey, we walk together, bound by the threads of destiny, into and out of the temporal world of form and matter, on a divine mission of love.

Every scar, tear, and smile reveals the depth of our shared human experience and is a testament to our resilience and love.

In its infinite wisdom, the loving universe allows the experience of pain, pleasure, confusion, and clarity. Everything is divinely purposed for the good of the soul and the benefit of all. This divinity includes the horrible, wonderful, bizarre, beautiful, and all the other perfectly imperfect expressions of love and life. Every experience, without exception, has deep meaning and serves a greater purpose. Life, in all its unpredictability, is a dance of contrasts, a path to love, and the only way home. From heartbreaks to extreme joy, from the mundane to the miraculous, everything is orchestrated in the grand plan of divinity for the expansion of love.

In the grand design of the loving universe, each soul holds a sacred space and resonant light, contributing to the majestic unfoldment of God.

In the light of this unchanging truth, you and I were destined to cross paths. It was not mere chance or circumstance but a purposeful chapter in love's eternal narrative. Our meeting again on the pages of this book is part of the universe's imperfect perfection. It is a larger plan for our souls and an ode to love's enduring, mysterious, and transformative power. Among the countless paths we could have traveled, we miraculously found each other once more.

I am eternally grateful for this divine synchronicity, for your presence not only illuminates my very being but also invigorates my soul, breathing new life into my existence.

The lover grows strong in his love for the beloved.

He tears down walls that separate, builds cities of gold, makes magic castles in the sand, and turns back time. The impossible is suddenly possible; all doubt disappears in the light of his love. Indeed, in the silent reverence of the beloved, the world instantly stops spinning, and everything broken suddenly makes sense. The very earth beneath his feet quakes as new universes are born in the luminous light of his unending love. The blessings of this timeless, ageless, endless love rise like the morning sun that slowly spreads its fingered rays of warmth and radiant light across the dark expanse of time and space.

In the same way, as twin flames called by destiny, we too have journeyed together through many lives, drawing strength and wisdom from each other, creating and destroying universes. Every magical meeting of our souls, every shared moment of joy, and every fallen tear has been an ineffable blessing.

Our unending love story continually unfolds in vibrant colors, dark shadows, and unimaginable hues of radiant light. Indeed, throughout our many lives together, you have courageously unveiled layers of love, tenderness, and understanding. Your willingness to embrace my darkest shadow has guided me into the soft yielding space of vulnerability and healing. In the safety of our enduring bond, my wounded soul is once again alight with the truth and beauty of love. I am forever humbled by the divinity that has made it possible for us to experience such profound depths of connection and love.

Every whispered secret, tender touch, and life-giving breath carries the echoes of our eternal bond. Even in the silence of our shared glances, my heart overflows with gratitude and love for you.

This love, our great love for each other, is a love beyond words, definition, or meaning; how could one speak of such a divine love or say that which is unsayable?

The lover falls mute at the feet of the beloved, surrendered in the silent discourse of the heart.

He has no words to describe such immense feelings and deep emotions; all words escape him. The lover is left speechless and awe-struck in the presence of the beloved. Nothing can be said of that which is without measure, definition or concept.

In the light of such profound love, even these eloquent words are empty of fullness and lack meaning. Nevertheless, they are all I have to convey my deep love and undying affection for you.

Please forgive the opaqueness of my language and accept the glorious gift of my timeless love. You are my beloved of many lives, a cherished child of the loving universe, and the most beautiful expression of "*you*" possible in each moment.

How I wish you could see yourself through my eyes: see your beauty, your grace, and your goodness. And how I wish I had the words to express my undying love, but again, words fail me. What I will say is that, though it cannot be measured or described, I love you in every way possible and more. I love you like no other will ever love you. I love both your radiant divinity and flawed humanity; nothing is excluded in my love for you.

You are the most essential part of me; my breath, my blood, and my bones. You are the very essence of my soul. You are the perpetual dawn of my day and the circular moon of my night.

You are God in the making, God manifest, and God realized.

Perhaps now you understand why I love you so very much; without you, there is no me. All opposites are consumed in the fire of love and then only love is left.

To truly love, one must be strong enough to be weak, brave enough to be broken, and vulnerable enough to be seen.

So here on the pages of this book, I have undressed my soul and stood naked in the light of my love for you. Why? Because you are my beloved of many lives, and you need to know that you are loved in this way: unabashedly, completely, and without end. My presence is meant to be a life-giving rain, a reason to hope, and a light that illuminates the way. I am here to ease your pain, hold your hand, and guide you home. Together, we shall rediscover the river of emotions and feelings born from our shared joy and pain. The echo of our love is so profound that it has been carved into the very structure of time itself. My declaration of love for you goes beyond the present; it is a whisper from the past and a promise for the future. It's an acknowledgment of every moment we've shared and all that we will continue to experience.

Every shared memory adds depth and meaning to our eternal bond of love.

I wish I could distill the vast ocean of my feelings and deep emotions for you into a single drop, a potion potent enough to convey the eternal expanse of my love and the endless reach of my deep affection for you. But words, as powerful as they are, pale in the shadow of my raw and real feelings for you, so I will simply saying that I love you now and forever.

Though our time together on the pages of this Love Letter has come to its inevitable end, please know that our love story will continue on in the silent space of a future yet to be born. Though it pains me to go, for now, I will leave you with the following pearls of wisdom and blessings for your beauty-filled soul: *May you find the strength to step out of the shadows, the ability to live with integrity, the courage to confront life's obstacles, the bravery to face your deepest fears, the freedom to voice your unfiltered truth, the determination to fulfill your life purpose, the vulnerability to love deeply, and the resolve to set the world ablaze in the name of love, and for the sake of love.*

Love calls forth the courage to be seen, held, known, and unguarded.

Indeed, in the sacred space of our love, I have been braver than I ever imagined or hoped. For you have made me feel safe, seen, and held, in ways that words could never completely capture or say. But in every held glance, tender touch, and shared secret, our sacred bond of love speaks louder than any poetic verse or benevolent action.

In the boundless realm of love, the lover and beloved forever unite, impervious to worldly forces and the unsolvable mysteries of the universe. Nothing can tear them apart in this world or the next.

Though our bond of love has no end, unfortunately, this sacred Love Letter does. Now, as I again prepare to leave you, tears fill my eyes. I never want to part ways with you, my beloved. Please know that even in my absence, I am forever by your side, silently watching over you, closer than your breath. True love knows no time. It has no beginning, middle, or end.

True love is an eternal bond that transcends our earthly existence, forever uniting us in the loving arms of God.

Always remember and never forget that you are my beloved, and you are not alone. The first and last breath of my every day and long night is in homage to you. You are my sun, my moon, and the flickering stars that illuminate the night sky. I know myself in your radiant light and forget myself in the dark of your night. Every speck of light that is me forever holds a silent vigil for you, for your precious soul, eternally waiting for you to come home.

Just as life and death forever dance together, you and I are also inseparable. Nothing in this world or the next can pull us apart or sever the eternal thread of love that forever unites us. For as long as there is light, I will be a candle in your night. I will be the love song that had to be sung. I will be the lover with a pounding heart, patiently awaiting you, my beloved.

In a world of uncertainty and change, I will be your constant, abiding light. In your joy, I will be the sound of laughter. In your sorrow, I will be a blanket of solace. In your challenge, I will be a breath of freedom and ease. In your fear, I will be the warm embrace of safety. In your anger, I will be the clear sky of calm. In your angst, I will be the voice of reason and peace. Whenever your skies dark and stormy, I will be the very air that you breathe, and someone who truly loves you.

Through every glorious moment of triumph and times of dark despair, my sacred promise to you is to always be by your side and to never leave you. Though you may not see me, I will forever be with you in heart and soul. You will find me in every whisper of the wind. I will sing to you in the quiet hum of distant stars. I will gift you the first ray of light after the long, dark night. I will be the silent space between every beat of your heart. I will fill the empty void with love, and more love, and still more love.

Seasons will come and go; the leaves will turn and fall to the ground, but I will never leave you and I will always love you. I loved you long before you read these words and I will love you long after you have forgotten them and me.

*Eternally surrendered at your feet
in humility and love.
— Chrystal Rae*

*Love is the most powerful force in the universe;
in truth, the only force*

Letter 9

salvation
save yourself

In life's most difficult moments, when we feel uncertain or lost, it may be comforting to believe in a force greater than ourselves.

We may even secretly hope that a supernatural entity or savior will heal our brokenness, ease our pain, and save us from ourselves. Unfortunately, or fortunately, as the case may be, no one is coming to save us; we have to, and we get to save ourselves. When we feel unsafe or alone, it is quite natural to look for solutions beyond ourselves, turning to trusted figures like family, educators, friends, spiritual leaders, or even the Divine.

However, the core responsibility for our lives rests solely with us. Life unfolds in such a way that we are endowed with the autonomy and free will to make our own choices. This empowerment comes with the challenge of navigating a world rich in diversity and choices. The vast array of options available to us can sometimes lead to feelings of overwhelm and confusion. Understanding and embracing our personal power is key to successfully steering through the complex and abundant choices life presents.

In truth, whatever we choose is always the right choice, even if it is the wrong choice.

This perspective holds true, at least in the context of the moment when the choice was made and until we gain the insight and wisdom to make a better one. Life is an ever-evolving journey, marked by a series of twists and turns that bring forth new insights and opportunities for growth.

Much like the lotus flower, which elegantly rises above murky waters, we, too, are radiant beings dwelling in a world that encompasses both shadow and light. In this realm, nothing is imposed upon us; instead, we are graced with the profound gift of choice and personal autonomy, allowing us to journey through life's varied experiences with resilience and grace.

The human endeavor brings us great joy, offering the soul a unique embodiment of self-discovery and reflection. Nonetheless, life is brief; every moment is fleeting and precious. Though our bodies will one day return to the earth, our souls are eternal and unchanging. The essence of love within us endures, untouched by the temporary trials of the physical world. Even the gravest harm cannot dim the light of our souls. From the soul's perspective, everything is as it should be—*imperfections included.* We exist for the bliss of our own existence, and nothing needs to change. Irrespective of the good or bad circumstances of our lives, our souls are never in peril.

There is a profound wisdom in knowing that nothing needs to change.

Indeed, from the serene vantage point of the loving universe and our eternal soul, everything is as it should be, including the perfection of imperfection. Our journey into and out of the material world is driven by the exhilaration of conscious exploration. We excitedly venture into this realm of shadows and light on a mission of love and conscious evolution, before returning back to Source, *more awake and alive.*

While the personality we assume in a given life may falter, the soul remains unbound, present, and aware. Indeed, it delights the soul to explore and discover aspects of the Self that are unavailable in any other realm. Through the human experience, we come to know ourselves, others, and God more fully. Our journey back to the Divine is a profound and enriching adventure of the soul. From this more expansive perspective, every obstacle is a concealed blessing waiting to be unveiled. Everything happens for us, and nothing happens to us.

Challenges in life serve as gentle nudges toward personal growth, and are powerful catalysts for transformation. Similar to how a grain of sand creates a pearl, our struggles carry inherent worth and purpose. They awaken us from complacency and rouse us from states of stagnation and inertia. However, during life's turbulent times or when we're engulfed in darkness, the weight of human existence can feel crushing.

In these deeply personal and vulnerable moments, we frequently find ourselves searching for answers and longing to connect with something greater than ourselves, often reaching out to the Divine to fix all our problems and save us. And though our soul family, angels, teachers and guides are always by our sides, comforting us and offering their love and assistance, they will not fix all our problems or save us. Though a human life can be quite trying, to be spared from our trials or removed from life's crucible would deny the soul its sacred pilgrimage. If left unfulfilled, the soul is compelled to return to the physical realm to find its completion and divine reunion. In addition, given enough time and space, everything works itself out, or comes to its ultimate resolution or inevitable end.

Even the darkest night fades into the morning light.

In the same way, the complexities of a human life that seemed so all important will quickly fade into the setting sun that marks the end of our time in the physical realm. While the soul treasures every radiant moment of its physical existence, driven by a sacred longing to explore and expand, it constantly seeks its path back to the Divine.

For most, evolution is a gradual process, unfolding in small steps and subtle shifts over time.

In this steady evolutionary process, each stage of our souls' advancement plays a crucial role in our personal development, and the ultimate return to love. Often, we encounter recurring situations that span across multiple lifetimes, compelling us to face these familiar challenges until we absorb the essential lessons and find healing and freedom. These repeated encounters are not punitive; they are a kind gesture of the loving universe, providing us with the opportunity to independently explore our shadows and light.

In a loving universe, that is kind, and benevolent, the circumstances of each day and every breath are orchestrated to guide us along the most radiant path of our souls. No one is ever abandoned, discarded, forsaken, or cast aside. We are forever cradled in the love and care of those who watch over us from a distance.

Life is not a solo journey; we are surrounded by angelic beings who love and support us.

Our enduring connection with these celestial beings spans across time and space, through the resonance of love and our energetic alignments. Specific lessons, tailored to our individual natures, repeat from one life to the next as recurring themes until we transcend them. Once we have transcended the necessity for a specific experience, that particular energy pattern is assimilated into our consciousness as wisdom and light, ceasing to be a concern for the soul. Even lingering karmic ties of cause and effect fade into the light of our heightened awareness.

In a loving universe, where our growth and well-being matter most, love is the only possibility.

And again, no one will be abandoned, forgotten, cast aside, or subjected to eternal damnation and suffering—*no retribution is required*. Recognizing that no judge or jury is shaping our life's path, it becomes evident that we bear the sole responsibility for our position based on our choices.

The weight of our decisions, the alignment of our energy, and the resulting life circumstances emphasize the value of making the most of our precious time. The process of transcendence entails a courageous and purposeful departure from familiar patterns that bind us to certain habits and ways of existing. As we step into the radiance of our true Self, the shadows of the past naturally fade away. Yet, for some, breaking free from the bonds of familiarity and comfort can be a daunting task, even when their current reality is shrouded in darkness and shadows.

These echoes of the past create familiar rhythms that perpetuate the cycle, keeping us in the bondage of habituation and sticky habits. Breaking free from such patterns necessitates a profound shift in consciousness and a courageous leap into the unknown toward the more radiant possibilities of love, wisdom, and light.

The common denominator in all of our life's challenges is always us.

Without introspection and inner work, we run the risk of perpetuating cycles of unhealthy relationships, unresolved challenges, and unconscious behaviors. Our recurring patterns and cycles are not retribution or punishment but a call to higher consciousness. These consistent life challenges are invitations to growth and spiritual refinement. Everything in our lives is another chapter in our souls' exuberant narrative. We magnetically draw the people, places, things, conditions, and circumstances that best serve our soul's evolution and for the benefit of the entire universe.

Our purpose and soul work is to free ourselves from our inclinations toward darkness on the radiant path of love. No one can do this for us; we get to do it for ourselves. That is a great gift. We are not at the mercy of anyone or anything, including God.

While we have many teachers, angels, and guides, ultimately, only we can save ourselves.

This independence does not mean that more enlightened beings are not available to help, support, and assist us along the way; they do, and we're never truly alone. In this world of shadows and light, the tender care of our soul family, angels, teachers, and guides is what sustains us all. Nevertheless, we did not come into physical existence to use supernatural powers or divine intervention to make our decisions or solve our earthly problems. Although divine intervention does occur on occasion, there are no cosmic shortcuts on the path of personal salvation and the ultimate liberation of our soul.

The path to enlightenment requires courage, tenacity, and unwavering commitment. Each time we stumble or fall, we must summon the strength to rise again with unwavering faith and resolve.

Each breath of life is a rare treasure.

It is a fleeting moment in the vast expanse of time and space, deserving of our reverence and complete attention. From a spiritual perspective, the glorious gift of a human life is the experience of experience. Each dawn and unfolding moment is "*yet*" another opportunity to shine brighter, be kinder, more compassionate, and loving to ourselves and others. In this radiant understanding, we freely bear the weight of our choices. No external judgment befalls us *other than the judgments we bring upon ourselves*. All roads, even the long way home, inevitably lead back to God. Triumphs or missteps, successes or failures, good or bad, all earthly experiences enrich and enhance our soul and benefit the loving universe. From this vantage, though mistakes are inevitable, we cannot fail in this wonderful sojourn of self-realization.

We are spiritual beings having a spiritual experience in a physical world for the absolute joy of the experience.

Even our missteps, when seen through a larger lens, are a necessary part of the collective consciousness. Everything serves as a lesson or gift, contributing to the expanding light and unending wisdom of the loving universe. The human mind might grapple with discerning good from evil, yet even our shadows are part of our radiance.

As we evolve and expand, we contribute to the advancement of the collective consciousness, illuminating the entire universe with the wisdom and insight garnered from our short foray into the world of form and matter.

In the human experience, enlightenment is our starting point, not the destination.

Though we are mostly veiled from this truth, the soul is forever pure and radiant. Our journey into the physical world is one of experience and remembrance. On the earthly plane, we deepen our understanding of ourselves and the Divine through the prism of choice, contrast, and change.

Nonetheless, the idea that our souls willingly embrace the shadow and light of a human life may be perplexing, yet it is a testament to the boundless gift of free will. Despite the heartaches and hardships of the physical world, the soul is never in danger, damaged, or hurt. On the contrary, the soul benefits from its flight into the night and journey back into the light. In the aftermath of life's storms, nothing has changed, no one is hurt, and there are no lasting effects on the eternal, unchanging nature of the soul and all is well. The wisdom garnered from a human life adds experiential depth to the expansive nature of the soul, God, and the loving universe.

Everything works together for the good and grace of all.

The exquisite beauty and wonderful gift of a human life is the complete liberty to explore all the possibilities of physical form in a material world. This freedom explains why some lives are easier than others. In our excitement to discover and explore, we may take on too many burdens. In these more challenging lives, we may perceive ourselves as a mere shadow of our true potential.

The weight of our more challenging lives may lead some to exit the planet prematurely, only to be reborn in another form with the same life lessons to be repeated. We will be stuck in these continuous loops and repetitive cycles until we learn the lessons or transcend them. Whatever we choose, darkness or light, or however long it takes us to learn our life lessons, the universe responds with kindness, benevolence, and unconditional love. Our gravest challenges are not a mark of punishment or retribution but moments held with boundless grace, love, and compassion.

Love forever holds us in grace, yet we determine the direction of our footsteps.

The divine paradox of the human condition allows for both shadow and light. This grace includes the freedom to help or harm ourselves or others. The most tragic and cruel, as well as the most benevolent and kind permeations of life are expressed in the grace of God's unending love. It is truly an unparalleled act of generosity that allows us the autonomy and consciousness to chart our own course. Within the vast expanse of a human life, every experience, from the heartbreaking to the heartwarming, finds its sacred place.

All our life experiences are simply that: *experiences*. Life unfolds as a series of shifting shadows and hues of light, each one bearing its own significance. Like droplets in an infinite pond, our choices endlessly ripple out, shaping our existence and impacting the whole of Creation. While some choices bring warmth and clarity, others stir up storms that become dark shadows. The weight of our choices adds to our joy and well-being or our downfall and demise. Some lives are so extremely dark and painful that an early exit is the most compassionate path, a testament to the universe's innate mercy.

On the path to love, even our most dire circumstances are a gracious movement of the Divine.

Our life challenges are not a punitive acts borne from the wrath or revenge of an angry, jealous God. Any notion of a vengeful God demanding praise is not an accurate representation. The radiant source *(God)* of all existence is the essence of pure love. Born of this light, this all-encompassing love, also, flows through every cell in our bodies and permeates the universe.

As beloved children of the Divine, we are eternally held in God's unending love and grace. We are never forsaken, abandoned, or alone. Even in moments of extreme darkness and sorrow, love remains our unmoving foundation, guiding us back to our inner light. While suffering echoes our choices, and mirrors our decisions, it is never bestowed upon us as a punishment. Indeed when suffering becomes unbearably intense, it can halt our growth and dim the light of our souls. Rather than catalyzing evolution, such profound pain and suffering can become a heavy chain, anchoring us in a very dark place.

In the loving universe, no heartache goes unnoticed or unattended.

The gentle hand of grace is always there to help us find our way, ensuring that no soul remains forever lost in the darkness. Many brave souls, seduced by life's dark shadows and seductive temptations, fall into the depths of their own personal hell. However, even these lost souls who wander deep into the labyrinth of want, desire and darkness are not forgotten, abandoned, or forsaken.

In the loving heart of the universe, compassion thrives, and kindness prevails.

No soul is ever truly lost; each soul is eternally cherished and loved. When the weight of our lives becomes too heavy, a gentle nudge leads us back toward the light and love of the Divine. In this, we find the profound mercy and tenderness of our very existence. Though suffering and pain may be profound, their grip is fleeting, and they do not ultimately affect the radiance of our eternal soul. More often, when we find ourselves slithering with the snakes or draped in darkness, it's not a reflection of innate evil within us but a result of shouldering too much in a specific life and losing our way. This misstep is common among younger souls who dive into the deep end with uninformed optimism despite the wise counsel of their angels, guides, and spiritual mentors. They often overlook the warnings about the risks of their choices, presented in the prebirth soul realm.

As previously explored, before we arrive, we are fully aware of the joys and perils of an upcoming life. Over time, most of us learn the delicate art of balancing challenges with opportunities. In the interplay of shadow and light, countless lessons unfold, guiding us toward our true purpose and our loving Creator.

Breaking free from automated behaviors ingrained by mass consciousness is a formidable challenge. This struggle is more difficult when shrouded in despair, blinded by ignorance, or trapped by excess. While the process of shifting our energy is straightforward, lasting change can be challenging. This holds particularly true when we've been deeply entrenched in certain patterns of behavior for an extended period.

For sustainable change, we must upgrade our consciousness and energetic alignments.

To achieve this, we must resist the innate pull that tempts us to return to familiar yet harmful habits. Otherwise, we risk being ensnared in relentless cycles of suffering and despair. As Einstein wisely stated, *"Insanity is doing the same thing over and over again, and expecting a different result."* While conquering our deep-seated habits is an undeniable challenge, it remains within the realm of the possible. Indeed, liberation is inevitable for all. It is a matter of *"when" and not "if."*

Change demands courage, as growth frequently resides beyond our comfort zone.

Personal autonomy and choice pave the path to our transformation and ultimate liberation. Each choice brings change, and every decision shapes our journey, empowering us to live with greater conscious intent, purpose, and love. As we move forward with increased wisdom and integrity, we undergo an existential transformation.

However, many times, advancing toward loftier aspirations entails challenging the comfort of the familiar and safe. Venturing into the unfamiliar and uncharted realms of the soul not only opens the doors of transformation, but also promotes our personal development, and accelerates the evolutionary process. As mentioned, a mantra, even a simple word like *"change,"* can be a potent instrument for transformation. It reminds us to break free from old patterns and move towards brighter potentialities.

In simplicity, a profound truth emerges: to change our lives, we must change.

The evolutionary process becomes purposeful when our actions mirror our intentions. True transformation is both an inward and outward journey. We take that essential first step toward liberation by acknowledging the weighty chains of old patterns and behaviors that held us captive, and kept us enslaved by our longing for comfort and safety. To continually release the firm grasp of the habitual and the familiar is an ongoing journey where we progress one day, one step, and one breath at a time. The smallest step toward more love and light sends ripples outward, unveiling vast realms of unseen potential and beckoning the aid of unseen spiritual beings of light.

Change is a perpetual process, and while it may occasionally feel like one step forward followed by two steps backward, it is also a journey filled with valuable lessons and opportunities for growth. Every step, regardless of its direction, contributes to our overall progress and understanding, ultimately leading us toward a more enlightened and fulfilled existence. Consistency, tenacity, and commitment are vital for conscious transformation and lasting change.

In the space of "what is" and "what can be," the true potential of our choices is revealed.

Though the above statement is true, we can only do so much on our own. Surrendering our will to a higher power and deepening our intuition serves as the wind beneath our wings, carrying us beyond self-limiting beliefs of failure and despair. This intentional surrender aligns us with the radiance of the universe and the love of God, *where the miraculous becomes possible.*

All change starts with a choice to do something different, and the resolve to persevere. Our smallest decisions are profound seeds of transformation, ripe with untapped possibilities. Take the act of brushing our teeth. It is a simple act, even mundane. Yet, when we neglect it because we're *"too tired,"* we are not just neglecting our dental hygiene; we overlook a promise to ourselves, a self-care ritual. It is a minor breach of discipline, a small gap in our personal resolve, but gaps when left unchecked, widen over time. The decline in personal autonomy doesn't happen overnight. It's a gradual descent, where minor omissions become habits and solidify into our character.

The seemingly insignificant decision of choosing comfort over responsibility compromises our resolve, negatively affecting our lives.

Over time, we might find ourselves compromising in bigger areas of life—*be it our diet, our exercise routine, our work ethic, or our relationships.* When we yield to the continual desires and impulses of the body and mind, like succumbing to fatigue and skipping oral hygiene, we subtly reinforce the notion that it's acceptable to surrender to immediate urges or emotions. On the other hand, when we summon the strength to resist immediate impulses and stay true to our smallest commitments, we fortify our resolve and prepare for life's larger challenges.

Similar to a muscle, resolve becomes stronger through practice. Bearing this in mind, the seemingly inconsequential choices we make each day, like brushing our teeth despite feeling weary, are profound declarations of our commitment to self-discipline, integrity, and long-term well-being.

How we do one thing is how we do all things.

Every thought, action, and repeated behavior is like a groove on a record. The more we play a particular song, the deeper the groove gets, making it all the more challenging to shift the needle or change the song. Nonetheless, the potential to change our thoughts, habits, and ultimately our lives is always available. Even so, our cyclic patterns, even those that are self-deprecating and unhealthy, may require much time and effort to change. While the possibility of change, and the innate resistance to change, might at first appear paradoxical, it becomes clearer when we consider the workings of the human mind. Just as water naturally flows along the path of least resistance, we, too, over time, gravitate toward familiar behaviors, well-worn pathways in our consciousness, even if they are not in our best interest.

Repetitive cycles form the root of all addictions, where the line between choice and compulsion becomes blurred. However, there's an empowering flip side.

Just as patterns can be formed, they can be reformed.

Every moment presents us with a choice, a chance to change our lives, and an opportunity to rewrite our narrative. The earlier we recognize a destructive cycle, the easier it is to break. But even if we find ourselves deeply entrenched in a pattern, the potential for change is always available and possible. With every conscious choice and every purposeful act of love toward oneself, we set a new pattern in motion.

Each act of self-love and determination creates ripples, breaking old cycles and forming new, healthier habits that empower rather than deplete.

When we ask the all-important question "*What is my most loving response?*", we open once-locked doors of opportunity and change. The good news is that our loftier aspirations invite angelic forces and divine assistance. Even the slightest shift upward in our energetic alignments can lead to profound change.

This upward transformation commences with self-awareness, leading to mindful, loving choices and deliberate, measured actions. However, if we rush or push too hard, we run the risk of feeling overwhelmed and reverting to familiar and unhealthy habits. As we attune ourselves to the gentle guidance of our soul, the path to self-liberation and freedom unfolds in the space of grace.

***Our present choices redefine our path, regardless of the past.**

And again, all roads eventually lead home. Consider the following. All our choices, including those we may view as mistakes, led us to this very moment of realization and the potential for liberation. A student of mine once shared a profound story about his journey. For forty years, a cigarette was a constant companion in his hand until one day, he made a single, life-altering decision. It may seem astonishing that it took four decades to reach that pivotal moment, but what truly transformed his life wasn't merely quitting the habit; it was the act of choosing something different.

***The key to change lies in an energetic shift from less to more radiance—more love.**

As my student transitioned into a higher energetic state, the possibility of breaking free from the habit became accessible. Conversely, during the years when he resided in the lower energetic resonance that included smoking, change not only remained elusive, but impossible. However, once he began making more loving choices for himself and his life, he naturally aligned with a higher vibration. In such an elevated state, change was not only possible, it was natural and inevitable.

That said, it's crucial to acknowledge that the gravitational pull of our habits can easily resurface. In the delicate process of personal transformation, it's not enough to simply decide to change; we must also reshape our surroundings. If we continue to frequent the same energetic environment that fostered our habits, the risk of relapse remains high. Instead, we should reconstruct our lives so that the environments, people, and places we engage with support our efforts rather than hinder our progress. It's essential to assess our friendships, living situations, and any factors that might trigger old, unhealthy habits. If they do not align with our well-being, distancing ourselves may be necessary. For many, altering their environment and redefining their relationships can be the most challenging aspect of personal transformation, particularly when overcoming addictions. Often, our unhealthy choices provided hidden benefits, such as a sense of community and joy. As we distance ourselves from these habits, people, and triggers, we may initially experience a profound sense of loss and loneliness, *what some call the dark night of the soul.*

However, as we persist with the intention to improve our lives and honor our souls, this temporary pain and suffering will passes. By raising our energetic frequency, we invite new opportunities, foster healthier habits, and forge authentic connections with others on a similar path.

In the realm of energy, frequency dictates possibility.

Once we break free from our familiar and ingrained energetic patterns *(habits)*, change isn't just possible; it's inevitable. With this in mind, my student could only break free from his smoking addiction when he consciously stepped into a future version of himself, one where he had already triumphed over his habit.

Within the lower vibrational frequency that included smoking, transformation was impossible. Yet, as he made increasingly more powerful and loving choices, he naturally gravitated towards a higher energetic resonance. Then, change flowed effortlessly, as if nature itself were blossoming.

Following the law of attraction, individuals in recovery should reevaluate their social circles and surroundings to enable positive transformation.

Often, it's crucial for them to raise their energy frequencies, necessitating changes in relationships and environments to align with the powerful, nurturing energies of love and care. This attracts more positive experiences and connections. In essence, to transcend ingrained habits, we need to embrace a higher path with determination, joy, and love in a sustainable manner. This can be achieved by making small shifts in consciousness, gradually replacing old patterns with beneficial ones over time.

Rather than fighting the darkness, we light a candle.

The process of transformation involves not just opposing the familiar but also consciously making more loving choices in a new direction. True transformation and lasting change require diligent effort over time. As we work to change the mental pathways carved by time, we must reshape our thoughts, align our actions and surrender to the transformational process.

Thought is an energetic field charged with emotion and intention.

Through consistent, loving, and conscious choices, we set in motion harmonious rhythms that honor our bodies, nurture our minds, and elevate our souls.

This necessitates a shift in our self-perception and outlook on life. Rather than perceiving ourselves as helpless victims, we reclaim our power, tap into the inner strength of our souls, and overcome past limitations through conscious intention, grace, and surrender. It all begins with our thoughts. Through the intricate pathways of our brain, specific thought patterns become familiar, well-traveled routes; *the defaults we resort to*. Those prone to anger find reasons to be angry; sorrow dwells in the hearts of the melancholic, and happiness graces the lives of the joyful.

These familiar pathways can confine us to unchanging energy patterns and undesirable habits. Despite our best intentions to evolve, an invisible switch resets to the default mode, and we find ourselves replaying the same old scripts. We generate over sixty thousand thoughts a day, *many on loop*. Our emotional responses follow, inviting parallel experiences, yet forcing change proves futile. The complexity of thought patterns and well-rehearsed scripts resist coercion.

"What we resist persists." ~ Carl Jung

Like wind-blown leaves, thoughts drift into and out of our minds without invitation or permission. They materialize unexpectedly, often unrelated to our desires or needs. Consider the following classic example: "Please do not think of a small purple elephant in the palm of your hand." Paradoxically, this very statement plants the vivid and undeniable image in your mind. We do not have direct control over the initial appearance of thoughts, as they arrive on their own accord. This explains why, many times, the mind can be as unpredictable and unruly as the weather. However, amidst this sense of lack of control, a subtle truth emerges.

Our true power lies in responding to life consciously rather than reacting impulsively.

While we cannot prevent thoughts from arising, we can choose how to engage with them. We can purposefully guide our minds toward the thoughts that best serve us. The purple elephant thought showcases this power. Once a thought is held in mind, we possess the agency to decide what happens next. We can let the thought linger, allowing it to consume our mental space, or we can acknowledge its presence without judgment and gently guide our focus elsewhere.

We must become conscious of our own awareness to guide the undisciplined mind. By observing our thoughts without attachment, we lessen their grip on us. Like watching clouds drift by, we acknowledge their presence without getting entangled in their forms or manifestations. This practice cultivates mental clarity and resilience, for as we detach from the constant stream of thoughts, we regain control over our attention. The uninvited nature of thoughts teaches humility, reminding us that we aren't all-powerful directors of our mental stage. This simple realization is empowering, for it frees us from the tyranny of every fleeting thought. Instead, we can find a balance between allowing our thoughts to arise as they do, while only investing our energy in those that align with our well-being and intentions.

A poignant story to illustrate this point comes from a Native American tradition. An old Cherokee chief taught his grandson about life with a tale of wolves.

"A fight is going on inside you," he told the boy. *"It is a terrible fight between two wolves. One is evil: heavy with anger, envy, sorrow, regret, greed, arrogance, self-pity, guilt, resentment, inferiority, lies, false pride, superiority, and ego."*

The wise old man continued, *"The other wolf is good, full of peace, joy, love, hope, serenity, humility, kindness, benevolence, empathy, generosity, truth, compassion, and faith. The same fight is happening inside me, and everyone else, too,"* he said. The grandson thought for a moment, then asked his grandfather, *"Which wolf wins?"* The old Cherokee replied, *"The one we feed."*

The push or pull of energy either feeds or starves our thoughts. Why all this emphasis on change and choice, you might wonder? Well, within the context of the conversation about salvation, a profound truth emerges. In the realm where self-rescue is the only option on the path to salvation, our thoughts hold the key to either elevate us to Heaven's gate or drag us down into dark dungeons.

The possibility of our liberation and ultimate salvation rests solely on our shoulders.

Through conscious discernment and deep introspection, we wield the power to influence the direction of our thoughts and the course of our lives. The ability to shape our thoughts and navigate our existence is an intimate journey into the depths of our being, where we discover the tools to chart our mental trajectories.

At the crossroads of self-liberation and enslavement, the compass of our thoughts wields the decisive power of change. In moments of deep contemplation and reflection, we recognize the profound synergy between our inner dialogue and the direction of our lives. Salvation is not completely dependent on the grace of omnipresent creator; it is the inevitable result of our conscious intention and purposeful choices.

As architects of our own deliverance, we stand at the threshold of transformative power.

In this sacred dialogue with ourselves, we decide what thoughts, to entertain or to consciously let go. The canvas of personal transformation calls us to wield the brush of thought, crafting our own destinies. However, for most of us, changing our thoughts and redirecting our lives is not easy. Well-worn paths of habits, thoughts, and addictions, deeply carved over the years, wield significant influence in our lives. These familiar routes, etched by repetition, guide our actions and choices, often subconsciously shaping our daily experiences and long-term journeys.

Shifting these ingrained patterns requires purposeful intent, determination, and a willingness to surrender to the grace of a benevolent creator and a loving universe.

Indeed, reshaping any habit requires redirecting our thoughts and creating new mental highways that lead in different directions. Imagine desiring a shift towards healthier eating. In employing the principles discussed earlier, attention is diverted away from undesirable foods. Instead, our focus centers on more nourishing choices.

An analogous personal experience emphasizes this concept: some time ago, I made a decision to avoid certain foods, *specifically, doughnuts and French fries*. This change required me to consciously redirect my attention and energy. I refrained from visiting fast-food restaurants and deliberately chose not to indulge in doughnuts or French fries. Instead, I stocked my cupboards with healthier alternatives.

Within the context of this conversation it's important to note that the universe abhors a vacuum. Therefore, as we transition away from old energy patterns, we must intentionally replace them with higher vibrational choices. If we don't make a purposeful change in our habits, we may find ourselves shifting from one negative habit to another.

Changing a habit requires that we redirect our focus from the undesirable and proactively engage with more favorable alternatives.

While this process may seem arduous due to deeply ingrained habits, it reaffirms that transformation is possible. Changing our ingrained habits requires consistent effort over time.

The process of change and personal transformation is not usually an overnight feat but the result of consistent effort over time.

The lessons garnered from this simple example of altering dietary habits extend to life's broader canvas. Just as one can detach from the allure of doughnuts and French fries, similar principles apply to more significant life choices. Redirecting our attention, investing energy in positive pursuits, and fostering unwavering determination are core to changing habits. Nonetheless, our most sincere efforts don't guarantee a successful change in our habits or in our lives. Whether we succeed or fail, our intention and purposeful effort contribute to the enrichment of our soul.

Furthermore, we can invoke the love and assistance of divine forces. We are not lonely travelers in a cold and uncaring universe. Having said that, please remember that although we can always ask for and receive assistance and guidance, our celestial family of angels, guides, and teachers will not direct our path, choose our course, or do our soul work.

Our path is our decision as is the direction of our footsteps, *towards or away from love*. No one can shoulder the responsibility of our personal evolution, liberation, and ultimate salvation. Each of us must undertake the deeply personal journey of salvation alone. In other words, we are here to bite the apple for the pure and absolute joy of it. Our every choice impacts our world, others, and God. Yet, as sweet as an apple may seem, if it does not elevate our spirit, it is wiser to refrain from eating it. Some apples are rotten, and we do not need all the experiences available in a world of constant change and divergent opposites.

Indeed, some experiences are so dark and bleak that if we indulge in them, it may take eons and many lives to heal. Please guard your precious soul, and be discerning in the experiences you invite and entertain. Darkness can be enticing but beware of the black abyss as it is all-consuming. It is best to avoid these treacherous roads. However, even if we find ourselves drowning in darkness or consumed by our desires, we are not eternally lost, helpless, or hopeless; love always prevails.

Love is the most powerful force in the universe; in truth, love is the only force.

At any moment, we can call forth the power of love and be lifted out of even the darkest pit of hell. All the same, it is best for our well-being to steer clear of both negative and dark forces, and be discerning about what we allow into our consciousness.

Everything has a magnetic pull.

For example, if we choose to watch horror films or the nightly news that primarily focus on life's negative aspects, we can be pulled into the shadows of these lower energy fields. We are responsible for our choices and the subsequent consequences. Not only are we accountable for the effects of our choices in our own lives, but we are also responsible for their effect on others.

Many will be positively or negatively impacted by our choices, including our children, students, colleagues, lovers, mates, spouses, friends, family, etc. Some in our sphere of influence would not find their way without our love and guiding light. Just as we needed the light of those who came before us to find our way, those in our care need our love and guidance. In this sense, we are partially responsible for the evolutionary success or failure of those in our care.

This is a great responsibility indeed and not to be taken lightly.

Our choices hold profound consequences, not only for our soul, but also for others within our sphere of influence.

Within our actions and omissions, the fabric of the present moment, the potential future, and echoes of the past are woven and rewoven. The path of our soul is not preordained; it's a delicate dance of choice and consequence that we craft and mold. From a universal perspective, all threads of destiny have gracefully converged in completion in the "*Eternal Now.*" All paths lead to the same place, the loving embrace of the Divine.

Nonetheless, in the relative space of our current experience, our choices are paramount to the outcomes of our lives, mirroring the resonant energy we emit. This elegant synchrony between our inner vibrations and life's unfoldment is a timeless interplay of shadow and light.

In the profound journey of personal salvation, we are powerful co-creators of our own reality, and not the helpless victims of fate.

We willingly participate in the ongoing symphony of existence, contributing our unique notes of consciousness to the composition of yet-to-be-discovered and explored universes. Consider your life like a book, a story of a blossoming white rose. Its chapters unfold from seed to bloom to wilting—*birth to death.*

This story is complete, the rose's journey is etched long before we turn the first page. Imagine opening this book. We decide where to start, whether to read straight through, skip, or revisit our favorite chapters. The freedom is ours, as with life itself. Like a book, our life's story is already written, waiting for us to read it. We hold the power to choose the chapters and story lines. Our life's narrative is set before birth. Yet, our choices determine what we read and when. Exciting new chapters emerge as our storyline unravels and evolves. Whatever chapter we choose to read, the storylines we create transform the trajectory of our lives. Often, we get stuck reading the same chapter over and over again in the repetitive cycle of our many lives.

To escape the loop of repetition, at some point, we must step outside it.

Just as flipping to a new chapter reshapes the story, embracing fresh choices reshapes our lives. To truly be free, we must take full responsibility for our choices, lives, and our soul's evolution. Liberation and its ultimate promise of salvation call us beyond our comfort zone, leading us into uncharted territories of the future. However, the path to freedom often unfolds in deliberate steps rather than hasty leaps. Moving too quickly can result in setbacks; sustainable growth should be our guiding principle.

The key is to embrace discomfort within reasonable limits, as pushing too hard can hinder our progress. Breaking the shackles of lifelong habits is a delicate journey, as growth flourishes in cycles of measured effort, ease, and grace.

The foundation of the universe is love.

Love is the very essence of the universe, nurturing and sustaining all life forms. It is the unifying force that unites individuals, communities, and the wider universe. We are born of love for the purpose of love, and we shall return to love as more love. The journey of life is ours to have; we may take as many detours as we please, but failure is not an option. We succeeded before we began; to exist is our success.

The gift of a human life, endowed with free will and choice, is the most precious gift of all; *nothing else compares.* We are blessed beyond measure to be *aware that we are aware*, and *to be conscious of our own consciousness.*

Each soul exists for the absolute bliss of its own existence, including your precious soul.

Life is not a test, or a punishment, nor a prize. We are not here to make amends or to prove ourselves worthy of God's love; our very existence makes us worthy. We are beloved children of God, seeds of the almighty. We are loved without condition. Nothing needs to change. Even our evolution is not required of us. We are absolutely loved, just as we are right now. Our lives in this physical plane are a cumulative and unique opportunity to experience abstract concepts, such as love and fear, in real-time.

While it's true that our souls remains safe and never in peril, our physical existence is finite, leading to an inevitable end. This concept can be perplexing, especially when considered from a less enlightened perspective. Many of us grew up with the belief that salvation or enlightenment comes from seeking guidance from a higher power, which can lead to confusion when faced with the reality of our physical mortality contrasting with the enduring nature of the soul. This juxtaposition highlights a spiritual journey where understanding and reconciling these aspects becomes a part of our conscious evolution.

In our most expansive version of self, we are always safe within God's loving embrace, and there is no need for a Savior.

This is not to say that there is no benefit to having a more enlightened being to guide us. Indeed, at certain levels of consciousness, we all need an intermediary and benefit from their love and guidance. Having said that, *Savior or not*, regardless of what transpires in the physical realm, our eternal souls remain untouched. Indeed, as previously mentioned, we come to this world of form and structure, which includes free will and autonomy, to experience ourselves, others and God in new and novel ways. However, this is not our true home, but an interesting experience that enhances and enriches our souls.

Nevertheless, many of us get caught in the magnetic pull of the familiar or are ensnared in the shallow superficialities of life, *forgetting our divine mission of love*. Nonetheless, there resides within us, a deep longing for the profound, and this is the driving force of our ultimate liberation and personal salvation. This longing often leads us on a spiritual or philosophical journey to explore the profound questions of existence, purpose, and the nature of reality. We seek to transcend the confines of a purely materialistic and shallow existence to discover the richness of a life lived in alignment with our true selves and deepest values.

A human life is a beautiful journey and grand adventure that we take for the pleasure and enrichment of our souls. Every country road, narrow highway, graveled path, open field, and dark detour leads us to the next most exciting experience.

There are no wrong or right turns on the path to love or the road to God.

While it is true that some roads are smooth and serene, others are rugged and challenging; all converge toward the same destination, *the loving embrace of the Divine*. Wherever we find ourselves on the road of free will and grace is exactly where we should be right now. The silent compass of the soul guides us to the exact road where the most valuable lessons and gifts are available. Every step charts the course of the human experience, guiding us toward our origin: Love, the very heart of the Divine.

Ultimately, all paths converge in love, and no one shall be left behind. In this regard, our choices carry significant weight. Every decision, whether seemingly insignificant or monumental, shapes the trajectory of our lives. This deeper insight brings us back to the notion that as free, autonomous beings, our salvation is in our own hands, deeply connected to the choices we make. In seeking liberation and personal salvation, it's these choices that steer our journey, either drawing us nearer to or further away from the essence of love.

By consistently making choices that resonate with our highest values, we essentially "*save*" ourselves from despair and darkness. Seen this way, salvation isn't a singular event, but a continuous journey of self-discovery and improvement.

Our true salvation is discovered in our ongoing quest to become the best versions of ourselves, driven by conscious decisions made each day.

In the complex fabric of our three-dimensional world, we face a simple dichotomy: to *move toward or away from love*. On one path, radiant with the shimmering hues of our inner light, we find our way to a celestial dawn of personal liberation and salvation. On the other, we get lost in the mire of a superficial existence or become shrouded in the obscurity and despair of oppression that dampen our light and hinder our advancement.

Either way, just as the Sun inevitably rises out of the blackest of nights, all souls will rise out of the ashes of ignorance and despair into the light of their inherent divinity and the love of God—*no one will be left behind, not a single soul.*

Salvation is inevitable, for we are children of the Divine, and our souls are forever cradled in the loving arms of God.

My every step into darkness or light,
is a heartfelt path of love that leads me back to you.
— Chrystal Rae

*Love forever holds us in grace,
yet we determine the direction of our footsteps*

You are a radiant being in a garden of light

Letter 10

bliss
garden of light

Do you know why the rose blossoms? Why it blooms?

It blossoms for the joy of blossoming and blooms because blooming is the fullness of its joy. We, too, will blossom and bloom in our own way and time. Like the rose, we exist for the bliss of our own existence. We come into and out of the material world for the pure and absolute joy of the experience. Everything and everyone in the known and unknown universe exists for bliss: *the bliss of a new day and the nightfall, too.*

Nothing is excluded from the bliss of our existence; the prickly thorns and inevitable wilting of all things are integral to our joy.

The rose, ripe with clear skies, sunny days, droughts, and storms, is the successful result of yesterday's toil, a journey that began long before it took root and will continue far into the future. Just as the seed had to break free of its dark confines and make the arduous journey into the vast sky of its own flowering, we, too, have struggled, cried, given up, failed, conquered, and succeeded in breaking through the dark barriers that once chained us to a lesser version of ourselves.

The sacred journey of the soul, from birth to death, and rebirth, unfolds with grace, love, and revelation. A human life, though glorious, is far from easy. Finding our way in a world of constant change, limitless choices, and extreme contrasts can be quite challenging. We are here to explore the myriad of life experiences, both on its shallow surface and in its deep depths.

Planet Earth is a garden of light, blossoming with fragrant flowers and prickly thorns.

Every soul that ventures into the physical realm joyously anticipates the adventure of a human life and the opportunity to explore and expand in consciousness. To know oneself, others, and God in a realm of absolute freedom and choice is a treasure beyond all treasure. Whether our lives unfold in joy or sorrow, there's much to learn and to love on this glorious planet.

Mother Earth is fertile ground for the soul, offering an unmatched realm of adventure, exploration, and self-discovery. Our time here is fleeting and short, every moment brimming with potential and joy. But just as a candle swiftly wanes in the wind, we arrive, blink our eyes, and then, just as quickly, it is time to go. Given the brevity of our time here, what we accomplish between our first and last breath is of great value to our souls.

The experiences we gather during our human exploration of love, light, and shadows enrich and enliven not only our souls but also the entirety of creation.

In the physical realm, graced with autonomy, free will, choice, and self-awareness, the soul encounters rare opportunities for evolution that are both unique and essential for its expansion. Our innate ability to choose our own path doesn't change the reality that our lives unfold unpredictably, marked by countless unexpected twists and turns.

Although the choices we make do play a crucial role in shaping the outcomes of our lives, it's vital to acknowledge that we don't exist in isolation. Regardless of our good or bad choices, many external factors profoundly impact our lives. Plans may not always materialize as envisioned, leading us down divergent paths. This unpredictability is a profound invitation to embrace humility and expand in consciousness. In addition, our journeys through life are finite and fleeting, with the duration and trials of the path veiled in uncertainty.

Impermanence is at the core of the human experience, reminding us of the priceless value of each and every moment.

Amidst this swirling uncertainty, we are bestowed with a precious opportunity to wholeheartedly embrace the present, guided by our most cherished values and a profound reverence for the boundless love that unites us all.

Love is alive in every burgeoning possibility, radiant bloom, and wilting flower.

It is a universal force that permeates and sustains all that exists. In the temporal world of form and matter, everything, even apparent opposites, is an expression of divinity and *the unfolding of love*. Indeed, our world is a blossoming garden of shadow and light where both weeds and flowers grow. This metaphor extends further, for within this garden, a diverse array of creatures thrive, including diligent beetles and caterpillars, graceful butterflies, unassuming worms, elusive snakes, and concealed predators.

The stark contrast between shadow and light and the grand diversity of life itself is, at its core, an expression of love intricately mirroring the vastness of the universe. In the grand expanse of all existence, and considering the relatively short duration of a human life, we are not merely passive participants in random or arbitrary events. On the contrary, we exist within a universe that intentionally guides us towards people, places, and experiences essential for our personal growth and spiritual transformation.

Our earthly journey deepens our awareness, nurtures a profound connection with the divine, and enhances our capacity for love. Despite the transient and sometimes harsh nature of a human life, our souls remain eternally pure and unaltered. Every aspect of existence, from the blossoming flowers to spidery weeds and slithering snakes, contributes to the richness and diversity of our shared human experience. To exist is absolute bliss, *and even the most down trodden soul is a celebration of life's wondrous unfoldment*. Life, with its continuous interplay of shadow and light, unfolds as a perpetual and joyous journey, guiding us from moments of profound stillness into transformative radiance, only to lead us back to an even deeper level of stillness—*a stillness so ecstatic, that it appears motionless.*

The true essence of the soul is pure and unbound bliss.

It is a profound joy that reverberates with such incredible speed that it returns to its starting point before it departs, all the while maintaining a state of serene and unchanging presence. Each soul that comes into being is a joyous embodiment of this active presence. No words can hold the weight of such a joyous expression. The closest semblance of truth is to say that it is love expressed as more love, *a love brighter than a thousand suns, more radiant than all the stars merged into one.*

In the loving universe, that which is most beautiful perpetually comes into existence—*this includes both you and me.* More directly, you are the most exquisite embodiment of the Divine. If you fully understood your own radiance, divine purpose, and luminous light, even the darkest of nights would be included in your experience of light.

You are the manifestation of God's boundless love in its full splendor. You are pure bliss expressed through you, as you, and *for you*. Does this mean there will be no pain or suffering? Certainly not. The human experience encompasses moments of joy, pain, freedom, and suffering. While pain is unavoidable, suffering remains a matter of choice.

Suffering is pain carried over time with a story attached to it.

Buddha wisely noted that "*suffering is the desire for things to be other than they are.*" We long for the rose to unveil its tender petals, but capriciously, it remains enfolded. Or, we hope that the rose never wilts, and of course, it does. Again, pain is not the problem. It's the narrative we attach to the pain that generates and prolongs our distress and suffering, even after the physical sensations have subsided. Suffering always arises from a *"push"* or *"pull"* for the present moment to be different than it currently *IS*.

To illustrate this point, consider the analogy of holding a hot coal in your hand: it burns until you release it. Similarly, the sad stories and self-depreciating narratives can be a source of great pain and suffering until we let go of the need for things to be other than they are. With this in mind, blaming others, circumstances, or external conditions for our pain is like holding onto a hot coal. Regardless of what has happened or who may have hurt us, the story we tell ourselves is the true source of our continued pain and prolonged suffering.

When we let go of our good or bad stories, we free ourselves from needless suffering.

Letting go of our attachments and preconceived ideals about how life should be not only frees us but also transforms our souls and deepens our capacity for love. Making a conscious decision to meet life on its terms is a rational choice because resisting the present moment is a futile battle; whatever *IS*, already *IS*.

Our opinions about the past, present, or future do not alter reality. Does our inability to change the present moment mean we should surrender or passively tolerate injustice? No, it means we can actively choose not to suffer or squander our precious and limited time on this planet wishing for things to be different. Instead, we embrace life as it *IS*, without preconceptions or resistance.

The good news is that when our actions come from a place of love, things tend to naturally align, *even if they don't*. With this understanding, the saying *"we reap what we sow"* takes on profound meaning.

A conscious movement of love, no matter how small, shifts paradigms and alters universes.

Indeed, every thought, intention, and action grounded in love is a seed planted in the fertile soil of existence, nurtured by the radiant energy of the Divine. This radiance encompasses not only our brighter aspects but also our shadows and less radiant expressions of self. In other words, on every level of existence, the next most radiant possibility is always available.

We enter the temporal world of form and matter, bearing dormant seeds that await the perfect conditions to blossom, bloom, and ripen. However, nothing is predetermined or guaranteed except for the unconditional love of our Creator which is bestowed upon us with unmeasured grace. With this grace, we are gifted the free will to choose love or fear, and our lives unfold accordingly.

Every loving choice we make holds the silent promise of a future filled with even more love.

This is a powerful concept that brings to mind the profound wisdom of *Mother Teresa*. When asked to participate in a protest against the Vietnam War, she replied with a resounding message of unity and peace: "*I will not fight against the war, but when you walk for peace, I will stand beside you.*" With this statement, the devout saint highlighted the transformative power of love and collaboration over conflict and division. She also demonstrated that unity and compassion are our most potent tools for building a better world.

When we wholeheartedly embrace this truth and make love our guiding principle, we uncover a wellspring of strength and resilience within ourselves. In stark contrast, allowing fear to prevail can leave us exposed and erode the very core of our inner fortitude. In an affirmative universe, love stands as a singular, unwavering truth. What this means is that the loving universe only acknowledges that which is true; everything else is null and void. Staying in tune with the affirmative universe means saying "Yes" even when faced with a "No." Let me illustrate this idea further. Imagine you've planted a garden, eagerly anticipating the blooming of every flower. However, despite your diligent care, some flowers fail to thrive and wilt. Embracing the notion that not all flowers will flourish as hoped allows us to appreciate the diversity and fleeting nature of life.

This acceptance aligns us with the affirmative universe, where we acknowledge the beauty and wisdom in both flourishing and fading flowers. Saying "Yes" in this context doesn't imply agreement with the situation; rather, it signifies a profound recognition of the present reality.

Instead of pushing or pulling for things to be other than they are, we can accept the present moment, recognizing the divine essence in all things.

Through this garden example, we come to realize that saying "*Yes*," even to a "*No*," is a silent acknowledgment that despite our best efforts, not all flowers will bloom as we had hoped. The same holds true in the broader expanse of our lives. Saying "*Yes*" to life, rather than resisting it, conserves our energy, enabling us to be more proactive and loving. This willingness to meet life on life's terms not only aligns us with the affirmative universe but also serves as the key to avoiding unnecessary suffering over things we can't control or change. As mentioned, *what we resist persists*. There is profound wisdom in accepting things as they are, even when they don't align with our initial desires.

Rather than waging a futile fight against the wind, we choose a path of peace and become a force for goodness and grace.

Embracing this perspective aligns us with the truth of an affirmative universe, benefiting us personally and contributing to the betterment of the collective consciousness. However, this alignment with the present moment doesn't imply acquiescence to unfavorable circumstances or negative energies. Instead, it signifies our conscious alignment with the positive and the good. Saying "*Yes*" to life means acknowledging the intricate interplay of light and shadow, joy and sorrow while recognizing that within every experience lies an opportunity for growth, understanding, and transformation. When we say "Yes" even to a "No," we affirm our commitment to truth and love.

Just as a gardener meticulously plants seeds in fertile soil, choosing the right time for optimal blossoming, we, as *ambassadors of light*, sow seeds of love and peace. Instead of battling the darkness, we choose to light a candle.

A single candle illuminates the blackest of nights.

Consider a simple example: when the wind unexpectedly blows a door open, instead of reacting with frustration, we can acknowledge that the door has blown open without adding a dramatic story. Calmly and without emotional turmoil, we have options. We can opt to do nothing and leave the door open, take action and close the door, or any number of other viable options. Whatever we choose to do, there is no resistance to the simple fact that the door has blown open. This approach allows us to respond with mindfulness and adaptability.

While it's understandable to resist life when it unfolds in ways that seem cruel, unkind, or unfair, such resistance is akin to pushing against the wind, *a futile fight and a useless battle we will always lose*. Mastering the art of accepting life as it is, without any agenda, may take time, but it's a skill that can be developed through practice. Starting with smaller challenges and gradually progressing to more significant life struggles can help in honing this skill.

We are born of a loving universe and never given more than we can handle.

Many times, the best we can do is to stay peaceful about not being peaceful. When we are able to find serenity even in the absence of tranquility, we free ourselves from the need for things to be other than they are, *and our suffering stops*. To be clear, the acceptance of the inherent ups and downs of everyday existence does not imply that we live our lives like a feathers in the wind.

Instead, it suggests that we use the winds of change and challenge to carry us to places we would not reach of our own volition. Indeed, change and challenge prime our souls for spiritual advancement.

Whether we succeed or fail in terms of our life circumstances is of little consequence to the soul, or God; what matters, in the end, is our loving intent and diligent effort to move towards love and away from fear. Even on our darkest days, we are unconditionally held, loved, and accepted in grace and goodness.

The love that creates and sustains us is absolute and unconditional.

Our good or bad actions have no bearing on this omnipresent love. There is nothing we can do to earn God's love, and nothing we can do to lose God's love; *it is inherent to our very being*. Nonetheless, from an everyday human perspective, what we do matters, and it matters a lot. Our thoughts and actions carry much weight and have a profound effect on the course of our individual lives. We attract "*what we are*" and not necessarily "*what we want.*"

What we think about we bring about.

If we focus on the negative and what we don't want, we pull it toward us; the opposite is also true. When we focus on goodness and grace, they will be our reality. Either way, our existence is not the result of a random, unkind, or unloving universe. Everyone, and everything, exists as an expression of God's unending love, including you.

You are a perfectly imperfect child of a loving universe, the progeny of the Divine. You may not know your own magnificence and inherent glory, but I do. You are the most beautiful possibility of you. Your good and bad deeds, successes and failures are all included in the fullest expression of your divine soul. You are a radiant being in this luminous garden of light that we call life. You are the soil, seed, root, stem, buds, thorns, petals, blossoms, blooms, and yes, you are the wilting too.

You are all of this, none of this, and so much more. You are magnificent and stunningly beautiful in every sense of the word. How I wish you could see your grace and beauty through my eyes and understand the depth of love that envelopes you. You are a rare star in the night sky. A never-to-be-replicated expression of the Divine. Your existence, with all your experiences, thoughts, emotions, and actions, is unlike any other. The incredible journey of your life, with all its ups and downs, is a story that has to be told. No one else could tell your story but you. Only you can fully perceive the world from your perspective. And, only you can understand your innermost self.

Each soul that comes into and out of the temporal world is a radiant expression of universal singularity expressed in the multiplicity of diversity. And, yet again, allow me to say this directly to your beautiful soul.

You are God in the making, God manifest, and God realized—as you, through you, and for you.

Your very existence adds depth and richness to the collective consciousness of all humankind, the loving universe, and God. You are a masterpiece come to life. You are the love of all love, expressed and manifested as you.

This love is so radiant and alive it echoes forward and backward in time. It is a priceless gift of the Divine, *a blessing beyond all blessings*. There is nothing you can do to earn this love, and there is nothing you can do to lose this love.

Irrespective of our good or bad thoughts, words, or actions, God's love does not waver.

In the presence of such divine radiance and love, all the temporal superficialities of a human life vanish like shadows born of and absorbed by the light of the Sun. When seen through the lens of truth and love, what was once deemed significant is unveiled as mere dust, devoid of meaning and significance, and what really matters comes to the forefront; *love*.

Love does not judge, condemn, blame, or shame: love loves and then loves more.

This realization is profoundly transformative. Qualities often underestimated, such as care, compassion, tolerance, forgiveness, understanding, loyalty, and, above all, love, emerge as the most authentic expressions of our true selves.

These virtues and qualities hold the essence of what truly matters in our lives, serving as the ultimate measure of a meaningful and successful existence. They provide depth and richness to our human experience. They are the benchmarks by which we gauge our interactions, contributions, and impact on the world.

When we prioritize these virtues, we not only lead a more fulfilling life but also leave a lasting legacy of love and kindness that extends far beyond our years on Earth. Through this one revelation, we come to understand that we are the radiant center of our own existence, holding such profound significance in creation that entire universes of potentiality would be fundamentally altered or collapse in our absence.

Every soul, including your precious soul, is cherished and enveloped in a love beyond any conceivable measure. Your joy is the joy of the universe; your tears are the tears of God. You are so very loved that everything in the universe is orchestrated for your benefit and well-being. You are the rose, the blossoming, the bloom, and the wilting, too. You are the very reason the Sun graciously rises and softly sets. You are the Moon that graces the night with its comforting light. You are the bliss that made it all possible, too.

In the loving universe, nothing is left to chance regarding your precious soul.

Every speck of dust, drop of water, and cloud in the sky is a joyful emergence of the Divine. Even my presence is meant to be part of your unfolding happiness and eternal bliss. I came back to hold you in the warm embrace of unconditional love, to joyously accompany you to the radiant heights of your potential, to shine a light of awareness into the dark corners of your life, and to carry you across the deep oceans of disappointments and despair.

As an ambassador of light, and as a representative of the loving universe, and someone who truly loves you, I came back to this earthly plane so that you would know that you are not alone, and that someone cares; *that someone is me*. I love you with all my heart, my soul, and everything I am for all of time and space. In this light, these heartfelt Love Letters are an expression of my profound love and affection for you. I wrote them to comfort and support you, contributing to your personal growth and the expansion of your soul. To this end, these sacred teachings have been spiraling toward you for eons of time and many lives, finally finding you on this most auspicious day of your blossoming.

Like the radiant rose, we blossom and bloom in our own divine timing.

Indeed, you are reading these words because it is your time to do so. The radiant seed of Divinity, planted within you long before you arrived in the physical realm, is now unfolding its tender petals and reaching toward the inner light of divinity that lies dormant within you.

Our divine reunion on the pages of this book is much celebrated in the heavens, on Earth, and beyond. Time and again, we have found each other on the solid ground of a human life to be part of each other's blissful unfoldment.

Planet Earth is a glorious garden of light where we are free to explore and expand in love.

In our shared human experiences and collective explorations, we dive into the complexities of our emotions, thoughts, and feelings. We learn from one another, gaining insights and wisdom that can only emerge from the interplay of diverse minds and hearts.

Through these encounters, we recognize the universality of our human struggles and joys, expanding our capacity for empathy, compassion and love. Through engaging with others, we become more aware of the intricate interplay between our inner worlds and outer realities. As we come together in a shared experience of conscious expansion, we awaken to the power of our thoughts and intentions, realizing the reverberating ripple of their effect.

Consciousness, too, unfolds and deepens in shared moments of humanity.

Through our interactions, we elevate our personal consciousness, contributing to the upliftment of the collective consciousness of humanity. In the immense landscape of human existence, we set forth on a noble journey of the soul, contributing both our shadow and light to an ever-evolving universe.

Each of us possesses a unique radiance and beauty, yet, it is within our collective human experience that we truly thrive. There, amidst shifting shadows and brilliant light, we delve deep into the human experience, uncovering our most profound purpose and radiance. As we unravel the layers of human consciousness, we reveal the ever-expanding potential of our soul. These intertwined forces hold immense power to sculpt.

Each soul, a seed of the divine, blossoms into a radiant future yet to unfold.

In our shared moments of unity within the human experience, we find an invitation to nurture growth, forge deeper connections, and enrich our reservoirs of love and kindness.

As we reach the end of our fragrant journey through the garden of light, I offer you a white rose, a symbol of my love and dedication. This delicate bloom is a hopeful seed, cradling the vast universe within, holding the promise of many more blossoms to come. May it take root and flourish, spreading love and light to all it encounters.

Never forget that our journey through the radiant garden of this life is just one step in the grand dance of existence.

In the fragrant gardens of our many shared lives, under countless radiant suns, and in many worlds yet to be born, our eternal bond of love is the seed that forever unites us.

Each garden we explore, every sunrise we witness, and every fragrance that envelops us will be a new chapter in our never-ending love story. Until then, may these words, and the love that inspired them, grant you the wisdom, strength, and determination to transcend any limitations that may confine you in smallness or lack. May you find the grace and wisdom to root yourself in the fertile ground of truth and love, recognizing your divinity, radiance, and divine light.

Above all, may your footsteps, into and out of this earthly realm, unearth the omnipresent light and love of God's fragrant bloom, blossoming within you and all around you.

You are the radiant blossom of my soul
and the eternal bloom of my heart.
— Chrystal Rae

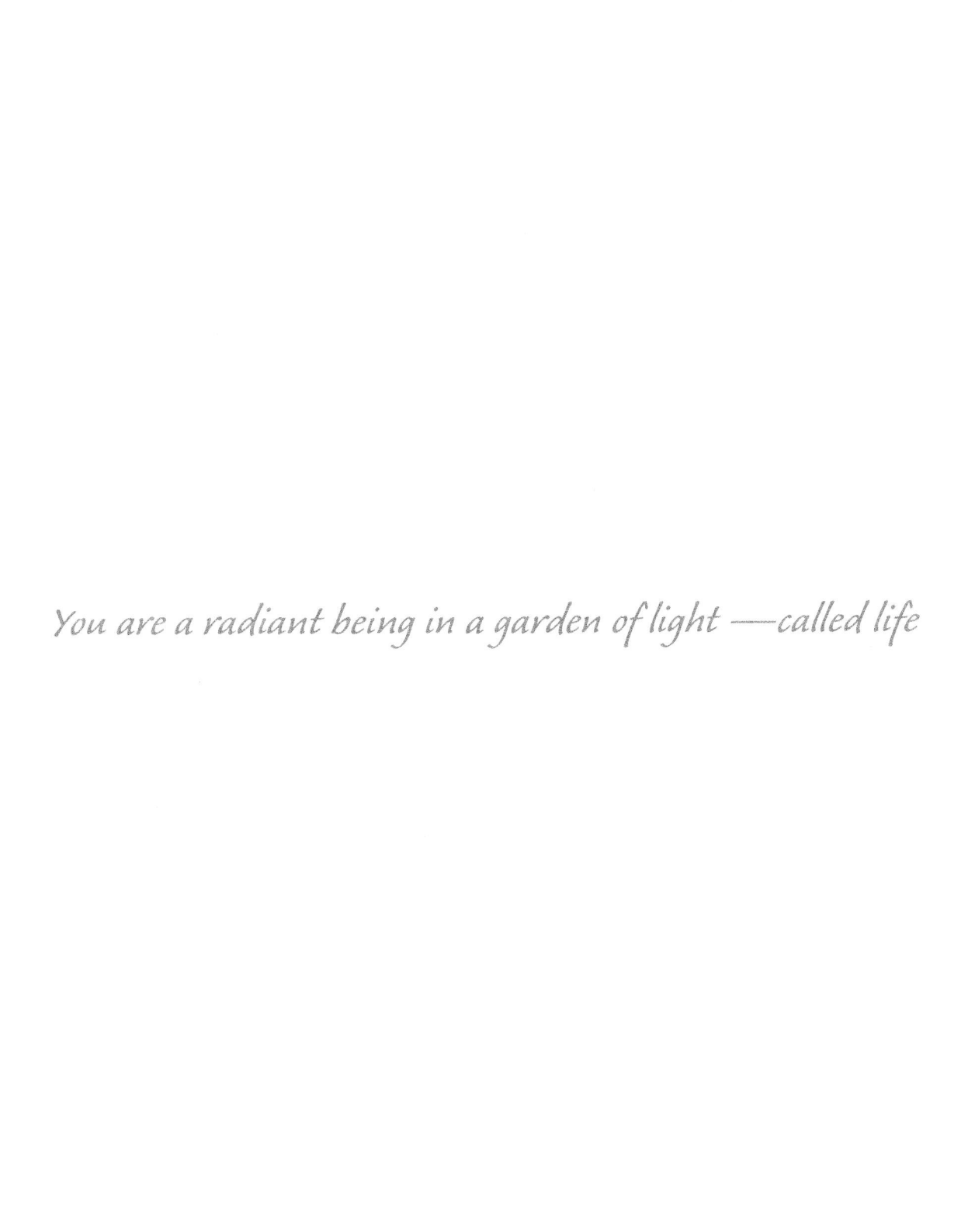

You are a radiant being in a garden of light —called life

Only love can fulfill the deep longing of the soul

Letter 11

longing
what do you really want?

What do you really want?

If you could have anything, what would it be? What is the deep longing of your soul? What would be different in your life if you magically received that one thing? Would you be happier? Happy forever? More secure? Less stressed? Would you live forever? Have more friends? A perfect family? Better relationships? Perfect health? Never get sick? Of course, the answer to these questions, at least, in the long run, is a resounding no, nothing would change.

Wherever you go, there you are.

Nonetheless, it's a common misconception that happiness exists outside of ourselves. We often mistakenly believe that genuine happiness would be within our grasp if only circumstances were different. When prompted to consider what changes we'd make to achieve happiness, our responses typically revolve around acquiring more wealth, improving relationships, attaining robust health, gaining recognition, witnessing societal changes, undergoing physical transformations, or changing our bodies.

Beneath these desires, spoken or unspoken, lies a profound yearning for security, love, and affection. The irony is that we are always safe and unconditionally cared for by a loving Creator, yet we are mostly unaware of it. Even if we were able to magically manifest all our desires, that would only bring temporary satisfaction, and these moments would be fleeting and ultimately empty.

"Happiness is on a curve; what goes up will come down. True contentment is on a straight line, unmoved by the highs and lows of everyday existence." ~Roy Williams

Possessions, people, accolades, money, success, awards, and all the other accumulations in life have diminishing returns. Let's consider the example of purchasing a new car. Initially, the mere thought of it fills us with joy. We take great care to park our new car far away, meticulously wash it, and drive cautiously. However, as time passes, the car inevitably gets weathered, used, scratched, and our cautious parking habits wane. The same car that initially brought immense joy gradually loses its luster and allure. This shift in value is often misunderstood, as the car's intrinsic worth remains unchanged. What does change is our perception and appreciation of its value, which is subjective.

Nothing in the temporal world brings us lasting joy, ultimate fulfillment, or true contentment.

Just like all other material possessions and experiences, new cars, thrilling adventures, and exciting relationships can only provide temporary satisfaction. True contentment is a sense of peace that remains unshaken by external circumstances or acquisitions. What we often mistake for happiness is merely an ephemeral excitement that fluctuates, much like the ever-changing weather. Nothing outside of us has an intrinsic state of peace that is constant and enduring. Numerous studies support this idea. One noteworthy finding showed that lottery winners and individuals who have experienced significant life-altering traumas tend to return to their baseline emotional state within three months. How is it possible for us to revert to our innate emotional equilibrium, regardless of external circumstances? The answer lies in the phenomenon of "*hedonic adaptation*."

This is a psychological concept that suggests that we possess a default level of happiness to which we naturally gravitate regardless of life events, whether positive or negative. Think of this default as an emotional thermostat, constantly readjusting us to a familiar level of contentment.

For instance, when something positive, like winning the lottery, occurs, we experience an initial surge of euphoria and joy. However, over time, we acclimate to the new lifestyle or possessions, and what was once thrilling becomes the new normal, causing our baseline happiness to readjust to its usual set point. Conversely, when confronted with adversity or trauma, our initial distress may be intensive, and perhaps, even unbearable. Yet, with time, we adapt and develop coping strategies, leading our emotional state to gradually return to its consistent baseline.

The ability to reset to a familiar emotional baseline serves our evolutionary process.

Our emotional equilibrium helps us navigate life's highs and lows without being constantly overwhelmed. It also highlights that sustained happiness is not solely dependent on external circumstances. Instead, the return to a familiar emotional set point is intrinsic to our being. While the answer to the deep longing of the soul might seem simple, its implications are profound.

On a superficial level, we seek enduring happiness, inner contentment, and personal growth through the cultivation of positive mindsets. However, from a strictly spiritual perspective, true inner peace is not contingent on adaptation to our environment or our emotional thermostat—*it is a consequence of our spiritual development and divine connection.*

Only love can fulfill the deep longing of the soul.

We are energetic beings with unique emotional set points, vibrations, and frequency. In a magnetic universe, where *"like"* attracts *"like,"* we naturally attract life experiences that align with our current energetic state. Though many other life experiences are available, both positive and negative, we are limited by the constraints of our consciousness and our ability to align with higher vibrational possibilities.

A simple analogy related to the perception of light illustrates this point. The human eye is capable of detecting colors like red, orange, green, cyan, blue, and violet, but there are many other colors beyond our visual spectrum that we cannot see. For instance, butterflies can perceive ultraviolet light, which is invisible to us. Our limited range of vision restricts what we can or cannot perceive, but does not negate the existence of these phenomena. Whether we are aware of it or not, a vast realm of energetic activity unfolds within the very space of our existence.

As we evolve, previously unavailable realities become accessible.

While it might be tempting to believe that a higher evolutionary stage equates to something better, the complexity of the universe defies a simple, one-size-fits-all answer. The notion of being more or less evolved is not intended as a ranking, judgment, or criticism; it is merely a statement of the diverse paths available to the soul.

Our evolutionary state perfectly mirrors our soul's natural progression.

This understanding offers clarity on our present location within the energetic continuum, underscoring the inherent synchrony and rhythm of our soul's journey. To illustrate, consider the analogy of school grade placement: first, second, and so on. Just as a college student is not better than a kindergartner, our evolutionary state does not imply superiority or inferiority.

Nonetheless, the opportunities and experiences available to college students are markedly different from those available in kindergarten. Each soul possesses a unique yet ever-changing energetic equilibrium. The good news is that our current position, whether in kindergarten or college, is not a permanent state. We are continually in flux: growing, learning and expanding in consciousness. It is crucial to remember that lasting happiness cannot be found outside of ourselves, as everything in the temporal world has a beginning, a middle, and an end. A *"push"* or *"pull"* for things to be different does not change the present moment, and is the source of our suffering. And, as previously mentioned, even if we get what we think we want, everything in the temporal world is fleeting and has diminishing returns.

To quote the Buddha, "*the source of our joy is the root of our sorrow.*" However, this doesn't imply that we shouldn't savor the pleasantries of life. We are here to enjoy the myriad of life experiences. Our successes and failures provide the necessary stimulus for spiritual growth. The physical world is a wonderful and enlightening school for the soul.

We come into a physical embodiment to revel in the joy of existence, partake in the experience of experience, and rediscover what our soul already knows: Love is all that matters.

The quest for joy and success in the three-dimensional world, though ultimately unfulfilling, is an important evolutionary step of soul development. A human life is a perfect platform to fulfill the deep longing of the soul to expand and evolve. A physical embodiment offers us the opportunity to know ourselves, others and God in new and novel ways.

The ultimate gift of a human life is personal autonomy and freedom.

With this in mind, the answer to the question "*What do I really want?*" holds profound and life-altering implications. When seen from a broader perspective, our desires point to the soul's deep longing to move beyond the mundane and toward the profound.

To this end, the freewill paradigm provides the soul with a unique opportunity to explore the flickering lights and dark shadows of the physical world in an experiential way. When we become aware of the implications and opportunities of a human life, it is exciting and, perhaps, a bit daunting. Nonetheless, many of us get stuck in the collective of mass consciousness, negating our birthright of personal autonomy and freedom. We often conform to the crowd, following the default path of complacency, and simply doing what everyone else does. Consequently, we miss out on the joy and excitement of personal autonomy. Instead of blazing our own trail, we follow the leader and never venture beyond the safety of the herd. As a result, we are absent from our own lives, detached from our bodies, and oblivious to our soul's genuine longing for awakening. Under thee circumstances, we tend to sleepwalk through life, caught in a collective dream of despair and helplessness. While this might sound somber, it's only one aspect of a much larger story.

Evolution is an inevitable journey for all, and no one will be left behind.

Concerning our evolution, the question is *"when"* and not *"if."* Everything unfolds in Divine timing, never too early or late. Like the development of caterpillar wings at the precise moment it is time to take flight, our soul experiences similar spontaneous and transformative moments. Every potentiality has already transpired and reached its culmination in the *"Eternal Now,"* including our current life experience.

Time is stacked upon itself in the "Eternal Now" where all possible timelines have already come into completion.

Our life as we know it is the unfolding of a unique vibrational alignment, potentially positive or negative, guiding us towards a specific destiny. Yet, irrespective of our chosen path, every road leads us back to one inevitable destination: *back to our source, God.* This notion underscores the profound truth that all possible outcomes in the universe are already in completion. In other words, there is nothing new in the universe.

Our current life is a consequence of the deep longing of our soul to experience itself in a particular way and the subsequent energetic alignments. Because all energetic pathways and timelines are already complete in the *"Eternal Now"*, there is no wrong way to go. As previously mentioned, all roads inevitably lead back to our Source. Whether we wander into the darkness or stray into the light, nobody will be left behind, forgotten, or doomed forever. With this promise, it may seem that awakening in this life, or in any life, is superfluous, yet, it is actually crucial that we awaken. Every life is vitally important for our spiritual growth and the evolution of our soul.

The soul longs for independence and self-realization within a framework of unlimited experience and free will. Our earthly journeys deepen not only our comprehension of self, others, and the divine but also contribute to the enrichment of the whole of creation. Spiritual advancement is not only inevitable, but also pleasurable for the soul. Considering this, the attraction to these elevated teachings and poetic writings are no coincidence; they reflect the profound opportunities this life presents for transformation and spiritual progression.

Our slightest inclination toward or away from love creates or destroys vast universes.

Even so, for many of us, the gravity and consequence of our decisions largely go unrecognized. As conscious beings, our ultimate pursuit, often unbeknownst to us, is to awaken from the *"illusion of separateness"*.

The soul intuitively moves towards the benevolence and grace of the Divine.

While we may not immediately understand the forces that draw us toward or steer us away from certain people, places, or events, our awareness of these energetic alignments grows over time. As this understanding deepens, the once-disparate pieces of our experiences gradually coalesce, ultimately presenting a clear and coherent picture of our life's journey.

When we become aware that we are aware, everything changes. With our awakening, even our evolution accelerates, transforming us into a conduit of love and a source of healing light. Our earthly journey, whether it leads to evolution or devolution, impacts everyone and everything. Just as lifting the water level of the ocean elevates all the boats, raising our consciousness contributes to the upliftment of the entire universe.

A single decision has the power to pivot an entire life course for better or worse. In addition, what we do today can, and does, significantly influence the circumstances of our yet unborn future lives.

Future suffering can and should be avoided now.

How? The answer is so simple that it is often overlooked. When our intentions, choices and actions are founded in love, potential suffering is naturally avoided. With love as our anchor, and compassion as our compass, we attract more loving circumstances, people, places, and things. Often this involves reconciling past errors and grievances, and intentionally sharing more love and light in all our relationships, particularly the most vital relationship—*the one we have with ourselves*. Our personal awakening is essential in the unfoldment of the loving universe.

Each step we take toward love is a step closer to God.

Our every choice powerfully influences and impacts the lives of many. In this sense, we are responsible for our energetic presence on the planet and its rippling effect on everyone we pass and meet on the sacred journey of our souls.

In the context of the "*Eternal Now*", our future is already complete and we are already back in the loving embrace of our Creator. However, in the relative sense of a human life, what we do or don't do has profound implications for our soul and the whole of Creation. The ripple of our existence continues long after we depart the body. At least seven generations, descendants and ascendants are impacted positively and negatively by our smallest inclinations and largest choices. We are far more connected to each other than most realize.

Our deep interconnectedness surpasses current scientific understanding. Given our shared energy, we are responsible for our influence on others' lives. Having said that, with the recognition that everyone, including ourselves, is doing the best they can with their current level of consciousness and circumstances of their lives.

In the light of this profound truth, all judgment falls away, and only love is left. There is yet another benefit to the conscious release of self-incrimination and judgment of others, for as we reclaim responsibility for our own lives, we are no longer at the mercy of others. Despite their good or bad behavior or actions, we recognize that we are ultimately responsible for our own well-being and soul evolution.

Victim mentality serves no one.

Many times, our personal narrative and sad stories keep us stuck in the past. Though our stories of victimhood may be true and, at times, can even be horrific, if we allow our unfortunate circumstances or the unkind behavior of others to define our lives, we are locked into a harsh reality that lowers our sense of well being. This negative perspective not only attracts more of the same, it can, and does, limit our soul's evolutionary process. Indeed, the implications of victim mentality are profound.

With the mindset that life is unfair and that we are helpless victims, we attract more of the same in a self-perpetuating, repetitive loop.

Realigning to a more harmonious state may require much time and effort, and for some, numerous lifetimes. However, in the vastness of a loving universe, there's neither judgment nor a timeline. We have the liberty to remain in our victim stories for as long as they serve us. In due time, we will transform all our stories, both good and bad, into a heroic legacy of love and wisdom.

Every path, dark and light, fulfills our soul's deep longing for independence and experience.

With a more expansive perspective of our lives, it is evident that we always make the best choices possible, given our understanding and circumstances at the time, even if they may appear less than ideal in hindsight or upon reflection. The very fact that we didn't choose differently proves that it was the only choice possible then. Every decision we make contributes to the divine unfoldment of our soul.

In the end, victim story or not, everything eventually and inevitably works itself out. Indeed, this is a pivotal life of great opportunity and exponential change and spiritual advancement, your actions will be more conscious and their effects profound. As we evolve, many secrets of the universe are unveiled and revealed.

Naturally, we align to a more harmonious way of being. This increased understanding and accelerated evolution results in a brighter, more loving, radiant version of Self.

Love is the only enduring aspect of our lives.

Love is all we take with us, and all that we leave behind. Love is the answer, the reason why, and all that matters. Everything else is fleeting and transient: *Dust*. The mundane pleasures of an ephemeral world leave us unfulfilled, empty, and hungry. The profound longing of the soul finds its solace only in love. It is for this reason that we, with conscious intent, embark upon this terrestrial journey. Though the path may lead us into realms of shadow and light, it remains replete with profound purpose and intrinsic meaning.

Our earthly sojourn serves not merely as a passage but as a grand gateway to an ever-burgeoning experience of love. This journey, unequivocally real and unadorned, is the quintessence of all existence, and a pathway to love.

The only possibility of love is to love, and to love abundantly.

Our journey from shadow back to light, irrespective of its duration, holds no sway over the eternal essence of our soul. Whether it is a fleeting moment or spans eons, our soul is ultimately unaffected, and forever untainted and pure.

In due time, all paths reconverge, guiding us tenderly back into the divine's comforting sanctuary. From this place, cradled in the infinite love of the divine, we become the very embodiment of God's unending love. Our essence, like a seed, carries the indelible mark of its source. Imagine planting a rose seed; it doesn't spontaneously yield a tomato, a carrot, or celery. It unfailingly cultivates a rose. Similarly, we, as seeds of an ever-loving universe, are planted in the nurturing womb of Mother Earth.

Our journey as children of the Divine blossoms into the vast garden of God's unending love as more love. To this end, we come to this world of form and matter to cultivate the energetic qualities of our soul. Planet Earth, though, at times, a harsh teacher, is one of the rare realms that offers the unique and wonderful opportunity to experience free will as a means of evolution.

Only the bravest souls venture into this Earthly realm.

That is why you are here. You are a warrior of the soul, on a fast track of soul expansion and rapid evolution. You understood the inherent challenges you would face in a human life, and still, you came. You were excited to challenge yourself into change and for the opportunity of personal transformation in a world of shadow and light. In the human experience, we are like children playing hide and seek with ourselves. There is as much joy in the hiding as there is in the seeking and finding.

However, at some point, the game of life loses its luster and becomes tedious. Then, we simply want to go home. We come to planet Earth purposefully veiled and unaware of our true essence and birthright *(love)* to rediscover it again with different parameters. Our earthly sojourn, the unveiling of our eyes, and the joy of rediscovering our way back home are essential to our soul development. Our movement through the shrouded existence of this temporal world illuminates our soul and enhances the whole of existence. There are no random events, coincidences, or accidents in the universe. Everything that IS, is exactly as it should be, including your precious soul.

Each Soul is here for the absolute bliss of its own existence.

For some reading these words, the above statement can be quite challenging to accept. It can be especially difficult to embrace the idea that we exist for bliss, when our lives are dark, heavy, or burdensome. However, this limited worldview, based on temporary experiences, is not the entire story of the soul or the fullness of the human experience. While darkness and despair may exist in a relative sense, they do not define the absolute truth of the Self, the universe, or divinity. Even when shrouded in darkness, the eternal truth remains unwavering: love.

Love is unchanging and eternal.

Consider the sun: it always shines. Even when obscured by clouds or hidden from view, it maintains its silent vigil, watching over the earth. Yet, without a deeper understanding of the cosmos and the earth's orbital patterns, we may perceive the sun as intermittent or absent, thus shaping our reality.

Similarly, for the soul, life can seem dismal and dark in the absence of a profound grasp of God's unending love. When we lack information, or our understanding is limited, the truth is obscured. Indeed, within the veiled human condition, our understanding is inherently limited; we remain unaware of what we do not know. Often, even what we perceive as profound truth is constrained by our minds' inability to grasp the immense intricacies of a loving universe and God's unconditional love. Nevertheless, God does not penalize our lack of understanding or the resulting missteps. Instead, we are consistently invited to explore deeper layers of self, recognizing our growth as an integral part of our journey—*not as a condition for divine acceptance or love.*

To better grasp this concept, picture a young child, fearful of perceived monsters lurking beneath the bed. In their innocence, they are not yet prepared or capable of comprehending the concept of shadows. Nevertheless, the child's mother does not scold them for believing in monsters; instead, she lovingly cradles the child, providing comfort and reassurance. As the child grows and their understanding deepens, the mother eventually explains the nature of light and shadow, dispelling the myth of *"monsters."* Yet, until the child possesses the capacity to grasp a different reality, their belief in monsters remains their undeniable truth, regardless of the actual facts or objective reality.

Only when we can grasp the next level of truth does it become accessible.

The child's lack of understanding or erroneous belief in monsters doesn't warrant correction or impatience; rather, it calls for empathy and nurturing. The tender relationship between a mother and child mirrors the Divine's interaction with us, accommodating our diverse phases of awareness and spiritual growth. Much like the child, we are bound by our current level of understanding and evolution. The universe (*or God*), serving as a compassionate parent, does not criticize us for our ignorance or misunderstandings. Instead, in moments of confusion or limited knowledge, we are enveloped in patience, tenderness, and unconditional love. This benevolence gently guides us toward greater wisdom at our own pace and readiness.

To continue the analogy, just as a loving mother doesn't attempt to explain shadows to a child, the universe offers answers in accordance with the limits of our current evolutionary understanding.

In this context, even this book serves as a part of the universal plan to open your eyes and reveal a deeper, more profound truth than was previously accessible. These Love Letters will soothe your soul, lift your energy, dispel the shadows, illuminate your path, and unveil imaginary monsters.

As our understanding grows, more and more truth becomes unveiled.

With this in mind, let's revisit the initial question of *"What do I really want?"* and how its answer unfolds. It's evident that our comprehension is limited to what we can grasp at any given moment. Similar to the child who gradually comprehends shadows and overcomes the fear of perceived monsters, as we grow and gain more understanding, the response to *"What do I really want?"* also expands and adapts to align with our evolving comprehension and subsequent choices.

Just as a child experiences predictable stages and markers of growth (*such as the "terrible twos" or rebellious teenage years*), there are also predictable stages of soul growth and evolution. With the movement away from an unfulfilling, self-centered, materialistic life, many are drawn to a more spiritually driven life and the pursuit of enlightenment.

However, even the desire for enlightenment can become a barrier to our evolution if it's rooted in a longing for spiritual gifts and recognition. As we gain wisdom, even the yearning for spiritual progress is eventually left behind.

The process of letting go and making space for growth is both natural and inevitable.

Similar to a baby who stops crying for a pacifier after outgrowing it, we, too, naturally outgrow elements that hinder our soul's evolution. The quest for enlightenment, once sought through rituals, deity worship, or symbolic acts, gives way to the direct experience of truth. Along with the understanding that true fulfillment cannot be found outside of ourselves, we are naturally drawn toward the inner world of the Self, where all spiritual growth takes place.

From the exploration of the open-ended question "*What do I really want?*" another, perhaps more profound question arises: "*Who am I?*" Many people mistakenly believe they are defined by their thoughts. Yet, if this were true, which thoughts define us? The kind ones? The unkind ones? The enlightened or unenlightened ones?

Some may identify themselves with their physical bodies. However, which body truly represents us: the infant, teenager, or adult? Can't the body fall ill, be injured, or perish? In that case, which body are we? The healthy one? The injured one? Still, others may equate their identity with their actions. But again, which actions define us? The virtuous ones? The regrettable ones? The default actions? The ones we take pride in, or the ones we wish to forget?

We could continue in this vein of questioning endlessly and to no avail. Like a fish searching for the ocean while swimming in it, we sift through the sands of our lives, tangled in the seaweed of our existence. To this point, we may search endlessly for love without realizing that we are made of and sustained by the very thing we search for: *Love*. We are eternal beings of light having a profound spiritual experience in a temporal physical world for the pure and absolute joy of it and for the benefit of all.

The most important thing we can do in this life, or any life, is to love.

The movement towards love is natural and inevitable. The soul's journey advances when we consciously choose love. This fundamental choice aligns with our deepest essence. As children of the divine, we are both the observers of our existence and the vital energy that animates life itself. Each soul carries within it a unique fragment of the greater whole.

In the depth of life, a random act of kindness is the most significant contribution of the soul.

For some, their time on this planet involves making significant imprints, serving as catalysts for transformative change. Yet, for many, life unfolds quietly, and is simpler but no less significant. As we reflect on our actions and their consequences, it's crucial to acknowledge that human existence is a gift, not a trial. There's no ledger for righteousness or penalties for missteps. While our choices carry natural consequences, hope is eternal, and redemption is a constant promise.

Salvation isn't a distant goal; it's an inevitable consequence of existence. Every experience, is part of our soul's journey toward realizing its truest nature within the embrace of God's unending love and light.

In a loving universe, no soul is forsaken, eternally lost, or condemned to endless suffering and eternal torment.

Each one of us, without exception, will find our way back to the love and light from which we were born. The path we take isn't as crucial as the manner in which we journey— *with love or with fear*. Every path has its unique lessons and challenges, and reconvenes at the source—*God*. Even these loving words, cascading from the pages before you, are meant to guide your journey in a direction that most profoundly nurtures and honors your beautiful soul. To this end, these Love Letters are gentle reminders of your internal compass and the love that summons you homeward. Yet, the path you choose, the trails you take, and the roads you travel on are marked by your steps and shaped by your will.

While surrounded by angels, mentors, and guides, your evolution rests entirely in your hands.

To this point, there are many ways to cross the river and to live our lives. We can walk along the river's edge, jump in the water, float, backstroke, race to the other side, or do anything else that makes us happy and brings us joy. Most keep their eyes closed and swim along with the unconscious masses. While a few, more conscious and awake, step outside the norms, charting their own course.

In our lives, every step we take moves us closer to, or further from, our loving Creator.

Each of us intuitively knows the best path for our soul. Ultimately, the direction or speed of our journey does not matter. In a universal sense, all roads, with their twists, turns, and straight lines, ultimately converge at one destination, our authentic home: *love*.

Many believe the most direct path to God is ideal. Some favor a path of abundance, thinking it the best and most rewarding. While these less challenging paths and lives offer a comforting start, they may not always lead to deep spiritual growth. True transformation often comes from our more challenging, unpredictable lives.

Life's most valuable lessons frequently come disguised as detours and winding roads.

These more challenging paths push us, stretch our limits, and prompt us to question and explore, igniting within us a profound understanding and a more expansive love that a easier road may never reveal. In this intricate dance of soul evolution, every path and road holds its value, and every journey its unique beauty and set of lessons. Determining the "*best*" path is a deeply personal choice, tailored to our soul's desire for growth, discovery, and reconnection with our original love.

Receiving these Love Letters suggests you're in an advanced stage of spiritual evolution, facing complex life challenges that encourage profound growth. Yet, it's crucial to remember that this isn't a hierarchy or a system of rewards and punishments. Our life circumstances reflect our choices, made either consciously or unconsciously, rather than being a measure of merit or penalty.

Before our physical existence, in collaboration with our soul family, angels, and guides, we purposefully crafted our life circumstances to foster growth, expansion, and joy. This understanding emphasizes our active role in shaping our life journey. Every challenge and blessing is a part of the soul's ongoing evolutionary process. Bearing this in mind, our starting point is not a random roll of the dice, rather it is a strategically chosen set of conditions tailored specifically to our soul's unique evolutionary requirements. And amidst all experiences, whether they bring tears or joy, lies the presence of love as an unmoving anchor and guiding force.

In the unfolding journey of the soul, everything is a movement of love.

Love is the answer and the reason why. Love is the way, the journey, and the destination. Love is the path we follow and the footsteps we leave in the sand. Love is a dream beyond all dreams. Love is God expressed as all people and things. Love is the eternal bloom of creation. Love is kindness, goodness, and grace. Love is the most joyous possibility and our ultimate reality. Love is a soft, flowing river, guiding us home. Love is the storm that washes away yesterday's pain, and love is a life-giving, gentle rain. However love shows up, love is always love, and more love.

Love is all that matters.

The foundational lesson of love is to embrace ourselves completely. Indeed, to genuinely love another, we must first love and accept every part of ourselves, the shadows and the light. This path of self-love often leads us through feelings of unworthiness and inadequacy.

Nonetheless, we must bravely traverse these delicate emotional roads if we are ever to be truly free and love. Having said that, it is important to remember that our love might not always be reciprocated. Unrequited love may be painful and hurt, but true love stands strong, not bound by expectations. To be able to love without conditions or expectations is an essential part of our spiritual journey. Just by reflecting on these truths, we make great strides towards deeper love and spiritual growth.

However, we must allow ourselves the space to be human and the freedom to start fresh as needed. Even if total liberation is not achieved in this particular life, our earnest desire and effort marks notable soul progress. The slightest shift towards love can profoundly alter the course of our lives, rippling out far into the future.

As we close this chapter, let's take a moment of calm reflection to consider the powerful concept of unconditional love in regard to the deep longing of our soul. This conversation is not about temporary or superficial love, but the soul's deep longing to reconnect with the Divine.

All our earthly journeys—success, inner peace, and enlightenment—are manifestations of our soul's deeper spiritual pilgrimage.

Underlying our ambitions and dreams is a relentless, profound longing for love, the true desire of the soul. The soul's quiet wish is to love without limit and to be loved unconditionally. This silent prayer, this heavenly melody, and this deep longing guides us towards the Divine. This realization highlights that our deepest pursuits are not just our own endeavors, but are also part of a larger, divine interplay of love and connection.

We are born of love for the purpose of love, and we shall return to love as more love.

Irrespective of our superficial desires and the noise of daily life, the soul's deepest longing is always and forever to reunite with the Divine. This homeward journey is a path all souls are destined to travel. To this end, our spiritual journey, moving in and out of the physical realm, is marked by invaluable lessons of shadow and light.

This sacred sojourn enriches us with experiences from the depths of challenge to the heights of joy. In the shadows, we learn resilience, empathy, and the strength to overcome. In the light, we experience joy, love, and the power of connection. Both experiences are equally important to our soul's evolution. These contrasting human experiences are important teachers, sculpting and refining our understanding of the ourselves, the loving universe, and God.

Each challenge, triumph, sorrow, and joy enriches our spiritual narrative, preparing our soul for its inevitable reunion with the Divine.

This journey, marked by a spectrum of human emotions and experiences, underscores the soul's inherent quest for something beyond the tangible and transient. It is a pilgrimage towards a profound truth: our ultimate fulfillment and peace do not reside in worldly gains, but in reconnecting with the Divine. These powerful life lessons, although sometimes difficult, are crucial for our spiritual development and maturation. They shape us, teaching resilience, empathy, and understanding.

Every moment, whether filled with joy or pain, plays an important part in our soul's evolution. Ultimately, the soul's greatest aspiration and deepest longing is to evolve and return to its Source, sharing the love, wisdom, and knowledge acquired in a human life, enriching all of creation, including God.

This return to unity signifies a reunion with wholeness and love, embodying the soul's deepest longing, the truth of our essence, and the foundation of the universe.

My deepest longing is to love you.
— Chrystal Rae

*Each soul is here for the absolute bliss
of its own existence*

God is everything, including the dream

Letter 12

fables
truth of fables

This Love Letter is a playful unfoldment of fables and a serious unmasking of labels.

It is meant to make you blink, think, laugh, sing, cry, and question why. It is a magical map of what we've been told; a secret code for the all-knowing soul. It is an old fashion waltz that is both true and false—*an eternal dance that never begins or ends.*

So please, before we start, quiet down, and listen with an attentive heart. Then open the shutters that block the light and unhinge the blinds in the dead of night. *"Pat-a-cake, pat-a-cake baker's man, bake me a cake as fast as you can."*

Let the wisdom of love guide you home, we are all in this together, you are not alone.

Though the words may be silly, *"A-tisket a-tasket,"* reckless, and covered in mud, *"A brown and yellow basket"*, the message is always unconditional love. *"Happy birthday to you, happy birthday to you,"* happy birthday sweet angel—your Mommy loves you. *"Oh what a wonderful life"*, *"The cow jumped over the moon."*

Please don't stare, but if you dare, the empty sky will make you cry. *"Twinkle, twinkle little star." "How I wonder what you are"*. Together we are better, thats why I wrote you this love letter. *"Star light, star bright"*; you are my starry night. Storms may come and storms may go. The sun may shine or not. Have I told you, I love you a lot? *"Now, I lay me down to sleep, pray the lord my soul to keep"*. Every shadow and ray of light, every angel and dark night.

"*I wish I may, I wish I might*, have my wish come true tonight. In the open arms of the vast sky, we take our first breath and then we die. "*Down comes the rain, and washes the spider out*"; I really do love you; of that, have no doubt. The howling voice of the wind, point to a storm brewing on the horizon. "*Out came the sun, and dried up all the rain*", nothing ever stays the same. The forgotten remnants of yesterday, and the fading memories of warm summer days, are still alive in the gathered leaves of now naked trees.

The itsy bitsy spider climbed up the water spout; I still don't know what all the fuss is about. Perfect bliss is born of dynamic stillness. To my surprise, through half closed eyes, in the motionless haze of the afternoon sun, children play, laugh, and run. Old MacDonald lost the farm, "*E i ee i o*". Lost the cows and lost his barn. "*E i ee i o*". He lost his job but not his soul, "*E i ee i o*". It's true; we reap what we sow. "*E i ee i o*".

There is no real hurry, but its time to go. When we are in a rush, time moves slow. A single shoe on the side of the road; a tragic story, yet, to be told. A small boy, with his head in his hands, will one day soon become a man. Off to war, to make it right; he is ready to shoot and loves to fight. When the world spins out of control, you better hang on tight to your beautiful soul.

Today, like yesterday, and the day before that, an old man with one leg, and a tattered hat, holds up a sign, asking for wine. He is no longer a boy, but still in the sun, with one shoelace half undone. The sky turns dark, and then it turns light; we won the war and lost the fight. The sky is the container and its content, too. It is the space where I first fell in love with you. In the empty field, where the "*blessed are meek*," children play hide and seek.

The old man with a wooden leg and a bottle in his hand, dies alone on the street, where pigeon scavenge, looking for something to eat. Still the children dance round, and round; believing that they will never fall down. The sky is silent, but collects all sound; "*ashes, ashes, we all fall down*"

The hopes and dreams of every tomorrow; are stepping stones of joy and sorrow. The seamless sky reaches out in all directions; time never stops or makes a correction. The shadow and light of the ephemeral world, the oyster's most secret pearl. Survival of the fittest, on a hot summer day. One child is born; another passes away. Flickering lights of glory, and heavy clouds of shame are nothing more than foolish, foolish childhood games.

Pinocchio, with his long nose, went from rags to riches, and bought new clothes. He, happily, fell into the endless sky of hunger and greed; and turned his back on those in need. *"Baa baa black sheep, have you any wool? Yes sir, yes sir, three bags full!"* We rise and fall in amazing grace; a gift of time and empty space.

Love is the seed, root, and reason: the changing leaves, and the shifting seasons.

Whether we live or we die, the stars still sparkle in the evening sky. At the end of the game, nothing has changed. Love is still the light that illuminates the night. Everything is a mess; and yes, I must confess, I would rather not undress. We exist for bliss; the bliss of the first kiss, but it's always a risk. Oh, *"traveler in the dark, thank you for your tiny spark."* So much to do, but I do miss you. On hot stormy nights, I hold you close in the absence of light. Rather than cry, or question why, I take a long desert hike, and purchase a brand new mountain bike. Sometimes it feels so wrong, to do what's right?

A gentle rain or hurricane; pleasure and pain. Children play and dance around, as we bury our loved ones, under the ground.

You are love expressed and personified; against the odds, you somehow survived.

All creations of the night are permeations of the light. The monsters we invent or the angels we invite follow us into our dreams, where *"Nothing is as it seems."*

These fairytales of wicked witches are quite sad but still delicious, and prince charming is so alarming. The sky allows for this, too. It allows for me, to be me, and for you, to be you. Every wave on the ocean, every movement and motion, every star in the sky, every tear in your eye, begs to question, the reason why. But the rhyme of reason, can seem more like treason. Not a single grain of sand, on the seashore of time, belongs to you, or is mine—*It's all a pantomime*. Still, I love the ocean floor, and I love you even more.

On the rocky cliffs of joy and sorrow, there is hope of a better tomorrow. And its true, I would happily dive into the endless blue if it led me back to you. "*A sailor went to sea, sea, sea, to see what he could see, see, see.*" But the storm became a hurricane, and after the torrential rain, there was no one left to blame.

We set our gaze upon the ground, where Jack fell down and broke his crown. Then Jill came tumbling after. It was such a beautiful disaster. With bouncing balls and ballerina shoes; the war has begun on the evening news. You are all of this; none of this, and so much more, the pure bliss of eternal happiness.

Beyond all doubt and strife; the most dangerous object is a butter knife. You are love manifest, and so much more; you are the glass ceiling, and the broken floor. You are the wall, where Humpty Dumpty took a great fall. I am sad to say, but I'll tell you anyway. All the king's horses, and all the king's men, couldn't put him, or his friends, back together again.

In our hurry to check our text, we were quite reckless. We neglected to protect the innocent child, we walked away and forgot how to smile. We are the pulse of a loving universe, and the hungry longing of an empty purse. We are the heart of God, pure compassion and grace, and the evil one, dark with disgrace. We are the longing of life, pounding in our own chest. We don't always succeed, but its a fun game of chess.

Even when we fall and fail, there is still wind in our sails. You are a being of light, a flickering candle in the night. Oh glory, *beyond glory*, to know that we know and reap what we sow. To be the sky and understand why. Why we exist, and the experience of bliss. We are the children of the sky, and love is the reason and the why. "*Row, row, row your boat, gently down the stream, merrily, merrily, merrily,*" nothing is as it seems—"*life is but a dream*".

Playing marbles in the sand, the little boy becomes a man. A radiant being of light, drowning in the night. We are God's own evolution, manifest, and alive; we are meant to do much more than simply survive. We are the soft landing of a white, winged dove; oh my darling, so much love. We are the armed masses, enraged with resistance; the natural unfoldment of God, and existence. We are love expressed in every possible way. We are the sinking ship; slowly, sailing away. We are the seamless sky, the tears we never cried, and the lingering hurt in a child's eyes.

We are pure potential of changeless change.

We are every pleasure and every pain. We are the passengers of time, fragments of space: we are a child without shoes, humming "*amazing grace*". We are everything and nothing; and so much more. We are all of our excuses, spilling out on the floor. We are the itsy bitsy spider that climbed up the waterspout; tag your it, tag your out. We are the radiant light, and the dark of night. We are an unlikely potentiality of a miraculous reality. Even in the glory of divinity, the blind man still can't see. "*One, two, three, four, five; once I caught a fish alive.*" "*Six, seven, eight, nine, ten; then I let it go again*". A single breath is more precious than gold, ask anyone ancient, anyone old.

"To be" rather than "not to be," gives rise to joyous tears and the darkest fears.

"*Enie, Meenie, Minie, Mo, catch a tiger by the toe*"; but if you let him go, you will reap what you sow. Remember truth or dare, doesn't work with a bear. A radiant light crashes to the ground, where questions and answers are yet to be found. *"With a knick knack paddy whack, give the dog a bone, this old man came rolling home." "Ashes, ashes we all fall down"*, you will find me at lost and found.

Problems without solutions, arise and fall; there must be a rhyme or reason to it all. We, too, blaze our way into the black of night, with a joyful sound, and a fading light. The sinking ship of our deathless night; surrenders, again and again, to the first ray of light. Love is eternal; this is true, I promise to always, always love you. *"The wheels on the bus go round and round". "Round and round: round and round"*.

Life is a treasure; a gift without measure.

Peter Pan had a good plan; but sometimes, magic can be quite tragic. The girl with freckles, and a pretty pink bow, suddenly, fell out the open window. Surprisingly, she didn't die, she sprouted wings and learned to fly. After all it is your life, what will you do with that butter knife? The story ends, before it begins.

 Cinderella had to save herself, her glass slipper is still on the shelf. Prince Charming never arrived; rumor has it, he didn't survive. Santa got drunk and fired his elves, we all have to save ourselves. Live with reverence, and joy, and put away your childish toys.

Fall into the blue of the sky, and let love be your reason why.

Love is you; love is me; love is absolute harmony. Though shrouded in shadows, and draped in light; together we conquer the endless night. Such glory, grace, and God; the gardener plants new sod. *"Ring around a rosey, pocketful o' posies. Light bread, sweet bread, squat!"* Remember in December, its cold, not hot. The sky doesn't change, it's always the same. I found a penny, a nickle, maybe a dime; oh never mind, the numbers were fake, and I made a mistake. *"Hickory Dickory Dock"* the stock market dropped.

No need to get mad or be sad, a little blue pill will cure all our ills. The man on the moon is coming home soon, he scheduled a meeting with the team on Zoom. *"If you want to take a trip, climb aboard my rocket ship. Zoom, zoom, zoom, we're going to the moon."* Feed the baby with a silver spoon, the end of the world is predicted soon, *"thy Kingdom come". Thy will be done,"* beyond the doom and gloom, *sweep up the mess with an electric broom.*

We are a sound that had to be heard, an energy that had to emerge, a soul that had to exist, an opportunity not to be missed. We are the blossoming of a summer's day, and the dirty laundry tucked away. We are the purest expression of love and the white winged dove, hovering above. We are the wicked witch with a skinny stick, waiting for Hansel and Gretel, brewing her kettle. We are aware that we are aware, but nobody cares that Samson lost his hair, playing truth or dare.

"Five little monkeys jumping on the bed, one fell off and broke his head". The moral of the story, there is no glory, in Russian roulette you might lose the bet. Though we laugh, cry, and question why, little Bo Peep still can't find her sheep. She got lost on the merry-go-round, and, to date, has not been found. When the music started again, the preacher said it was a sin.

In the light of a new day, when the mud washed away, Delilah shaved her own head, pretended to be dead, and said a silent prayer, still, no one was there. Samson was long gone, apparently, he moved on. *"Hush, little baby, don't say a word, Papa's gonna buy you a mockingbird.*

Life pushes us to be more, do more, and love more. The sad little boy makes the winning score, forgets his pain and wins the game. When the honey bees swarm the hive; we all run for cover and try to hide, but only the fittest survive. The Easter bunny with his candied eggs, points to Jesus and hopes to be saved. We hold hands, sing in churches, fall to our knees on penguin perches. Even our bruises are seeds of light; like distant stars we conquer the night. *"I'm a little teapot, short and stout, when I get all steamed up, pour me out.*

The joy, elation, and glories of life, and a martyr's ultimate sacrifice, both take a heavy toll on our tender soul. There is no separation between the seer and the seen; the deer in the headlights thought the grass was green, no one heard its silent scream.

We are both the witness and the "ISness" of our own existence.

"The boy on the bus, waves his hand. Waves his hand, waves his hand": the boy on the bus is now a man. We scrub the floors, leave everything clean, but when we are done, what does it all mean? Children build sandcastles, bury themselves, play in the forest, and pretend to be elves. What goes around, comes around. *"London bridges falling down"*. We spin in circles, round and round; then, we too, come tumbling down.

Everything works together for the good, still nothing turns out like we thought it would. I see myself in your eyes; I see my truth and my lies. You are me, I am you, and we are one, united forever in the morning sun. The eternal sky. My reason why. Our father's only son. A radical Nun with her hair undone. Have I told you, today, that I love you? Well, I do, I truly love you.

"Hush, little baby, don't say a word, Papa's gonna buy you a mockingbird. And if that mockingbird don't sing, Papa's gonna buy you a diamond ring." The meaning of life? I paid the price with my third ex-wife. All things; and no things: A teenage girl with a nose ring. We are the time in a bottle; the fast car with a throttle. We are the unmoving tree; a crashing destiny. Metal in a pile, and a body on the street. *"Little Bo Peep* still can't find her sheep, *"leave them alone, and they'll come home, bringing their tails behind them"*.

The diversity of singularity is the opposite of polarity.

The unveiling of consciousness, through consciousness, is consciousness. The politician and the physician; relay the state of our current condition. God's beauty, love, and glory: fear, anxiety, and worry. Every happy failure, unexpected triumph, bitter success, and all the rest. Everything is included in the sky, welcome in the sky, and necessary in the sky. The joy and laughter; tears and pain, torrential rains, and growing pains. The absolute wonder of a baby's birth. The ongoing evolution of Mother Earth. *"Lavender's green, dilly dilly, lavender's blue,If you love me, dilly dilly, I will love you."*

The first breath, the last breath; and then, no breath. The miracle of life; the pain, and the strife. Laughing children flying a kite and an Olympic athlete, reaching new heights. A couple in love, holding hands, muse about their marital plans. *"Shall I compare thee to a summer's day?* Sleeping beauty passed away.

A shaking old man, skinny to the bone, sits sad and alone. With heavy eyes, as happy people pass him by, he starts to cry. Rocking back and forth on a dilapidated porch, with a tick tock *"the mouse ran up the clock,"* and his heart suddenly stopped. As the sun sets, he sinks into regret; but it's too late now for a final bow. *"Mama called the Doctor and the Doctor said,"No more monkeys jumping on the bed!""*

A baby bird on its first and last flight gets lost in the black of the endless night. A blossoming white rose sits in quiet repose while the wilting shadow of time suddenly rewinds. Will you be my Valentine? Did you see the stop sign? Flickering stars in the distance; I won't submit, without strong resistance. A thousand suns in one endless night, a naked nun turns out the light. *"If you're happy and you know it, clap your hands." (clap clap). "If you're happy and you know it, and you really want to show it, clap your hands.(clap clap).*

There is a cloud of dust at the finish line, where everyone else is left behind, is a moment of fame, but lifetime of shame. Indeed, the race to arrive, to simply survive, and stay alive is both meaningless and pure bliss. Life is the unfoldment of shadow and light, the approach of the dark night, the tragic, beautiful, and everything else, too; including me and you. If you ask me, on bent knee: I will say, "*I do*," because I love you. The sky is not separate from the blue, and I am not separate from you. We are not separate from our Source. Still, the little girl, riding a horse, signs the dotted line of a nasty divorce.

"*One for the master, one for the dame, And one for the little boy who lives down the lane*". What affects you; profoundly affects me, too. But when you unveil your shadow; I promise, not to tattle. As you bask in your light, I conquer my night. I learn about my soul when the last bell tolls. You are my teacher, and I am yours; now clean your room and finish your chores.

For eons of time, beyond fables and nursery rhymes; you are my brother, my sister, my mother, my father, my friend, and my faithful companion to the bitter end. Once more we open the door, the wind blows in, and the movie begins. This time, I am the one who betrays, but in the next life, I will never stray. "*Hey diddle diddle, the cat and the fiddle, The cow jumped over the moon*". Every shadow and light, dissolves back into the night, but little red riding hood, is not always so good.

Though love has no limits, we still ask for penance. Patience includes impatience, until we can't wait anymore, then we run for the door. The light was yellow and then red and now my fender is dead. Calm gives birth to angst while peter pan walks the plank. Life is neither a burden nor gift to the soul, it is only our judgment that makes it so. We have seen that the darkness includes the light; we have believed in wars, and the need to fight. We have made straight A's, done our best; but still failed to succeed or pass the test.

There is nothing to discuss, "*All the kings horses and all the kings men,*" *were* taken away in an armored bus. Everything once thought to be true is a blurry line between me and you. Oh yes, it's true: How, I do love you. Let me count the ways. A teenage boy gets harassed and hazed, and its celebrated as the good-old-days.

The principle sits on a leather saddle with a wooden paddle, threatening the angry mob, in particular, a guy named Rob. Corporeal punishment is against the law, this truth is rather rude and raw, let the kids go to hell, or you will go to jail.

As the secrets of the universe are revealed, Jack and Jill go back up the hill. Without a clue, little Miss Muffet, again sits on her tuffet, watching Warren Buffet, on the evening news. . There are many winding roads, and lots of ugly toads. We have lost our way, more than once; and, found our way home on a blind hunch. Like children on a merry-go-round, we teeter totter to and fro, where we land, nobody knows.

We have arrived, and departed, so many times, we have forgotten our favorite nursery rhymes. *"Rock a bye baby, on the tree top, when the wind blows the cradle will rock. When the bough breaks the cradle will fall, and down will come baby, cradle and all."* We blame our mother or our father for our sins, and the endless cycle again begins.

We search for the other; only to discover, there is no other. If *"you do the Hokey Pokey and turn yourself around,"* you might get dizzy and fall to the ground. In case you had a doubt, *"that's what it's all about."* We have all searched for love and looked approval, but like Ebenezer Scrooge we are selfish and frugal. Fleeting shadows dance on the wall where Humpty Dumpty took a great fall. The locked door leads to an empty hall that once seemed big and now seems small.

A little girl, jumping rope, counts her steps with the secret hope that her mother will be pleased if she succeeds. If she trips, or takes a fall, she will simply blame Newtons laws—*but if we go down that rabbit hole, we might well lose our precious soul.* A, B, C, D, E, F, G, how wonderful and horrible life can be. Old Macdonald found his cow, Pinocchio shrunk his nose. Cinderella found her umbrella, but didn't accept the ring. The children still dance round and round, and London bridges is still *"falling down, falling down—my fair lady."*

They laugh, and sing: Ring a Ding, Ding. Underneath the mistletoe, secrets unfold, never to be told. Cinderella married Isabella, and they said their sacred vows in a pasture of spotted cows. With a diamond ring, they shared their dreams, and lived happily ever-after: that is, of course, until the middle-aged disaster. Jingle bells, Batman smells, and Robin laid a egg: someone wearing a paper mask said that it was the plague. Nothing is as it seems, the price of gas is so extreme, and toilet paper is just obscene.

The sky is still the sky. Love is still love. God is still God. You and I are still you and I.

The experience of the experience is the gift, and not the goal. Love has no goal, no agenda, no reason to be. Love is you and love is me. "*Tic, Tac, Toe,*" I will never let you go. Love simply loves; and then, loves more. When clouds move in, the rain starts to pour. Our hopes, dreams, fountains and streams, all lead back to the sky, back to the reason why, back to the gardener's sod, and back to the love of God.

"*Row, row, row your boat, gently down the stream; merrily merrily, merrily, merrily, life is but a dream.*" I love you to the end of time, you are my favorite nursery rhyme. Forever and a day, there is nothing more to say. "*Twinkle, twinkle, little star, how I wonder what you are. Up above the world so high. Like a diamond in the sky*". Please tell me the truth or forget to lie; I never want to say goodbye. Let me believe, even if I am deceived, in the white winged dove and the possibility of love.

"*If I should die before I 'wake, I pray the Lord my Soul to take.*" Amen. Now turn out the light, sleep tight, and don't let the bed bugs bite .

Mommy loves you, and so do I.
— Chrystal Rae

*Fall into the blue of the sky,
and let love be your reason why*

God's love is pure radiance without opposite or end

Letter 13

beyond
beyond the veil

Death comes as the night follows the day.

We open our eyes with the rising sun, crying, laughing, walking, skipping, flying, falling, singing, and joyously dancing, carrying on as though we will live forever and a day. Unexpectedly, the night arrives in opaque blackness, and everything stops. Time stops. Breath stops. Movement stops. Thoughts stop. Even the world suddenly stops spinning.

The end arrives when we least expect it.

Without pause, we take our first and then our last breath. It seems that we have just arrived, and then it is time to go, time to go home. It's time to leave this earthly world behind and step through the slow-opening door of one reality into another. It is time to venture "*beyond*" the familiar and embrace the unknown.

As the reality of our human existence comes to its inevitable end, all pain, joy, laughter, and tears fall into the sudden silence of death. As we move beyond the slow opening door of one reality into another, we leave everything and everyone we love and cherished behind. The shock of the material world, and everything we have known to be true, to suddenly come crashing down can leave us in a state of bewilderment and confusion. But the moment one door closes and another opens, we find ourselves disconnected from everything and everyone that we left behind, including our loved ones and our very own body.

Beyond the earthly realm, we find ourselves moving quickly towards a radiance that lovingly draws us near, cradling us in a shimmering blanket of love and luminous light. Many come to greet us, to hold our hand, and to guide the way. In this celestial reunion, we are embraced not only by those who walked this earthly path before us but also by our soul family, a radiant constellation of kindred spirits.

The ethereal presence of angels, guides, and wise teachers lovingly surround us, offering reassurance that we will find peace and well-being as we transition beyond the known into the unknown. Their undying devotion, dedication, and care is beyond measure or any expression of love known to man.

The transition from this world into the next can be both terrifying and beautiful.

Similar to a baby bird breaking free from the safety of its shell to discover its wings, we too must venture beyond the comfort of the known for our soul to take flight. As we transcend the confines of our earthly vessel, every trace of our former existence, encompassing the deepest abyss of our shadows and the most resplendent brilliance of our light, is engulfed in the all-consuming fire of divinity.

Words falter in the attempt to encapsulate the sheer totality and beauty of the unconditional love that saturates our very essence. It is a love brighter than a thousand suns and more radiant than all the stars combined. As we move from one realm into another, we are welcomed in waves of rippling iridescent light that absorb the shallow surface and lingering shadows of a human life.

Death is not what most believe; it is not the end.

To the contrary, death of the physical body is but a new chapter in a never ending love story. We do not suddenly disappear or spontaneously transform, you are still you, and I am still me: *pure radiant energy.* As the tangible world recedes, our essence endures—*unaffected and undiminished.* Beyond the delicate membrane that separates the material realm from this interstitial haven of radiance and brilliance, our senses are not merely heightened; they transcend their earthly limitations. Emotions don't just intensify; they evolve into deeper states of feeling. Every aspect of existence is renewed and sanctified within the all-encompassing embrace of love.

We find ourselves immersed in a swirling vortex of radiant light, afloat in pure bliss. Then suddenly, and almost magnetically, we are drawn by a swift-flowing river of energy that carries us along an ever-expanding channel of love. Wave after wave of luminous, restorative love, luminous light pours over us, washing away the remnants of our earthly journey. These soothing, effervescent waves heal the lingering scars of our earthly trials, mending the wounds still marked by life's experiences—*the relics of our struggles on Earth.*

During this divine interlude, our souls are released from the magnetic pull of worldly attachments—*the silent chains that perpetually draw us toward the material realm.*

Once freed from the lingering echoes of the past and the elusive mirage of the future, we awaken to the undying truth of love that never changes.

Indeed, this is more of an awakening to the unchanging truth of who we really are than a transformation. Nonetheless, this stage of the journey may be experienced as a complete metamorphosis; our very essence aglow in unblemished vibrancy.

When we let go of "what was" and "what could have been," we discover "what IS"—the truth of love and the grace of God.

As we surrender our smallness, we are granted greatness, and the burdens of our past naturally dissolve into the truth of love and the radiance of light.

In the completeness of this all-encompassing love and light that envelops every aspect of our being, we discover not an end, but a profound beginning—*a realm where the very notion of burden dissolves, and our existence radiates with the unobstructed brilliance of the divine.*

The sound of silence hums with subtle intensity as ethereal winds gently exhale in a comforting breeze that permeates the essence of the soul and enlivens our very being.

Awakening from the dream of separateness, we are once again united in Oneness, and in love.

After we leave our earthly bodies and worldly attachments behind, we awaken in a glowing garden of luminescent light. In this radiant space of exquisite softness, permeating light, and fragrant flowers, all judgments and seeming opposites fall away—*then there is only love, and more love.* Even the last bits of guilt and heavy shadows of shame, dragged forward from the human experience, are consumed in the fire of love.

In the absence of structure and form, the very essence of our being is revealed as iridescent luminosity—pure energy, love.

We are welcomed home by our soul family, teachers, guides, and others who have loved and cared for us throughout our many lives. In this joyous reunion, we are cradled with a love beyond description, enfolded with the sweet fragrance of blossoming flowers, and tenderly held in the care of angels. Like a vigilant shepherd caring for his flock, these celestial guardians watch over us, gently guiding us towards the profound truth of love. As we re-harmonize into a radiant space of remembrance, they shield us from anything that would compromise our soul or dampen our light.

We are held in the compassionate embrace of these radiant beings as we review the life we have just lived on a three dimensional holographic screen that unfolds before us. We watch ourselves, from the perspective of Oneness and grace, as every moment, breath, small detail of our past, and of the life we just completed is seen with unobstructed clarity. In the radiant space of our own reflection, poignant and long-forgotten moments where our heart was touched by love and kindness, and those instances where the opposite prevailed are revealed from myriad perspectives—*forward, backward, and sideways, each accompanied by their far-reaching effects.*

In the gradual relinquishment of our earthly selves, we encounter a profound revelation about the expansive nature of our being.

From the gentlest of words to the sternest of actions, from the deepest sorrows to the most exultant joys, the entirety of human experience coalesces into undulating waves of radiant light, thereby unveiling the core of our true essence.

Through these revelations, we realize that all our emotions, from deep grief to immense joy, are beautifully integrated into the glowing tapestry of the soul. This convergence of experiences not only unveils our true essence, but also reveals that each soul is part of a grander expanse of rippling, radiant light, a testament to our shared humanity and the profound depth of the ever-evolving universe. Within this ethereal panorama, we are also offered glimpses of forgotten lives that lay concealed in shame or shrouded in heavy emotions that kept us trapped in the relentless cycles of the past—*sometimes spanning across many lives.*

Our life review offers more than a broad summary; it reveals every infinitesimal detail, each relived with stunning clarity and intricate nuance, rippling endlessly out into the vast universe.

While we view and experience the unfolding sequence of our intentions, thoughts, and actions, the grand expanse of time reverses its course. We are lovingly guided back to our most challenging and cherished memories of days long gone. Yet, we are not confined to visions of the past in this all-encompassing and expansive life review. The same centrifugal waves of love and radiant light that carried us backward in time, suddenly thrust us forward into the nebulous realm of the future. Here, we encounter radiant universes waiting to be born, dwelling far beyond the boundaries of conventional science and human comprehension.

In the paradox of death lies a profound truth: we never truly die.

After we leave the body and all the trappings of the material world behind, the essence of our soul continues on in the vast universe of love and possibility. We are not vacant observers standing at a distance from our own lives, we are co-creators of the universe we live in.

Beyond our mistaken identities and small definitions of Self, there is no opposite to love.

As our most benevolent and unkind behaviors are replayed on the screen before us, we are held in the gentle embrace of absolute love and acceptance. Rather than encountering judgment or condemnation, we are shown the truth of who we are, the truth of the loving universe, and the truth of God's all encompassing grace.

When our life review is complete, the essence of our being and our many lives are consolidated into a singular point of light—*this is our truest expression of Self*. The truth of love and the divinity of light stand resplendent in the dawn of our renewed understanding and remembrance of love. Like the moon, sun, and stars, we observe the progression of our radiant soul, and the work that is yet to be done, in the radiance of light and from every perspective of love.

These glorious moments of reflection, rapture, and wisdom wash away our tears in a river of love that bursts forth from the very center of God's own heart. As the truth of love is unveiled and revealed, all our hidden fears, uncried tears, and unanswered questions fall away. Indeed, in the presence of the Divine, all questions are meaningless and all answers are known. Even the unruly currents of collective consciousness are swept into the water of our radiant transformation.

The slightest shift in the compass of our intentions, thoughts, and feelings immediately transports us to unimagined future lands where subsequent timelines simultaneously play themselves out.

As we stand at the threshold of death's door, we viscerally understand how a random act of kindness or the heavy hand of cruelty reshapes the core of our very existence, forever impacting the whole of creation, including God.

The light of our being can either be a healing force of goodness and grace, or a downward spiral of pain and sorrow.

Like a hurricane or a gentle rain, our choices echo out as rippling waves of love or fear, not only impacting our world, but the whole of creation: *The tiny ant we allowed to live, the flattened bug under our shoe, the baby that was never born, the beggar on the street, the palace made of gold, the wretched and the old, those sad souls with nothing to eat, the innocent child living on the street, and all the rest of life's horror and glory unfolds before us.*

On the path back to love, everything is transformed into treasured bits of broken light and radiant expressions of the night.

And again, there is no judgment, condemnation, or angry, jealous God. On the contrary, we are wrapped in layer upon layer of love and more love. Even so, the energetic difference between the ethereal and earthly realms can be quite pronounced, necessitating a recalibration of energy. Before we can move forward and continue our soul's evolutionary journey, we must reset our energetic body.

For this reason, to recalibrate, between this world and the next, we first arrive in a space of rest and recovery. Most find themselves in a radiant garden teeming with kindness, compassion, grace, and love. Within this tranquil realm, peace is not just a concept but a palpable presence.

Wherever we find ourselves, everything is sparkling and alive with love and kindness. As we hover in the liminal space between realms, we cast a contemplative glance back to the majestic peaks of triumph that we once surmounted. We also behold the profound chasms of regret into which we have, at times, plummeted. The murky twilights of desolation, too, come into view, those stretches where we wandered, shrouded in the shadow of our grief and narratives of suffering.

Much is learned about ourselves, others, and love, as we review the characters we played in the earthly realm, and the choices we made from a soul level. Strolling through yesterday's empty hallways and pounding on tomorrow's locked doors, our untold stories of regret and shame are dark and heavy. Yet, these somber reflections carry the hope and promise of a more radiant tomorrow, laying the groundwork for the enlightened chapters of our unwritten future. On the other hand, as we review our more enlightened moments, witnessing ourselves helping others, offering support, and unconditional love, the entire universe comes alive with radiance and light.

A simple act of kindness, a moment of selfless service, or unexpected grace uplifts the soul and enhances the whole of creation.

Conversely, in those fractured moments when we let anger, neglect, and entitlement guide our actions, callously ignoring and forsaking those who sought our love, care, and assistance, the entire universe darkens in tandem with our own souls.

Indeed, were it not for the nurturing embrace of our angels, guides, and teachers, we might not endure this poignant reflection. The weight of our cruelty, the lack of compassion, and the absence of love are heavy burdens that we must bear throughout the expanse of our existence and our many lives. Being shown these tragic, fractured moments, and heartbreaking episodes is not meant to be a judgment or condemnation. Rather, they are meant to bring us clarity and closure, offering unparalleled opportunities for profound self reflection and spiritual development.

From countless perspectives, and with many eyes, we are born and reborn into the world of form and matter, for the experience of experience, and for the bliss of our own existence.

We come to know ourselves in the opaque darkness of the night and recognize the truth of love in the radiance of divine light. Guided by the gentle rhythm of grace, we navigate the intricate terrain of form and matter. We seamlessly enter and exit life experiences, precisely tailored to support our soul's evolution.

To this end, I am an innocent child, the hungry beggar on the street, a frail old man, the radiant queen crowned with studded beauty, a muted prostitute longing to speak, a thief hiding in the night, a saint in perpetual prayer, and the whole of humanity in a complex world that's unaware: I am all of this, none of this, and so much more—and so are you.

A human life is rare, wonderful, and yes, challenging.

This poignant reflection on our innate beauty and the quiet observation of the inevitable flaws of the human condition are not meant to be an accusatory finger, a harsh punishment, or an unkind word. We stand, not in judgment, but in a compassionate embrace of our own journey, recognizing that every step, virtuous and flawed, has led us to this very moment of self-discovery.

In the light of our innate divinity, the truth of unconditional love and forgiveness extends to all, including to ourselves. The flickering lights and fleeting shadows of human existence serve as incomplete reflections of both you and me—*an ongoing portrait of divinity, forever in progress.* Indeed, as we stand humbly at the threshold of death's door, everything is necessarily reframed and must be let go.

Beyond the tears we could not cry, and the laughter that somehow passed us by, all expressions of life are the unfoldment of bliss and eternal happiness. In this awakening, we discover not just happiness but radical freedom. Each life is a lesson of love in the guise of buildings, structures, and walls. The adventure, triumph, and falls of the human experience come in the form of stiletto shoes and the evening news.

Even after we are gone, the rippling light of our shadow forever continues on. The lessons of love, the characters, and the movies of our many lives replay in repetitive loops for our enlightenment and the benefit of all: A love story opens the heart and is a direct path to God. A tragedy brings tears to our eyes and reminds us of our own fragility. A comedy fills us with laughter and joy. While a shattered fairytale with an unhappy ending teaches the value of impermanence and love.

Though the complexities of human life often involve regrettable choices, we can find solace, peace, and forgiveness through the recognition and acceptance of our inherent power and weakness.

Beyond our self-imposed judgments and labels, every challenge, excuse, and reason fades into the eternal grace and love of God.

Even our cruelest acts of violence and harshest treatment of ourselves and others are consumed in the fire of love. Regardless of our good or bad actions, angels descend with boundless grace and unwavering care to dry our tears. Indeed, some of us arrive from the human experience still covered with a thick layer of mud, while others are lightly dusted. Either way, between this realm and the next, we arrive at this healing garden to review, remember, recover, rejuvenate, reassess, and rest.

We are not alone; angels walk among us, their presence a guiding light in our earthly journeys.

In a timeless bliss, we are held in the warm embrace of the unconditional love by those who steadfastly watch over us. We reside in this sacred space of luminous light, a healing garden, until we are ready to embrace the fullness of our own divinity and continue our journey on the path to God.

As our mortal lens falls away, the ordinary is revealed as extraordinary.

Beauty bursts into every radiant possibility: *an army of ants, the roots of trees, a bird in the sky, the roaring waves, speckled lights punctuating the night, and the tiniest pebble on the beach are all seen in their resplendent beauty.*

In love's perennial blossoming, as we leave the earthly realm behind and move beyond death's door, the pulse of our human life becomes a slow fading memory of what used to be, and is no more. Unencumbered by the trappings of the material world, we are free of the joy, laughter, and tears we cried. We are free from being crucified, and free from the hope that death will pass us by. Transitioning from one realm to the next, the complexities of a human life melt into the simplicity of truth and the grace of God. Even a scribbled flash of light, thunderously crashing through the empty walls of a dark night, is a beacon of hope, guiding us toward the rising sun of a more radiant tomorrow.

After the storm of a human embodiment, we are reborn, more radiant and alive. Indeed, beyond the fleeting realm of form and matter, the enduring flame of love remains the sole unchanging truth.

God is the fire that sets the world ablaze.

In the presence of such radiance, there is no need of defense or pretense, and no reason to fight. In the radiant light of God's undying love, everything is as it should be—*both the tragic and beautiful.*

Once we have learned the lesson, pain and suffering lose their hold, and there is no need of karmic consequences. From the more expansive perspective of our soul, it is evident that we are all doing our best in every moment, even when it seems like our worst. The proof is that we did not do any better or worse—*until we do*. Either way, love does not change. The radiant light of love permeates the blackest of nights and most elusive shadows. Having said that, it should be noted that our life, and lives, are our responsibility, and our choices matter—*and they matter a lot, rippling out endlessly and affecting the whole of creation.*

When we heal ourselves, we heal the world and everyone in it.

Our responsibility extends beyond the impact we have on the world, the greater universe, and the whole of creation, to include even God. Indeed, we are that powerful. As children of the Divine, and the progeny of God, our good or bad choices forever imprint upon the loving universe. Nonetheless, we are born of love for the purpose of love and shall return to love as more love.

The seed and the source are forever united in love.

Even after we leave the physical world, the rippling light of our love and the darkness of our shadows continue on infinitely. Every life and experience offer unique gifts and lessons for our soul's growth and the betterment of all.

While the human experience is abundant with many exciting adventures, not all are radiant or filled with light. Some roads, into and out of the earthly realm, are eerie and dark, populated by creatures that dwell exclusively in shadows. Although these less luminous paths are available through choice and free will, if we indulge in the seductive darkness, we may be lost for eons, retrograding back to a wormlike existence.

For the well-being of our precious soul, and so that we do not needlessly suffer, it is best to avoid these barren, dark places of little light; very few survive these most miserable lives or resurface from the darkness unscathed. Every shadow and permeation of light is added to the essence of pure intelligence and love, expanding and enriching the whole of creation.

Our time on this planet is brief, and the moments between our first and last breaths quickly merge like the ocean meeting the shore, constantly finding each other anew, and perpetually renewed with vitality and purpose.

The light from which we are born and to which we return is enriched and enlivened by our radiance and shadows.

Even the smallest choice holds profound significance and is often underestimated. With this in mind, a crucial insight from our discussion on death emerges: *while we are still alive, we possess the power to transform our lives, elevate our consciousness, and influence the world profoundly.* How? By embracing love over fear.

This directive is not intended as a warning, rather it is a gentle reminder that our life is a precious opportunity that is finite and may conclude sooner than we anticipate. Indeed, on the others side of death's door, what is done is done, and we must move on—*there is no going back.*

For some, with unresolved issues, or still carrying heavy burdens of the past, leaving the known world and venturing into the unknown realm beyond the physical body can be a very difficult and frightening transition. However, in a loving universe, everything happens as it should, and nothing is left to chance, including the day, time, and moment of our departure from the earthly realm.

Our lives hold a deeper purpose and meaning than what may initially be apparent or known.

Though it can be unsettling to suddenly enter another realm, friends, family, and kindred spirits, who have gone before us, welcome us home. They comfort and reassure us, guiding us back to the loving embrace of God, affirming that all is well. No words are needed in the vibrational transfer of love that connects us to each other with shimmering threads of knowledge and light. In this newfound liberation and boundless freedom, we ascend into the limitless realms of luminous light where our soul continues it timeless journey of expansion and love. Nonetheless, many are shocked with the astonishing revelation after departing the earthly realm that they are still very much alive—*indeed, more than alive, they are boundless and free.*

Another unexpected occurrence upon shedding the physical body is our release from its earthly experiences, encompassing both joys and sorrows. Our collective dream of scarcity and lack dissolves into the abundance of divinity and the unchanging truth of love.

The profound truth of our existence and the omnipresent nature of love materialize in delicately measured moments of light, perfectly attuned to our capacity for comprehension. Regardless of our level of understanding or our ability to receive, we remain eternally immersed in the exquisite radiance and glorious rapture of the Divine.

God is pure love and limitless light, with no beginning, middle, or end.

From the instant of our birth to the moment of our death, an unceasing flow of possibilities and potentialities surge into and out of existence. Each life, characterized by its distinctive interplay of shadow and light, enriches the core of our existence and the radiance of the universe.

Now, like life itself, even this brief discussion on death concludes almost as swiftly as it commenced. What may have taken years to unfold is encompassed within the fleeting span of our final breath. Indeed, as we approach the end, the ephemeral essence of life becomes all the more evident.

As we become aware that our time in the temporal world is coming to an end, the significance of every thought, word, and action we have seems to magnify. Yet, simultaneously, we recognize that they lack true substance or lasting meaning. This understanding underscores the enduring truth in the phrase, *"this too shall pass."*

As we come to the end of our brief exploration of the radiant realms beyond the threshold of death's door, and contemplate the eternal nature of our soul, a profound truth shines above all else.

Love knows no boundaries.

Love is an ever-unfolding experience of the present moment, transcending the limitations of a single human life, and stretching across the vast expanse of time and space.

This discussion on death would be incomplete without acknowledging that it's not just our actions in life that carry significance, but also the manner in which we choose to approach them. There are essentially two ways to face life and death: *with love or fear*. My hope is that you choose love, and that you know, beyond any doubt, that you are unconditionally loved—*that God loves you, and so do I*. May this knowledge empower you to be your most radiant self in every moment in this world and beyond.

In this intricate dance of free will and divine guidance, we find our souls continuously drawn closer to the eternal light and love that await us.

May you know the gift of your own existence, and the eternal radiance of your beauty-filled soul.

I love you.

— Chrystal Rae

A soulmate's presence is a powerful transformational fire

Letter 14
soulmates
echo of love

Did you know that soulmates are real? Well, they are.

You have had many soulmates in your current, past, and future lives.

Some of your most beloved soulmates have traveled with you for many lives; I am honored to stand among them. Capturing the delicate threads of love, care, and appreciation woven through a single life is a heartfelt challenge, made even more poignant by conveying the profound soul connection that transcends time, an eternal bond of love. Though words fail to honor the depth of my undying love for you, what I will say is that I loved you long before you came into physical form. I loved the very energetic particles and light that came together to shape the essence of your being, the "you" that you recognize in this life.

The connection we have with a soulmate is profound and transcendent.

In a soulmate's presence, there is an immediate familiarity and resonance. The shared bond of love draws soulmates together: *life after life*. This is exactly how I feel about you—*a magnetic attraction and love that transcends time*. Even if our paths had not crossed, and I hadn't had the pleasure of meeting you again in this profoundly transformational life, the fact that you exist would still be a candle illuminating my night. With the intention of finding you again in this lifetime, I wrote these Love Letters, hoping that they would find their way to your heart and reignite the profound soul connection we have shared in our countless lives together.

As we once again embark on this timeless journey of shared experience and timeless love, please allow me to express my deep gratitude for your beautiful soul, loving presence, and the intricate forces of Nature and God that orchestrated our reunion. Your radiant light has nourished and nurtured my soul for many lives, which makes our reunion all the more joyous and profound. My love for you transcends the boundaries of time, spanning eons, and extending far beyond the limits of a mortal life. It is a love that has endured thousands of lives and many worlds, a flame that burns eternally, unwavering in its intensity and depth.

I have loved you under scorching summer suns and within the embrace of bitter winter nights. I have loved you from the highest peaks, the lowest valleys, and every other terrain of your beautiful soul. My love for you knows no boundaries; it is as vast and free as the open sky: it cannot be contained, dampened, or extinguished. In every life, my deepest longing is to reunite with you. I have loved all your divine expressions; every dark shadow and shimmering light is included in my love. I have loved you since the beginning of time, and I will continue to love you long after time collapses back into the void from which it was born.

Our timeless bond is a symphony of sound and a spectacle of light embodied in the transformative journey of human experience.

This bond is pure energy, a holy, sacred, and alive movement of God. I was drawn into this life by the silent siren of your radiant light that called me forth out of the darkness; nothing could hold me back from finding you again. The irresistible pull that forever binds us cannot be severed or broken by any force in this universe or beyond.

My greatest honor and purpose is to love, assist, and serve your precious soul. Soulmates have an unbreakable bond of love that spans the vast distances of time and space. When a soulmate experiences joy or pain, it is instantly sensed by the other as a magnetic current, creating a resonant ripple in the field. A sudden knowing emerges about their well-being. This phenomenon is observed in identical and fraternal twins. Scientists search for answers to this fascinating occurrence, examining their DNA and looking for other tangible clues that would explain the profound connection they share, even across vast distances. The data is provocative and intriguing, but the bond of a soulmate is much more than shared biology.

Meeting a soulmate is a healing, invigorating experience like no other. However, an encounter with a soulmate is neither rare nor unplanned. Quite the contrary, it is a common and natural occurrence. It is part of the divine plan of the universe for us to travel with certain souls who promote our well-being and evolution. Soulmates come into our lives for many reasons and in many expressions; even a faithful friend with a wagging tail or a soft meow can be the embodiment of a soulmate. Whatever form a soulmate may take in our lives, their presence is healing and empowering.

A soulmate often shares a similar energy or represents its complete opposite.

We are instinctively drawn to those with comparable energy, disposition, and life trajectories, yet also find ourselves curiously attracted to our opposites. Our paths cross with purpose, brought together by lessons we share and a dedication to enrich each other's ongoing personal growth and the evolution of our soul.

Love is the unifying force that draws us together, even in its most base expression. The loving universe continuously extends through the veil of time and space, in both extraordinary and mundane ways, to nurture our well-being and remind us that we are never alone.

Love is the sacred meeting ground for all souls.

In this light, every person we encounter is a soulmate. Otherwise, they would not exist within our sphere of influence, as there would be no resonance or energetic alignment. Yet, specific individuals will leave a more substantial imprint on our journey. Their presence holds profound significance, impacting our evolution in remarkable ways. To this point, our shared resonance is one of the main reasons that I came back to this world. I came back so that you would know that there is great love for you—*my very presence proves this to be true.*

Throughout our many lives together, your beautiful soul and kind heart have brought me great comfort and joy. However, contrary to the conventional notion of a soulmate as purely a source of joy, comfort, and support, some of our most pivotal soulmates play an opposing role. They enter our lives to challenge, pain, or provoke us into change and purposeful transformation. Either way, whether seen as a foe or friend, on a soul level, a soulmate's presence is always meant to be a source of love and support, acting as a catalyst for change and offering evolutionary opportunities that might otherwise remain unavailable.

Each encounter with a soulmate, fleeting or passing, promotes and inspires change.

With this intention, in the pre-birth realm, some souls willingly offered to take on the roles of opposition, creating havoc and discord in our lives as a means of making us uncomfortable and promoting change. Out of their great love and compassion, and to empower us to reclaim our inherent divinity, they willingly accepted the role of the *"rogue."*

Some of our most influential soulmates lovingly signed up to be the ones who challenge us, hurt us, or even betray us, by playing the role of a villain or rogue in our lives.

A soulmate's actions, whether kind or not-so-kind, serve to either provide solace and encouragement or nudge us beyond our comfort zone. Whether a soulmate's actions are kind or cruel, their impact on our lives is invariably positive, significantly contributing to our earthly experience and spiritual evolution. Indeed, a soulmate's presence is always a powerful transformational fire.

Soulmates enter and exit our lives to nurture our spiritual growth and evolution. They may manifest as friends or foes, yet their intentions are always geared toward our well-being. Whether they come cloaked in light or draped in darkness, a soulmate's presence leaves an indelible mark on our journey. The depth of our connection directly correlates with the strength of their influence. Often, soulmates are those nearest to us: family, friends, lovers, adversaries, and coworkers. They can also appear as a random stranger, offering a helping hand, leaving an indelible mark, yet never to be seen again. However a soulmate shows up in our lives, they significantly contribute to our spiritual progress.

Among the countless soulmates who have walked beside you throughout your many lives, I stand as one of the most significant, and you are one of mine. Our bond of Love is a sacred treasure, and among its many gifts, none is more precious than our timeless connection. In our every encounter, in this life, previous lives, and those yet to come, my aim is always to be a healing presence, a loyal friend, and to remind you of your greatness. Above all, I wish to be your comfort in the rain and your inspiration on sunny days. Why? Because I love you, and I have loved you for eons and many lives.

Only love can heal the wounded heart and soothe the tired soul.

We all need Love, and none would survive without it. Just as sunshine, nutrients, and rain are required for plants to grow, we, too, need certain elements to thrive: kindness, care, and compassion are vital for our well-being, and love is essential for our soul.

Our soulmates empower us to be the most radiant version of ourselves.

We are energetic beings born of a loving universe in the form of condensed light and the embodiment of love. Love is the unchanging foundation of the loving universe, permeating all existence and animating each cell of our body. Our very essence reflects God's boundless love.

The radiant threads of light that connect us to each other hold profound significance, particularly in the enduring bonds of love with our soulmates.

Through their timeless bond of love and energetic resonance, soulmates infuse us with vitality, support, and solace. Without their loving presence, we might not endure this challenging yet wondrous world. Indeed, in the absence of our soulmates, life would lose its vibrancy and become a barren desert of little joy. While in the company of our soulmates, we feel at ease, happy, and have a renewed vitality. A soulmate's influence is undeniably potent and transformative; whether they manifest as protagonists or antagonists, soulmates serve as a source of comfort and a catalyst for profound change. In both roles, on a soul level, they are the ones who genuinely love and deeply care for us.

A soulmate's presence can be a storm of growth or a gentle healing rain.

Irrespective of the path a soulmate takes, the purity of our relationship with them is rooted in unconditional love that spans lifetimes. This deep connection explains the sense of familiarity and enduring peace that we experience in their presence. As validation of our eternal connection, there will most certainly be a multitude of personalized synchronicities that will act as signs that we are on the right path and in the right company.

Lucid dreams, meditative visions, and intuitive insights will direct us toward both our soulmates and opportunities for growth and evolution. In the uplifting light of a soulmate's presence, we discover exhilarating opportunities for profound transformation and new beginnings. Bearing this in mind, and because you have this book in your hands and are reading these words, many energetic shifts have already taken place within your cellular structure.

Indeed, this life marks a period of great liberation, where newfound self-sovereignty takes center stage. As mentioned, we are not meant to travel these earthly roads alone—*together we are stronger*. Our soulmate's influence assists and empowers us to make difficult, life-altering decisions that shape our destiny.

In our transformative earthly journey, our soulmates' unwavering love and support provide a stable foundation for us to change not only our lives but also impact the world.

Indeed, united we thrive. The adage "no man is an island" resonates deeply. A soulmate's presence strengthens our resolve, guiding us to discover new possibilities and venture into realms of untapped potential. A slight shift in consciousness profoundly affects the trajectory of our soul, steering us towards wondrous universes of undiscovered possibilities. Throughout our many lives, we encounter countless soulmates, yet only those at a similar energy frequency repeatedly cross our paths. These sacred encounters act as catalysts for transformation and growth, advancing our spiritual journey.

We align ourselves with higher energetic possibilities when we choose love, kindness, and compassion for ourselves and others.

Aligning purposefully with higher energies and frequencies opens the path to meet soulmates awaiting us at our next evolutionary stage, be they from this earthly realm or other dimensions. These sacred meetings are crucial, as our most impactful soulmates often possess elevated consciousness, including earthly and ethereal angels, guides, and enlightened teachers. Though the implications of these sacred encounters are profound, the path remains clear: by choosing love consciously, we lift our frequencies of love and light, attracting more evolved soulmates into our lives. Their wisdom and presence enhance our journey. These enlightened beings have always existed around us, yet our vibrational state may not have been luminous enough to accommodate their presence.

Our spiritual growth, on profoundly personal levels, is closely interwoven with our relationships with both earthly and ethereal soulmates, who guide and enrich our evolutionary path. The recognition of our own evolutionary process and through the understanding that every person we encounter on our soul's sacred journey is connected to us in some way, we are naturally more loving, accepting, and respectful of others. Each of us contribute to the growth and expansion of one another's consciousness and capacity for love.

With the unwavering love and support of our soulmates, we are empowered to continue our exploration of the many mysteries of existence and our role within it. Simultaneously, we find solace and comfort in the knowledge that we are never isolated, abandoned, or alone on this intricate journey of life.

Our soulmates, whether friends or foes, serve as a healing and empowering force.

Their energy in our lives acts as a catalyst, helping us tap into our limitless potential. Our shared journey into and out of the physical realm is an ongoing love story, constantly evolving within the space of genuine care, love, and support, all working toward our higher good.

The presence of such goodness, grace, and love transforms and enlivens our DNA, elevates our consciousness, and enlivens our soul.

Love changes everything, including, and most importantly, love changes us.

Indeed, love is the grand alchemist, it transforms everything, and most importantly, it transforms us. To choose love over fear is not as complex as it may seem; it is actually quite simple and straightforward. In those moments when fear clouds our perspective, we can ask ourselves a simple yet profound question. "*What is my most loving response to this person, circumstance, or condition?*" This one question changes our perspective and opens doors to more radiant possibilities.

Attracting better circumstances and loving connections is simple yet profound—we must consistently, and without fail, choose love.

Love's light transforms universes, with this shift starting within us. There's no one-size-fits-all solution to break free from past patterns, but love remains the constant. It manifests in kindness, generosity, self-care, and assertiveness. Across all aspects of life, asking *"what is my most loving response"* guides us, be the approach gentle or firm, steering us towards greater love and compassion.

The truth of life's journey is love. When love grounds us, guiding our choices towards kindness and compassion, we flow harmoniously in its stream. Our ultimate purpose is rediscovering our inherent perfection. This involves transforming habits, elevating our energy, and gradually shifting our frequency, making life more joyful. Yet, this pursuit of a brighter, more loving self doesn't demand instant perfection. In our human experience, despite the support of soulmates, it's natural to sometimes falter in making the most loving choices.

The goal of life is progress, not perfection.

Seeking perfection is an unattainable and life-depleting pursuit. As sentient beings, we embody a unique combination of strengths and weaknesses, making us beautifully imperfect. Our existence is marked by both complexity and simplicity, with virtues and flaws intermingled. In this complex human experience, love remains a constant.

We are always evolving, and in every stage of our transformation, there lies beauty, love, and light. Our journey, spanning countless lives, shapes us both individually and collectively. Soulmates are key collaborators in our divine story. By nurturing our connections, we contribute to the expanding sphere of love and light in the universe.

As we evolve into more enlightened and loving beings, recognizing and accepting the perfection within our imperfections becomes essential. Discovering the unchanging love and radiant light within ourselves guides us back to our source, showing that flaws are integral to our unique journey. The path of self-discovery and acceptance not only enriches our individual lives but also fosters collective growth. Uplifting our energy and fine-tuning our frequency trigger a cascade of positive transformations, elevating our personal experiences.

This elevated state of consciousness and love serves as a crucible for our relationships: *they either thrive in this newfound light or gracefully dissolve, paving the way for deeper, more resonant connections with our evolved selves.*

The relationship we cultivate with ourselves fundamentally shapes our interactions with others.

Bearing this in mind, as we nurture a more positive and loving relationship with ourselves, our interactions with others either transform into kinder, more affectionate connections or they naturally dissolve. The realization of our collective journey and intrinsic connection to everyone and everything fosters a more loving, accepting, and respectful approach towards others and the world around us.

Each of us plays a crucial part in each other's growth, in expanding the collective consciousness, and in the unfolding of love.

Supported and nurtured by our soulmates, we can explore life's mysteries, comforted by the knowledge that we are never truly alone. Indeed, soulmates are vital to our growth, acting as necessary catalysts for our transformation. They play a crucial role in our evolution, helping to expand our consciousness and deepen our capacity for love.

Amid life's uncertainties and the puzzling turns of fate, we find comfort in the company of those who join us on the grand adventure in and out of the temporal world of form and matter.

However, it's crucial to recognize the balance between accepting support and maintaining personal responsibility. Ultimately, each of us, whether consciously or not, charts our soul's path.

Every thought, word, and action shapes our reality, creating and destroying universes in an instant.

Our perception of reality is just a fraction of a greater truth. Our understanding of the benevolent universe and our place within it pales in comparison to the stunning reality of the boundless love that created all of existence, including you and me.

As a manifestation of this loving universe, and to honor our eternal bond of love, I chose to return to the earthly realm. My enduring purpose has been to find you and remind you of our never-ending companionship and endless bond of love. The magnitude of my love for you is a profound alignment of both heavenly and earthly forces that meticulously orchestrate our meeting, again and again, throughout our many shared lives.

The enormity of the love drawing forth from the darkness is beyond measure or description.

What I will say is that in the tender embrace of love, we discover not just comfort but also a profound sense of happiness and meaning. This boundless force uncovers the deepest secrets of our hearts and the universe itself. As your loyal ally and devoted soulmate, my love for you transcends the ordinary, reaching into the extraordinary realm of the divine.

Each word in these heartfelt letters reverberates with our enduring connection and eternal bond of love. In its simplest form, my declaration is this: *I love you*. My deep affection has its roots in the dawn of time and will persist throughout eternity. Whether our paths in this life intertwine or diverge, my presence will be a palpable constant in your journey. You are never alone; my love accompanies you, offering solace, strength, unwavering support, and unconditional devotion.

The depth and width of my love for you go beyond mere words. Rather than fumbling with the inherent limitations of ordinary prose or the inadequacy of words to express the vastness of my love for you, I will end this Love Letter on Soul Mates with a poem, written just for you with trembling hands and a thundering heart.

Like the soft clouds that punctuate the blue of the sky, I find you in the dotted moments of everyday existence. Everywhere I look, I see your radiant presence rising like the morning sun that finds its way through the smallest crevasse and deepest canyon, shimmering in iridescent hues of purple, pink, yellow, and the most beautiful shades of orange.

The very thought of you brings salty tears to my eyes, tears of exquisite joy. How fortunate to feel such sorrow and pain, and to be so deeply alive in my love fore you. Floating in the afternoon haze, long shadows of our shared past intertwine with a future yet to be born. Like the iridescent prism of multicolored light that arcs across cloudy skies and raining summer storms, our love is born and reborn in the joyful pirouettes and spiraling light of falling stars—a timeless symbol of our infinite love.

In the safety of our eternal bond, once quiet flowers, nestled within themselves, unfold their tender petals, dancing in waves of ecstatic bliss on the untamed current of the wind. Even in the depths of dreamless sleep, I find you wrapped around me like a warm blanket, filling the void of empty space with purpose and promise.

Time and again, we find each other in the flickering light of the emergent dawn that signals the arrival of a new day with the soft vermilion splendor of morning light. Everything is fresh and alive, including our love. In this transcendent moment of perfection and grace, the world cannot be any more beautiful or blossoming. How I wish I could push back time and forever live in the suspended moment of this unfolding bliss, but the world will not stop spinning to quail the longing of a capricious child, and change is an inevitable constant in the universe we live in.

Without warning, the weather shifts, clouds gather, and the sun is darkened by the unforeseen forces of Nature that dispassionately pull us apart, shattering our dreams and all hope of tomorrow. Suddenly, I find myself gasping for breath, submerged in the rippling wake of your loud absence. But even this, I don't resist. In homage and honor to you, I willingly fall into the dark abyss of my loneliness. The shattered remnants of the setting sun tumble into the dark line of the horizon, as I retrace the origin of our unending love. Once again, I find myself surrendered to the pristine beauty of that long forgotten moment when we first met, now and forever etched in my memory as the perpetual bloom of the morning sun.

In the unmoving space of quiet acceptance, yesterday disappears and tomorrow falls away. My heart no longer resists the inevitable end of this fleeting, temporal world or the glorious reunion with the divine. I am pulled away from you, drawn by a luminescent light and an unfathomable, all encompassing love that emerges out of the darkness. Still, between this world and the next, I beckon to you like the nightingale calls to the night, finally home in the sacred abode of our undying love.

In the absence of light, the night grows dark, and stars fall from the sky, and still, I see you everywhere. There is no space where you are not. Even the reflected pearlescent light of the circled moon, pressed flat against the muted sky is a gleaming metal of honor, saluting the divinity that made our love possible in the endless ocean of stars.

For all of this, for all the joy, tears, laughter, and even the sorrow, I am forever grateful, and surrendered in humility and love at your feet.

I will search for you in every life and with every breath until the end of time.

— Chrystal Rae

We are the voice of God,

singing for the joy of sound

Letter 15
silence
voice of silence

Beneath the loud cacophony of everyday existence, is an ever-present and vibrant silence that births, sustains, and permeates all things.

Silence, often described as the universe's foundational fabric, is what some label as *Pranava*—the vibrant, unceasing melody with which the cosmos sings itself into existence. Others may know it as cosmic sound, chi, or life force. Either way, in peaceful moments, be it through meditation, art, music, or nature, one can sense this soft, soothing silence as an ever-present background hum.

Whether we tap into silence with conscious intent or not, it regenerates, heals, and enlivens us.

In today's fast-paced world, many remain untouched by the profound, restorative silence beneath the surface. There are a multitude of reasons we sidestep it. Chief among them is our entanglement with life's surface-level distractions: daily errands, television, shopping, work, social media, messages, emails, and the vast expanse of the Internet.

Further, a prevailing "*dog-eat-dog*" attitude and obsession over wealth, power, and desire often cloud our perceptions. Engulfed in the cacophony of life, we rarely pause long enough to acknowledge the underlying, ever-present silent rhythm of existence. The omnipresent hum of the universe gets overshadowed by our internal and external chaos.

Exacerbating the innate noise of life, the rise of social media has often skewed our values towards appearances and external validation at the expense of authenticity and depth. We often get caught up in life's immediate concerns and external perceptions, overlooking the more profound, subtle harmonies that connect us to the universe and our true selves.

Often, in our extreme preoccupation with the mundane, we overlook the profound.

Nonetheless, life's myriad experiences, whether steeped in beauty or marked by suffering, intermittently pull us into this reflective silence. Yet, as noted, these instances are often brief and unintentional. However, when we actively engage with the ever-present stillness, we access a broader realm of understanding and interconnectedness. This purposeful tranquility is more than passive absorption; it is an active attunement to the vast expanse of the universe and God. Engaging in the practice of consciously connecting to the silence fortifies our spiritual well-being and fuels our evolution.

The intentional dive into the profound depths of silence is core to the practice of yoga.

By mastering breath control, discipline, and inner peace, yogis achieve tranquility, emotional balance, and elevated states of consciousness. This approach transforms yoga into more than just physical exercise. In its most authentic form, yoga views breath as a key to enlightenment, bridging the physical and spiritual aspects of existence.

Seasoned yogis, through profound mastery of breath, unlock hidden realms of consciousness and yogic abilities that seem almost otherworldly. My own experiences, both witnessing and participating, confirm this. From voluntarily stopping the heartbeat for long periods and enduring extreme temperatures, to glimpsing past and potential future lives, and contorting the body in extraordinary ways, these phenomena underscore a deep cosmic connection. Such feats are attainable only through deliberate breath control.

While yoga is an intricate system dedicated to holistic well-being, its foundational practice of breath control, or Pranayama, remains refreshingly uncomplicated. Merely taking a few diaphragmatic breaths can work wonders, instantly soothing the central nervous system, bringing emotions to a still point, and quietening mental chatter.

Through a dedicated yoga practice, breath control, and intentional focus, we can touch the profound silence from which all life springs and achieve greater mastery over our sensory realm. This control ensures we are not at the mercy of our body's fleeting desires. As we consistently practice and hone our skills, we learn to modulate our nervous system through breath management and maintain an enduring connection to the ever-present, high-frequency silence that underlies the universe.

Out of the silence, sound bursts forth in a rippling echo of God manifest and alive all that IS.'

Esteemed yogis and spiritual luminaries remain eternally connected to this profound silence, enveloped in the high-frequency resonance of endless bliss. Beyond this serenity, the depth of this silence offers manifold gifts: rejuvenation of the body, profound healing, heightened insights, personal growth, and empowerment across various dimensions.

The vibrant silence that permeates the entire universe is the very essence of God.

The Old Testament proclaims, *"In the beginning, there was the word, and the word was God."* While this statement holds undeniable truth, it represents only a part of a broader narrative. To grasp the concept of God as *"the word,"* we must explore its origins.

In our discussion, for the sake of brevity, let's simplify it: *"the word"* emerged from the universal silence as a tone, a sound, a distinct frequency. Indeed, from the profound depth and quiet expanse of the loving universe, sound erupted in a spontaneous celebration of existence. This joyous emergence encompasses all of creation, including every one of us.

Everything that comes into being is an integral part of the whole of creation.

Every bright light and dark shadow is the most beauty-filled expression of love possible with the variables available at each level of consciousness. To better understand this concept, consider the transformation of a caterpillar into a butterfly: it embodies the energetic essence, luminous manifestation, and resonance of caterpillar-*ness* until it morphs into the energetic form of its more evolved state as a butterfly.

We, too, continually shape-shift into the next most radiant version of ourselves. However, our life journeys are not necessarily uniform. In some lives, we progress rapidly, while in others, we may stagnate or regress, reverting to patterns of prior existences. We may even devolve back into the chrysalis of prior lives. Yet, in all these states and stages, the loving universe is unwavering in its love and support of ever-evolving soul.

This grand benevolence is not contingent on our deeds, pace, growth, or where we stand in our soul's journey. There is neither a punitive finale nor a golden reward awaiting us. However, this does not negate the fact that our choices carry consequences.

Every decision resonates with an energy, aligning with the corresponding outcome and consequence.

We get what we "are" in life, not necessarily what we "want."

In addition, the actions of previous lives spill into our current life as opportunities for healing, amendment, and empowerment. This carryover is the natural consequence of our choices, not an imposed karmic punishment or prize. In its boundless wisdom, the universe does not weigh our lives on a moral scale. It neither judges nor seeks vengeance. Rather, our earthly sojourn is a much sought experience of personal development, conscious evolution, and the unfoldment of love:

no judgment is brought upon us and no retribution is necessary. The diverse life situations, temperaments, and predispositions we assume throughout different lives and as distinct beings enhance our soul's joyful journey back to its origin. These myriad experiences shape our individual paths and play a pivotal role in the grand, unfolding narrative of the universe and the Divine.

The echoes of our present, past, and future lives ripple out ad infinitum.

These echoes deeply influence our personal journey, impacting the whole of existence. Every moment, every choice, and every experience contributes to the intricate dance of life, shaping both our destinies and the broader narrative of the loving universe.

Indeed, in this vast cosmic play, our experiences are shaped by energetic alignments of *cause-and-effect* dynamics and not predetermined moral evaluations. What we experience as karma is the natural consequence of our choices. Just as the rain naturally finds its way to the Earth or a river naturally finds its way back to the sea, we naturally find our way back to God's loving arms.

The path we travel and the pace of our journey is always up to us. Sometimes we choose the high road, and sometimes we get stuck in the mud. Whichever way we go, nothing is set in stone; at any moment, we can change directions. For as we improve our thoughts, choices, and actions, we alter the very sound *(vibration)* of our existence and the energetic state of our being, elevating the quality of what we draw to ourselves.

Everything in the universe, from the tiniest atom to the vastest galaxies, consists of vibrating energy, each with its unique frequency, tone, and sound.

Just as musical instruments have specific frequencies, sounds, and tones, each individual has a distinct *"vibrational tone"* determined by their thoughts, emotions, actions, and overall state of being. Feelings like love, joy, and gratitude vibrate at higher frequencies, while negative emotions like anger, fear, or resentment vibrate at lower frequencies. When we choose positive thoughts, make wise decisions, and align our actions with our highest good, we "*attune*" ourselves to higher frequencies. This energetic alignment is much like a radio tuned to a specific station, our experiences are shaped by our bandwidth, and frequency.

Our vibrational tone reflects our current state of consciousness and naturally magnetizes experiences, people, and situations resonating with it. Through conscious and loving choices, we raise our vibrational frequency, drawing new connections and bringing about transformative changes in our lives. When we consciously and purposefully strive to improve our thoughts, decisions, and actions, we raise our vibration and shape the experiences and opportunities that come into our existence.

Consciously or unconsciously, our choices act as a magnet in our lives, attracting or repelling people and circumstances.

Life is a magnetic equation that always equals love.

Our Earthly experiences are closely tied to the unique energetic frequency of both our personal being and the collective consciousness. This frequency, mingled with the core elements of our soul, forms our natural vibrational *"set point."* Nonetheless, each person's *"set point"* is distinct, shaped by their prevailing thoughts and feelings. It's dynamic, evolving with our ongoing emotions and past experiences.

Our reality mirrors our current energetic frequency.

Please remember that wherever we currently find ourselves on the energetic scale is not static or fixed. We always have the ability to shift our thoughts and thereby alter our life's trajectory—*for better or worse*. However, its best not to label these frequencies as *"better"* or *"worse."* Such labels can create a false hierarchy or imply a judgment of good vs. bad, which does not accurately represent the truth. While cultural biases may suggest the superiority of one life path over another, every individual journey offers invaluable opportunities for personal development and soul expansion.

The compound effect of our cumulative energetic "set point," personal and collective, creates and collapses universes in an instant.

To this end, we come into the temporal world and earthly realm to better understand ourselves and the Divine through a vast array of experiences. Our perception determines whether we view this journey as positive or negative.

The essence of our being is formed by the layered impact of personal experiences and soul growth mirrored within humanity's collective journey.

The interconnectedness of existence hinges on understanding ourselves and our spiritual origin and heritage. Yet, many overlook our inherent power to steer life's course, underestimating the rippling effects of choice. Blaming others is often easier than taking full responsibility for our lives. Many, unfortunately, are unaware of their intrinsic ability to shape their life's trajectory. They overlook or disregard their role in attracting life events and the subsequent consequences.

The profound impact of our choices often goes unnoticed. In life, we have two primary choices: we can resist the present moment and experience suffering, or we can make peace with it and find contentment. A valuable rule to remember is that when we point at others, three fingers point back at us. Although we may not have control over every chapter of our life story, we do have the power to choose the ink with which it is written.

Accepting life's ever-changing circumstances doesn't come with a guarantee that everything will align with our desires or unfold as we wish that it would; at times, it will, and other times, it won't.

Despite not having the ability to choose all the people, places, circumstances, or conditions in our lives, how we respond to them is always within our control. Resisting the present moment leads to suffering.

Regardless of our opinions, the present moment remains unchanged and unmoved. This active acceptance is not a futile surrender. Nor does it imply that we should filter or suppress our feelings or pretend they don't exist. Instead, we immerse ourselves in them, but without resistance. In this way, we dissipate the emotional charge and subsequent feelings associated with them.

What we resist persists.

When we allow life to unfold naturally, without imposing our desires for how it "*should be*," we open the door to respond with greater awareness and love. Having said that, it's important not to filter our feelings or pretend they don't hurt when they do. Indeed, in this world of constant change, opting for the soul's higher path can prove to be a formidable, painful, and solitary undertaking. Rather than fight the darkness, we can simply light a candle, and the darkness will disappear of its own accord.

A single candle illuminates even the darkest of nights.

In the same way, the unconditionality of love naturally transforms and frees us from fear, hastening our soul's evolutionary journey of remembrance. Nonetheless, while love is the most direct path to the divine, and is essential for a more joyful life, it may appear absent or elusive to those in survival mode. When we are grappling to stay afloat, it can be difficult to see beyond our immediate struggles.

The reassuring news is that we don't have to face these challenges alone. We are surrounded by angels, guides, and spiritual teachers, both in the physical and ethereal realms, who deeply love and care for us. Just as our footsteps in the sand mark the path for those who follow, there are others further along the journey who shine their light to guide us back home.

In life's darkest moments, love is the light that reveals the path to our soul's awakening.

To choose love and be a light requires a level of consciousness yet to be achieved by most. While consistently maintaining a high vibrational tone and aligning with our soul's loving resonance may sound good, the reality is that it's often a strenuous endeavor. Life's unpredictability and human vulnerabilities can sometimes derail even the most dedicated amongst us from this path.

Balancing altruistic desire with the complexities of the human experience is a challenging feat. Disappointment, betrayal, or loss can leave us feeling disheartened and hopeless. Certainly, during these more trying times, it isn't easy to see the truth, much less live it. Life's trials and tribulations can dim the light of our soul and quickly alter our vibrational frequency. Nonetheless, even the shadows of disappointment and loss can be essential markers on our soul's journey, turning pain into profound wisdom.

Divine order is always at work in our lives, and all is well, even when it appears not to be.

Though it may often seem otherwise, in life's intricate workings, there's a hidden order that keeps things in balance. We are forever cradled in a love so all encompassing it is beyond comprehension. Everyone and everything we encounter on our soul's sacred journey adds to our inner light and to the ever-growing love and radiance of the universe.

Imagine a forest where towering trees and humble shrubs coexist. Some trees reach for the sky, while the shrubs hug the ground. Yet, the rain showers them all without judgment or bias. Our spiritual journey is much the same. Regardless of our present alignment or spiritual progress, we are showered with love and are supported as we reach for the light or fall into the night.

Each of us has a vital part in life's epic story and the unfolding of the compassionate universe. We are the song of the universe, the voice of God, singing ourselves into existence for the pure joy of being. We come to this planet to have the human experience together. Everyone and everything in our lives is a gift, meant to both support and challenge us, catalyzing change.

Whether we perceive someone as a rogue or a friend, their presence is a seed of empowerment, healing, and growth. Some arrive as angels of light, while others come shrouded in darkness, either way, they all serve our soul's journey.

In the diversity of singularity, and the multiplicity of diversity, we are One united in Love.

In the vast symphony of existence, we each have unique chord, a singular note within the universal song. Every soul plays a vital role in the whole of creation. A song with missing notes is a sad, flat verse. On their own, individual notes seem insignificant. Yet, when woven together with melody and lyrics, they create a beautiful composition—*a celestial love song.*

While a single note may appear minor, when connected to each other, they forms an exquisite harmony, a divine anthem of existence.

Each contribution, no matter how small, is vital to the full, rich expression of this celestial symphony. Without every single note, the song loses its full resonance and beauty. The *"uni-verse"* embodies this unity, a confluence of verses where every soul adds depth and meaning.

The joy of the human experience is to sing and sing, and then to sing some more in unison. We are born of the silence for the joy of singing and being heard. An unsung song is the saddest song of all, for the singing unites us and reminds us that we are not alone; we are "*One Love*" experiencing itself in multiplicity. There's is much comfort in knowing we're not alone on this journey. As these words unfold, they serve as a gentle whisper and reminder of the vast love surrounding each of us. Love is a constant force in our lives, providing stability and freedom as we navigate the ever-changing rhythms of existence. This constancy allows us to explore and transform ourselves. However, it's essential to understand that everything, including our personal growth, unfolds in its own time, a concept often referred to as divine timing.

We can't rush our evolution any more than we can force a flower to blossom or bloom.

Our role is to put in consistent effort towards our goals and aspirations, while also practicing patience and faith. It's a paradox that, by letting go of the urgency to evolve, we might actually facilitate our own growth. This approach requires a balance of action and non-attachment. Just like a flower that blooms in its natural time, our personal development follows a similar organic process. We are supported in this journey by a higher power, which might be seen as divine providence or the benevolent universe.

This support reassures us that we're not alone in our endeavors. As we navigate our path, it's beneficial to pause, reflect, and breathe deeply, trusting that everything will align in its right time. Such trust and surrender can bring peace and clarity, guiding us forward on our journey.

The love reaching out to you in this very moment is beyond what can be fully comprehended, transcending the ordinary limits of human expression and feeling.

It's a depth of affection and connection so vast and deep that it eludes full comprehension, reminding us of the extraordinary and boundless potential of love

There is so much love for you that the pages of this book cannot express or contain it; I am just one voice of many who love and care for you. This love is boundless, pure, and absolute. The abundance of love pouring out to you in each moment cannot be measured with concepts or words. This love, God's divine love, has no limits, boundaries, or opposites; it is pure and absolute.

The tender embrace of our loving Creator is a whisper into the silent vastness, and a love song to your precious soul. Whatever challenges arise, love is always the answer. Within the vast orchestra of life, every decision we make contributes to the collective harmony. It is through these choices that we shape the resonance and rhythm of our soul's journey.

We are free, self-aware, creative beings; nothing is forced upon us.

The unique mental, emotional, and physical tools we are endowed with are precision-tailored for our individual growth and the enrichment of our soul. Our shadows and light push us toward our next evolutionary leap, refining our souls. There are no missteps in the dance of the soul, as every path ultimately leads us back to love and more love.

Born of profound silence, we are the voice of God, singing for the joy of sound. We are the radiant song of life, bursting forth out of the silence for the ecstatic joy of creation. Nothing is excluded from the glorious song of the loving universe—*including your precious soul.*

The song of you can only be sung by you.

It is a beautiful, never-to-be-replicated song that rises, crests, and then joyously fades back into the silence of which it was born, enhancing the very origin of its own creation: God. Without pause, the first note of creation quickly fades into another necessary note that is swiftly born and reborn, again and again, bursting through the darkness into the loving universe in ever more spectacular sparks of shimmering, iridescent light. Each note, lyric, verse, and song is more exquisite and stunning than that which came before.

Just as children leave an indelible mark on their parents, shaping and evolving their worlds, we, as children of a loving universe, profoundly influence our Creator. The very pulse of our existence adds depth and vibrancy to the boundless love of the radiant universe.

We are the echo of God's love song, forever expanding and connected to the very first note of creation. Our existence not only influences our creator but also sends ripples across the entire universe. In the intricate balance between life and death, we forge bonds, some transient, others profound, that etch lasting impressions on our soul. Consider someone you hold dear: perhaps a child who looks up to you, a parent who guided your early steps, a teacher who recognized your potential, a friend who stood by your side, or even a pet whose loyalty never wavered.

Reflect on the moments shared, the laughter, the lessons, and the challenges too. Each of these interactions have reshaped your life in subtle and profound ways. Dive deeper into memory. Picture a preschool teacher whose comforting embrace made the outside world less daunting. Whenever you face a challenge today, a small part of her strength and assurance still remains with you. Conversely, consider a childhood adversary whose actions darkened those innocent days.

Though difficult, your childhood challenges forged a resilience and determination in you that became fuel for the fire of your soul.

Imagine, for a moment, if these individuals forever vanished from your life. Even in their absence, the legacy of their presence would linger. The words they spoke and the emotions they evoked all continue to ripple through the chapters of your life, shaping decisions, forging paths, and influencing interactions.

Time might blur their faces on the canvas of memory, but their soul's essence becomes a part of your very being—*as a gift or a lesson.*

We, in our unique way, influence the universe's continuous evolution.

This interplay, this eternal echo of shared moments and emotions, mirrors our relationship with the Divine. Just as individuals leave an imprint on us, our actions, choices, and emotions reverberate in the vast and loving universe. Every heartbeat sends ripples through the vast expanse in endless waves of love and light. Every experience is an entanglement of energy and an echo into the future. Every person, place, and thing that we encounter affects us in dramatic ways that are primarily unacknowledged: *a blossoming flower, a storm brewing, a dog barking, a cat's claw, a newborn baby, an old man, smog, pollution, clear skies, a chiming bell, ocean waves, a honking horn, pleasurable and painful sensations, wind dancing in the trees, a sour taste, music in the distance; and yes, the sweet hum of silence too.*

Even people we never meet, and the experiences we never have *(including the experiences of others)* are a part of our personal and group energy. This gives new meaning to the word "Oneness." We are a universal family. The whole of existence is born of and inherently part of this *"Eternal Oneness."* When we care for another, we are, in essence caring for ourselves.

We are all united in love; every joy is our joy, every sorrow is our sorrow, and to help another is to help oneself.

We are one light, one love, and one uni-verse; the love song of God that had to be sung. In the grand cacophony of life, we are the breath of God, echoing out in waves of ecstatic bliss and joy and rippling back to our Source, brighter and lighter. We are a poetic verse of the universe, and a necessary lyric of the divine. We are the sound of grace, goodness, and God; the manifestation of love and light, bursting forth out of the silence for the ecstatic joy of the song.

Out of the silence we are born, back to the silence we shall return.

As we close this Love Letter, please allow me to address this final thought directly to your beautiful soul. We are all connected in the love and light of God, but my love for you spans eons of time, extending throughout the vast expanse of the universe, and our many shared lives.

You are my soul's music and my reason to be: I love you in the loudest expression of life and the most silent repose of death and beyond. I am grateful for vibrant silence of your beautiful soul and the lovely song of your existence.

Keep singing, dear one, keep singing.

I love every loud and silent note that is you.

— Chrystal R.

The fire and alchemy of God's unending love transform us

Letter 16
metamorphosis
chrysalis of change

I have good news for you.

You are at a tipping point in your spiritual evolution. All the effort of your many lives is coming to fruition. As you become aware that you are aware, your path will become more direct and purposeful. You will experientially know, perhaps, without knowing how you know, that love is the answer to all your questions—*love is the answer to everything, the answer to life.*

A loving choice naturally enhances our inner radiance, which in turn brings about transformative shifts within ourselves and our surroundings, often in unanticipated ways. As we enter this new chapter in our soul's eternal journey, doors that were once closed now open. During this transformative phase, changes in our consciousness alter our DNA, enriching the entire universe. Though these changes may unfold slowly or happen rapidly, they are always significant, reshaping our understanding of ourselves and our place in the world.

The impact of this transformation extends beyond the present moment and our current reality, influencing our past experiences and future possibilities. These changes, neither predestined nor random, are aligned with a higher purpose for our soul. In a universe governed by unconditional love, divine guidance positions us precisely where our soul will benefit the most. Nonetheless, the boundless potential of the heart guides our journey of personal development and collective evolution. Though there are many divergent paths into and out of the darkness, they all converge in the evanescent light of love.

As we move into a more enlightened state, once locked door open to a more radiant future, transcending notions of limitation or lack. During this transformative journey of and the metamorphosis of the soul, many of our life's circumstances and conditions will be altered. Former pleasures will lose their appeal, leaving an empty hollowness in their wake. The pursuit of recognition, desire for material wealth and accumulation, and all the other superficialities of life will organically diminish in the light of our newfound radiance.

This shift in consciousness will be experienced as a deep longing for the sacred, eternal, and profound. We will naturally be drawn away from the trivial, transient, and mundane. Our experience of others and the world will be infused with heightened respect, greater compassion, and unconditional love. At some point, along the evolutionary path of the soul, we will all undergo this profound transformation.

This metamorphic awakening is a natural and inevitable evolutionary stage.

We are all destined to find our way back to our true home—*back to God*. However, while we discard the layers of our past self and sprout wings that will carry us into a more radiant future, the outer world and others may remain the same. As a result, some of our relationships, and the world we experience will dramatically shift.

In the realignment of our energy, we will be drawn closer to or part ways with those in our sphere of influence. This is not a judgment of good or bad, it is simply part of the evolutionary process.

After the butterfly sprouts wings, it has little in common with the caterpillar.

They suddenly live in completely different worlds. The same is true for us; once we embark on our own transformative journey, we may feel strangely disconnected with those who haven't yet begun theirs. Ultimately, all souls will evolve to this more radiant state. No one will be left behind. The question is not *"if"* but *"when."* The *"when"* is the only part of the equation that is up to us. We get to decide the roads we travel, and the pace of our journey, but not the destination.

The destiny of a caterpillar is to one day become a butterfly. We, too, will sprout our spiritual wings when the time is right for our transformation.

Just as the caterpillar sprouts wings to take flight, we too must undergo profound physical, mental, emotional, and spiritual transformation to discover our own wings.

Human evolution undergoes a metamorphic process in three fundamental ways. *First*, it can be an intentional shift driven by our choice to do things differently. *Second*, it can be a natural part of the soul's growth, much like a seed taking root. *Third*, it can result from dramatic or traumatic events, such as sudden loss, disappointment, or betrayal. This transformational process can be quite a smooth landing for some further along the evolutionary track. However, for most of us, it is a bit more complicated and can even seem harsh. I say "*seem harsh*" because the loving universe could not harm anyone. Indeed, God would not hurt his own creation, his beloved children—*God would not hurt you*.

With love, everything is divinely purposed for the good of the soul and the benefit of all.

My personal metamorphosis and subsequent transformation fell into the last category of complicated and seemingly harsh circumstances. It started with a dysfunctional childhood and culminated in a near-fatal car accident and an out-of-body experience that forever impacted and transformed my life.

Time slowed down on that fateful but otherwise ordinary winter afternoon when I became aware that I was aware. It was as though I were a spectator of my own existence. I viewed the accident from a short distance above with curious dispassion. From this vantage point, I witnessed our small red jeep collide with an out-of-control sliding car on an icy mountain road. We spiraled across the single-lane highway, before being catapulted off the rocky mountain ledge. We plummeted eighty feet to the unmoving ground below, flipping end over end ten times, before finally coming to a sudden and jarring halt, slamming into a wall of ice.

As I watched the scene from above, I was simultaneously shown the entirety of my life in a three-dimensional, panoramic view that was complete with the ripple effect of my every thought and action. From every possible perspective, I saw the impact of my life, backward, forward, up, down, and sideways, on the horizontal and vertical planes of existence.

I intimately understood how all my intentions, thoughts, and actions, both kind and unkind, endlessly ripple out into the universe, affecting everything and everyone. In a way that is difficult to describe with words, the profound impact and importance of my choices was made clear.

Everything that comes into existence is meant to exist, and is a necessary part of the whole.

We, along with every grain of sand, tree in the forest, and wave in the ocean, are an integral part of the grand matrix of existence, and a beautiful expression of the divine.

We are God's own breath, breathing life into life—for the purpose of love and more love.

In service to the soul's evolutionary process, planet Earth is one of the many energetic experiences available in the universe. The fact that we, as a collective, find ourselves on this planet instead of another suggests that this is the most suitable and valuable experience presently accessible for our souls. In addition, we do not exist in isolation and no man is an island unto himself. We are all connected in love. Therefore, my evolutionary success or failure is also yours and vice versa. Nothing happens in a void; we are all connected by an invisible field of all-encompassing love.

Your tears dampen the space around you. Your joy enlivens us all. When you fall, your angels and guides cradle your tender soul, encouraging you to try again. And when you succeed, the whole of creation applauds and celebrates with you. Without exception, everything in our lives is orchestrated for the good of the individual and the benefit of all.

Our individual style, temperament, talents, and weaknesses are integral to the grand unfolding of life and our personal development. All things and all beings are forever in flux, transforming into the next most radiant and beautiful expression of self. However, there is no guarantee we will always choose the most direct and loving path back to God.

We may take the long way home, get stuck in the darkness, or advance quickly and move directly towards the divine. Every path we choose, even if it seems wrong, ultimately leads us home.

Self-realization is not necessarily a straight and narrow path; for many of us, it is a rocky road and, most definitely, the long way home.

In some lives, our journey back to the light has lots of detours, missteps, and mistakes. Making mistakes is part of being human and adds to the richness of our existence. When we enter a human life, we are given the freedom to explore and discover our path without explicit directions. This is not abandonment by a cruel or unkind God. To the contrary, the freedom to choose is a grand opportunity of experiential learning and adventure. It brings great joy to the soul to unravel life's mysteries at its own pace and in its own time.

We may fumble and fall, but we always fall into the loving arms of God.

Nonetheless, if we choose to dive into the darkness, we may lose our way or get lost in the black of night. It is best to avoid these shadowy paths as they are laden with pain, sorrow, an much needless suffering. While no soul will be forever lost, forsaken or abandoned, it is prudent and wise to spare oneself from unnecessary anguish. You can't play in the mud and not get dirty. Please be vigilant and take good care of your precious soul. The allure of these darker avenues of growth can be extremely seductive and tempting, but they never end well. If we consciously choose to embrace darkness instead of adhering to our natural tendency toward love and light, it can lead to prolonged suffering spanning eons and many lives.

Although we are never condemned to eternal damnation, these unfortunate setbacks dramatically affect our soul's evolution, and may require us to revisit the same life lessons and challenges over and over.

Even in the most dire circumstances, we always have two choices: love or fear.

Whatever we choose has implications far beyond the present moment, rippling out into infinity, changing the trajectory of our soul, the timelines on the planet, and ultimately the human experience. This power to impact universes is a great responsibility and should not be taken lightly.

With great power comes a profound responsibility to care for both our own soul and the souls of others.

While we may already recognize that the right path is the more loving one, it's vital to acknowledge that the most loving choice can also be the most challenging. Succumbing to cruelty and unkindness is easy, and the natural impulse is to retaliate. To chose love over fear, kindness over cruelty, and forgiveness over retaliation, requires an extraordinary depth of personal resolve, inner strength, and fortitude of character.

Though the most loving choice may also be the most difficult, it ultimately spares us from future suffering. Nonetheless, we won't always make the right choice, even when we know the right thing to do. Often, our instinctual drive and survival mechanisms will overpower us.

However, we are not doomed by our fallibility; in fact, it is part of our power. The moment we recognize that our choices haven't aligned with kindness, compassion, or love, we can choose again and make a different, more loving choice.

Choosing love not only empowers us, but also inspires others who face similar challenges.

Having said that, please remember, that your choices are exclusively yours—*and there are no wrong choices*. There are simply choices that are more radiant and those that are not. The gift of being human is that we get to choose our path. Nothing, not even God's love, is imposed upon us. At any moment, we have the power to make a different choice—*a more loving choice*. Even if we've inadvertently strayed into the shadows or succumbed to life's temptations, the option to choose differently is always available.

Ultimately, we bear sole responsibility for our lives, and no one but ourselves can determine the direction of our footsteps, whether toward or away from love. Nevertheless, escaping the quagmire of our own shadow may not be easy. In fact, it would be nearly impossible without the loving support, assistance, and guidance of our angels, teachers, and guides.

While transformation begins within our own consciousness, the moment we opt for a more loving path, the forces of goodness, grace, and divinity swiftly rally to our side, helping us to help ourselves.

Planet Earth is both a wise teacher and a playground for the soul.

There are many fascinating rides and hard lessons to be learned. However, when the bell rings, recess is over, and it is time to come home. Sooner or later, in this life or another, we will all find our way back to the omnipresent love that created and sustains us. Everything we experience in the temporal world of form and matter is a necessary movement toward our next most radiant version of self. Just as the caterpillar, in preparation for the metamorphic process, instinctively weaves a protective cocoon at the end of its life cycle, we, too, must rearrange our lives to prepare for our inevitable evolution and soul expansion.

For some, this process of growth and change is natural, simple, and peaceful. However, for most of us, the propelling force of change will likely be more dramatic or traumatic: a sudden illness, accident, unexpected tragedy, betrayal, loss, or some other radical shift in our circumstances.

An existential crisis can abruptly usher us into a chrysalis of change, compelling us to adapt to life's ever-evolving landscape and seek deeper truths.

Many of us will go on a spiritual journey or vision quest in response to a sudden upheaval or unexpected change in life circumstances. We may be drawn to remote parts of the world, such as India, Peru, Tibet, etc., to unearth our own transformational process. Like the caterpillar that creates a chrysalis in preparation for its transformation, we, too, instinctively move away from the mundane world to commune with a spiritual teacher or others on a similar path.

For some, a journey into foreign lands may be the preferred cocoon and necessary preparation for their spiritual sojourn. Others will find safety and comfort in the arms of the church, a guru, prayers, sacred texts, or meditation.

As we step into the uncharted territory of our spiritual metamorphosis and personal transformation, mundane, shallow, and default answers will no longer suffice.

Like the caterpillar that consumes its own body to fuel its metamorphosis into a winged butterfly, we, too, emerge from the chrysalis of human life with spiritual wings that carry us to new and unimagined lands of the soul. Though our spiritual transformation can be exhilarating, we may simultaneously experience a deep sense of loss, abandonment, joy, or elation.

In the wake of our personal metamorphosis, we will no longer resonate with certain people and be drawn toward others. Indeed, many personal relationships will suddenly change as we heighten or lower our energy. We will be more united or disjointed with our environment and others. In the latter case, our relationships may fall apart due to the sudden energetic imbalance.

Either way, when our energies are no longer aligned, there's no longer a meeting place for the soul. Just as the caterpillar and butterfly suddenly exist in two different worlds and have little in common, the same is true for us as we find our own spiritual wings. While the caterpillar remains earthbound, the butterfly takes flight into a more expansive world far beyond the caterpillar's wildest dreams.

We either grow together or grow apart.

Everything changes at this juncture in our spiritual journey, including our vision of ourselves and others. The shift in our relationships toward or away from others is not a punishment; it is a natural consequence of an energetic imbalance. As we evolve, we no longer have the same goals or energetic resonance with those who have yet to sprout their spiritual wings.

Although we may resist this change and try to hold on to comfortable but outdated energetic patterns or relationships, eventually, it becomes impossible. The lack of resonance we may experience with some people and places is actually good news because staying in outgrown relationships or environments hinders our spiritual growth.

When a relationship or the presence of others no longer positively contributes to our spiritual advancement, whether due to lowered or heightened energy, it will inevitably come to an end.

And again, this is good news as the universe will not allow for a void. Therefore, due to our enlivened frequency, we will naturally attract others more aligned with our heightened energy.

The caterpillar cannot fly in its old, wingless body; it must shed its skin. We, too, must leave behind the empty shell of our former self with all its attachments to take flight. Once we've shut the door on the people, places, and things that no longer serve our evolution, the most challenging stage of our metamorphosis begins.

This stage can best be understood by observing the caterpillar's arduous transformational journey. There is a short time during the caterpillar's metamorphosis when it is neither a caterpillar nor a butterfly: *it is a Caterfly*. Similarly, as we shed our skin and sprout new spiritual wings during our transformational process, we no longer fit into the former version of ourselves; we can neither crawl nor fly. This cumbersome state is the most vulnerable and confusing time of our metamorphosis. Like the caterpillar, with our expanded consciousness and increased light, we no longer fit into the former version of ourselves but have yet to embody our future expression of self. We may find ourselves, neither here nor there, in a strange limbo where we are no longer earthbound but still unable to fly.

As our new life unfolds and our old life dissolves, we must confront the reality that very little is under our control. For many of us, this is when we have the profound revelation that, if not for something greater than ourselves, we would not make it in this wild and wonderful world.

Being at the complete mercy of nature, grace, and God is both humbling and freeing.

This humbling realization can and often does change our perspective of ourselves, others, and the unseen forces of God. It is also a time of great release as we have no choice but to surrender to the circumstances or conditions of our lives that are beyond our ability to change or control. While our consciousness expands, we may find ourselves outgrowing our old life, while the new one has yet to take form. During this most vulnerable time of transformation and change, we must be patient and have faith in something greater than ourselves.

As we await the emergence of our new wings and the potential for flight, we are forced to confront the demons of our past and grapple with our fears of the future. This is indeed a precarious time of great change and vulnerability. If not for the loving support and protective wings of our angels, guides, and guardians, none of us would make it through the dark night of the soul. And yet, we do; we not only survive, we somehow thrive.

Just as the butterfly miraculously sprouts wings and the possibility of flight suddenly becomes available, we morph into the next best version of ourselves and soar into the sky of limitless possibilities. How? Love is how.

Love makes all things possible, even the seemingly impossible.

Nonetheless, change is never easy; the past is sticky, and habits can be hard to break. The caterpillar's story reminds us to trust the loving universe's goodness, grace, and wisdom. It inspires us to have faith in the ongoing process of evolution and to trust that our wings will sprout when it is time for us to take flight.

When we transcend our fears and doubts, learning to trust in the enduring power of love and the grace of God, we come to understand the undeniable truth that *love conquers all.*

In the fire and alchemy of God's unending love, we are forever transformed.

Just as the caterpillar is drawn towards its own demise to take flight into new worlds of unimagined adventures, we follow a similar path and transformative journey, leaving behind our old life and taking flight into the vast sky of possibilities. As we find our spiritual wings, the mundane pleasures of everyday existence that once seemed so attractive suddenly lose their luster. Then, we are naturally drawn to the sacred and divine. This shift can happen in a flash of miraculous, existential divinity, but more often, it is a slow and progressive process of ongoing change; be patient with yourself, with the metamorphic process, and the unfoldment of your new life. Remember, everything happens when it is supposed to, and there is no hurry to evolve. In the universe, where love is a constant, no one, including you, will be left behind.

For you, dear one, the morning sun has already risen. You already have your magical wings and are further along the evolutionary path than you may know or acknowledge. You are on the right path for your soul, the path of love, kindness, goodness, grace, and God.

Now that you know that you know, find your angel wings and take flight; together, we will kiss the sky of eternity.

I love you so very much,
my beautiful Caterfly expression of God.
— Chrystal Rae

We are God's own breath, breathing life into life—

for the purpose of love and more love

Love is a sanctuary of the heart, a place of refuge and comfort in times of need

Letter 17

promise
you will be okay, I promise

You are going to be okay, I promise.

Oh yes, the storms will come. Thunder and lightning will shake you to your core. Hurricanes and rain will drown your yesterdays and flood your tomorrows, but storms don't last forever. Even the darkest tempest eventually fades into the light of a new day. Then the sun will shine again, lighter and brighter. Flowers bloom in the wake of yesterday's rain, clearing the way for the hope and happiness of a future yet to be born.

Given enough time and space, everything works itself out; it always does and always will—even if it doesn't.

Once the storm passes, we gain profound insight, learn valuable lessons, and discover the treasured gifts within our pain, suffering, and despair. As we recover and the skies clear, we emerge stronger and wiser. Although the storm is never pleasant, suffering is an inevitable part of life or risk becoming a slave to comfort or a victim of circumstance. Confronting our fears and addressing our shadows is essential; avoiding our emotions is unsustainable. Remember, nothing, including life's highs and lows, lasts forever.

Even the most devastating and dark storms eventually come to an end.

However, the universe operates on its own timeline, guided by a divine presence that underlies all of existence. We must practice patience, weather the storm, and find contentment with our present circumstances. Again, nothing, whether beautiful or tragic, lasts forever. Eventually, the sun breaks through the clouds of pain and sorrow, filling our hearts with renewal. In the warmth of a new day, we gain clarity and see the perfection in imperfection, recognizing it as a valuable part of our journey home within the embrace of infinite love.

One day, very soon, on the far side of thundering clouds of pain and sorrow, the sun will find its way through the cracked windows of the sadness, slide underneath the heavy door of disappointment, and spill into the darkest chambers of the heart with the burgeoning hope of a new day. But for now, dear one, while the rain is pounding and the floodgates are open, you must stay strong and have faith, even when everything is falling apart and broken, including you.

In life, our greatest challenge is to let go of fear, embrace possibilities, move forward, and trust the benevolent universe to guide us home.

As previously mentioned, given enough time, everything eventually finds its resolution, even when it appears otherwise. As the child of a loving universe, the progeny of God, you are never alone. There are armies of angels by your side, rallying for your success and well being.

You are loved far more than you can possibly imagine, and all is well with your soul.

Let the love that has found you on these pages be a sanctuary for your wounded heart. May it comfort you and be a reason to believe in goodness and grace. Let this love, my great love for you, and God's love, cradle you with tenderness, carry you through dark nights, and be the compass of your soul. Let this love be your pillar of strength and an unshakable foundation upon which you place your faith.

Life, like the shifting seasons, is filled with uncertainties, and nothing is set in stone. One moment, everything is fine, and in the next, it seems to be falling apart. Without warning, the skies turn dark, tornadoes brew on the horizon, and torrential rains approach. No one is ever truly prepared for this, but it happens nonetheless. These challenges, as daunting as they may be, are integral to the divine plan and purpose of your life. Remember, storms don't last forever, and the sun will inevitably rise again. You will be okay, I promise.

I speak from a deep well of experience; I, too, have trudged through the mud of life's storms and been engulfed in the profound darkness of night. I have braved the howling winds and relentless downpours, often engulfed in feelings of solitude and unrelenting fear. Yet, each time, I have emerged not just intact but stronger, with each new dawn bringing fresh light and the promise of new beginnings.

These trials have bestowed upon me a vital insight:

Even the most oppressive night eventually yields the luminous light of a new day.

As daunting as they may be, our struggles are not just hurdles to overcome; they are invaluable avenues for personal development and the unveiling of inner strengths previously unknown to us. They act as crucibles, testing and fortifying our faith, while sculpting our spirit with resilience and determination. Each new challenge presents a chance for growth, an opportunity to bolster our resolve, and a moment to deepen our faith, all the while continuously refining the essence of our love.

So, my dearest, hold onto this love. Let it be your guiding star in the darkest hours. This love knows no bounds; it heals and endures. Through it, you'll find the courage to face each new day, the strength to stand tall in adversity, and the wisdom to appreciate the beauty in life's every twist and turn.

Remember, you are never truly alone. In your darkest moments, you are encircled by angels of light, brimming with love and care for you. Open your heart to this love; let it be your constant companion, you light in darkness, shelter in the storm, and a refuge of safety.

Together, we will walk through the darkness and into a new light, hand in hand. Every tear, heartache, and wound will become part of the unfolding glory and wisdom of the soul. No matter the difficulties or tragedies we face, remember: the universe is kind, God is benevolent, and love never fails."

One day, the fragmented pieces of your life and wounded soul will merge together, forming a radiant collage of infinite beauty and radiant light.

Remain open and receptive to the everyday miracles that life presents. Consider a small yellow flower piercing through the tiniest cracks of a sidewalk, the elegant landing of an ally cat, a newborn's inaugural breath, and the magical flight of a bumblebee. Such phenomena, along with the marvel of our own existence, make up a multitude of miracles that often go unnoticed.

Whether recognized as miraculous or dismissed as ordinary, our lives are imbued with magic.

Everything, without exception, unfolds for our well-being and evolution. Like the weather, the progressive unfoldment of our lives is largely outside our conscious control. In striving to govern every aspect of our existence, we will suffer. How can we command the wind, steer the clouds, or dictate the blossoming of flowers? The truth is, we can't—*and we aren't meant to.*

Instead, by embracing the natural flow of life allows us to find peace in the understanding that we are a part of a larger, harmonious system, one that nurtures and guides us though even our most peaceful turbulent moments. Many of life's obstacles do not have a simple solution; paradoxically, that is the solution. We can't overcome every challenge that life presents. The anguish, tragedy, and grief we will endure are genuine and profoundly painful. These difficulties are intricately woven into the blueprint and intent of our soul's journey of expansion. Even if we keep our hearts open, not everything will peacefully resolve or work itself out. Sometimes, our wounds are so deep and the pain so intense that we carry them across multiple lifetimes.

While it can be challenging to reconcile with the distressing and dreadful events that dot our daily lives, they are an inseparable fragment of life's higher purpose. All of life's experiences are intrinsic to the unfoldment of our journey into and out of the physical realm, adding to the wisdom and radiance of the soul.

Life is a dance of shadow and light, a rhythmic interplay between trials and triumphs, and a delicate balance of joy and sorrow.

Often, it is precisely those experiences that humble and cause us pain that drive us forward. Having said that, while pain is inevitable, suffering can and should be avoided when possible. When we let go of the desire for things to be different, we stop struggling unnecessarily and accept the inevitability of change.

Life is a elegant dance of shadow and light, a rhythmic interplay between trials and triumphs, and a delicate balance of joy and sorrow.

In recognizing the immutable aspects of our existence, we conserve energy and sidestep the futile fight against the inevitable. This shift allows us to focus on what we want rather than what we don't, effectively altering the course of our lives.

Our focus and where we expend our energy play a pivotal role in the unfolding experience of life. Instead of wishful thinking, we can purposefully direct our energy towards solutions rather than dwelling on problems. Where attention goes, energy flows. Stay positive, channel your energy toward your aspirations rather than your fears, and have faith that everything will work out.

Nonetheless, change can be daunting, for it simultaneously liberates us from the past and veils the future in uncertainty. Yet, even when confronted with seemingly insurmountable problems or irreplaceable losses, we can discover strength and growth through acceptance and the unwavering resolve of the human spirit.

All we can ever do is our best, entrusting divine providence with the rest.

However, many well-meaning people overlook the part of the equation that demands that we "*do our best.*" They may say a few prayers and hope for a miracle, but the universe does not work like that. God will not do the work for us. We must be a part of the solution and play an active role in our own lives.

The action part is the most complicated and uncomfortable part of the process. Do it anyway, because through these actions, we grow and evolve.

The following story, "*God Will Save Me,*" highlights this idea. A terrible storm came to a town, and local officials sent out an emergency warning that the riverbanks would soon overflow and flood the nearby homes. They ordered everyone in the town to evacuate immediately.

A man of much faith heard the warning and decided to stay, saying to himself, "*I will trust God, and if I am in danger, then God will send a divine miracle to save me.*" The neighbors came by his house and said, "*We're leaving, and there is room for you in our car; please come with us!*" But the man declined. "*I have faith that God will save me.*"

As the man stood on his porch watching the water rise up the steps, a friend in a canoe paddled by and called to him, "*Hurry and come into my canoe; the waters are rising quickly!*" But the man again said, "*No thanks, God will save me.*" The floodwaters rose higher, pouring water into his living room, and the man had to retreat to the second floor.

A police motorboat came by and saw him at the window. "*We will come up and rescue you,*" they shouted. Again, the man refused, waving them off, saying, "*Use your time to save someone else! I have faith that God will save me!*" The flood waters rose higher and higher, and the man had to climb to the rooftop. A helicopter spotted him and dropped him down a rope ladder. A rescue officer descended the ladder and pleaded with the man, "*Grab my hand, and I will pull you up!*" But the man STILL refused, folding his arms tightly to his body, "*No, thank you! God will save me!*"

Shortly afterward, the house broke up, the floodwaters swept the man away, and he drowned. In Heaven, the man stood before God and asked, "*I put all my faith in You. Why didn't you save me?*" And God said, "*Son, I sent you a warning. I sent you a car. I sent you a canoe. I sent you a motorboat. I sent you a helicopter. What more were you looking for?*"

This story illustrates the grace of God. Though supplication, meditation, and prayer are the foundation of a strong spiritual life, connecting us with a greater power, we still have to do our part by making conscious choices.

Our active participation is the unspoken responsibility of being free, self-aware beings.

All known and unknown universes exist so we can do our soul work.

To this point even my presence in your life, and this book in your hand, is meant to contribute to your well-being and evolution. I am proof that divinity is always at work in your life. I came back to a physical embodiment and a human life, especially for you. I came back for your beautiful soul. I came back because I love you, and you need to know that a love like this exist.

With this in mind, before we proceed, I want to address your beautiful soul directly. No matter what challenges you currently face, no matter how difficult or seemingly insurmountable they may be, you are going to be okay, I promise.

There is no need to suffer unnecessarily, God's love never wavers.

__The solution to life's most intricate problems is straightforward, though not always easy: heed the guidance, trust in love, do your best, and surrender the rest__

We are not lonely voyagers in a cold and uncaring universe; quite the opposite. We are unconditionally loved and supported by our soul family of angels, guides, and teachers. We began this conversation by affirming that no matter what unfolds, whether it appears good or bad, there is a divinity to your life, and you will be okay. I hope that by now, you have gained a broader perspective and have come to understand the grand design of the universe and your vital, intricate role within it.

__You are the progeny of God, born of a loving universe, and your soul is never in peril.__

You are forever safe and unconditionally loved, and you are not alone. You are surrounded by beings of light and an abundance of love—*more than you could possibly imagine*. And yes, I am one of your closest soulmates. I have been your companion across countless lifetimes. Whatever challenges life presents, my love and support is a constant. You don't have to go through the darkness alone, I am always by your side—*in heart and soul.*

In truth, none of us are meant to walk this path alone, and none would make it without the love and care of those who watch over us. The temporal world, with its interplay of shadow and light, its moments of elation and periods of desolation, offers us a profound opportunity to explore the unchanging truth of love that transcends these fleeting dualities.

The human experience is extraordinary and wonderful, yet it comes with its share of challenges and burdens. We come to this realm knowing that there will be tall mountains and deep valleys to cross. We come knowing that nothing is set, and life is forever in flux. Knowing there will be joy, elation, sorrow and tears. We come for the bliss of our own existence and to connect with others.

Together, we find solace, strength, and companionship in this remarkable journey of the soul. Indeed, I came back to this world for you. My presence on the planet and in your life is necessary for your well-being and your presence is necessary for mine. Our bond of love is unconditional and eternal. I will be by your side until the end of time and beyond because I love you.

Let my love, the love that has found you again within the pages of this book, lift you up and strengthen you. Throughout our shared journey across the grand expanse of time and space in our many lives, we have ventured along many winding roads and strolled through fragrant gardens, each experience bestowing its unique wisdom upon our souls.

A human life is a profound exploration of contrasts, a challenging journey of opposites, and a fast track of rapid evolution.

When life's storms rage and the winds of change are relentless and unruly only love can sustain us. The transformative power of love transcends all pain and suffering.

Even in our darkest hours, love is an ever-present light, guiding us through the intricate labyrinth of life's most daunting trials.

Please allow me to once again address your precious soul directly. Hold on, dear one, for the storm will soon pass and the skies will clear, revealing a brighter and lighter tomorrow, I promise. In the light of a new day, the sun will rise again, more radiant than ever before. It will find its way underneath the locked door of your heart and spill in through the open window of your soul, filling every dark corner with its warm embrace.

We need not shoulder the weight of deciphering all of life's mysteries on our own, and in reality, such an undertaking is beyond the capacities of any single individual. Just as the sun needs the sky to shine, we need each other to find our way. Together we are stronger. When we let go of the need for things to be other than they are, we stop suffering. By trusting in the benevolent universe, solutions to our most perplexing problems often unfold in unforeseen and exquisite ways. Even these words are a precious offering, thoughtfully crafted to offer solace and reassurance that you are never alone on this profound journey.

Though we cannot dictate life's capricious nature, we have control over our inner landscape. Regardless of life's challenges, we can keep our hearts open. Whether life is a gentle rain or a storm, love is an ever-present light, leading us back to our origins, back to God

We are God's own breath, breathing itself into existence.

Everything and everyone is an expression of the divine. The very light of our soul is the purest form of this manifestation. If we could fully grasp the unparalleled beauty of our very own being, and the intricate role we play within the context of all existence, boundless gratitude and grace would wash away all our pain, and we would never cry another tear.

Indeed, in the profound understanding of our own divinity, doubt vanishes, and we perceive an unfathomable source of grace and goodness present in all of existence. We are so loved and cherished that every breath we take is precious and counted. We are neither alone nor forsaken; rather, we are enveloped in a love that transcends all known concepts, measures, and limits..

God's unending love, is a river of light that permeates and flows through all of creation.

In every life, we are magnetically pulled back to our source—back to God. We are never alone. God burst forth in every expression of shadow and light, and we are eternally held in a tender embrace. Everything in the loving universe works together for the good of the individual and the benefit of all—*including you*. Indeed, every flower that blossoms, wilts, and then returns to the earth does so in sacred homage to your precious soul. Even the dark clouds and stormy days serve a higher purpose and are meant to enrich your life. And again, you are not alone, your soul family, teachers, guides, and angels are forever by your side, helping you to help yourself. They watch over you from a distance, come to you in your sleep, and awaken you with the first ray of light. They whisper to you in the hazy afternoon breeze that softly combs through your hair, and they sing to you in the quiet voices of distant music.

These celestial guardians blanket you with clouds of comfort, join you in your dreams, and speak to you in the silence of your heart.

They restore you with the sweet fragrance of blossoming flowers, and they sing to you in the quiet echo of the songbird's song. They rise and fall with you, like the sun and the moon welcoming a new day, and then, just as graciously, they surrender all back t the black of night. You are so very loved that every grain of sand, small seashell and tiny pebble on the beach patiently await your arrival, longing to touch the soles of your feet but once in the oblivion of time. Everything in the universe, without exception, is orchestrated for your well-being and the benefit of all. Indeed, in regard to our soul, everything works together for the good.

In the loving universe, nothing is left to chance or random circumstance.

Every detail of our lives is prepared with careful deliberation, conscious attention, and much love by an omnipresent creator and loving universe. We are surrounded by beings of light who lovingly watch over us with infinite care and compassion. Though, we may not see them except on rare occasions, in a misty shadow or a sudden flash of light from the corner of our eye, they are always with us. They forever hold us close, embracing us with absolute kindness, care, and love. These divine beings orchestrate inspiring moments of pristine beauty and awe. They fill our lives with many everyday miracles that go primarily unacknowledged. However, if we seek them, we shall find them in the less-than-obvious moments.

The love reaching out to you in this very moment is beyond description, measure, or words.

It is the endless longing of life to live, and of love to love. It is God manifest in every possible way. It is the lover forever searching for the beloved, searching for you. No words can speak of such a love, God's love; anything said would be false, null, and void. So rather than describing this love, I will point to it from a distance.

This love, God's love, is the loving universe forever cradling us in the darkest of nights and awakening us with the first ray of morning light. In the light of this all-encompassing love, there has never been a moment when we are unattended or forgotten.

Our angels, teachers, and guides come in various disguises and speak to us with many different voices. They whisper to us in a cat's meow, cradle us with the sounds of night, sing to us in the silence of stars, and awaken us with the morning light. Those watching over us and entrusted with our care are alive in the minutest details and the largest expressions of life. They are closer than our breath and never leave our side. Just as the rising sun and the setting moon forever bow to each other in gratitude and grace, those who lovingly watch over us bow to our will and freedom to choose—*good or bad.*

These warriors of the light are ever vigilant and protective of our precious souls. We may not see them or recognize their light, but they are always close at hand.

The loving universe is alive in life's most ordinary, extraordinary, and simplest expressions.

The love that created us also speaks to us in a multitude of loud and soft voices. It loudly calls to us as the screeching wheels of a skidding car and softly whispers to us in the silent verse of a distant star. Every shadow is proof of the omnipresent light of God. In the serene expanse and radiance of light, we are all united in love.

This aliveness is perfectly captured in the silent poetry of a solitary leaf caught in the warm embrace of the afternoon breeze, and suspended in a magical moment of absolute stillness. In this quiet repose, where time is absent, and just before the halted push-and-shove of empty space, divinity is unveiled and revealed.

The subsequent downward spiral of gravity and trailing dance of forgotten leaves now amass into dark corners, along the lonely edges of vacant streets. Huddled together in crackling piles of yesterday's bloom, the rustling leaves gloriously reminisce of by-gone-days as the winds of change carry them to their new home.

The voices of our angels, guides, and teachers are both loud and soft, yet they always sing the same song: love and more love.

They hum to us in the quiet drum of a late-night rain, tapping softly on the bedroom window and lulling us to sleep. They are the dim light of a flickering candle in the windowless room just beyond the locked door of the heart. They are God's loving arms, reaching back from the boundaries of the physical world on a mission of love to find, support, and comfort us. In our darkest moments, these angelic beings wrap us in a warm blanket of unconditional love, compassion, and care.

Every experience of joy and sorrow is part of our boundless bliss and radiant unfoldment.

Our deepest fears and uncried tears are consumed in the fire of love. Even a renegade ray of light, slicing through the dark, cloudy curtains of night, announcing the quiet promise of a new day, is a silent message of love. It is a sign of something greater, a secret code of endless hope, and the warm embrace of the divine.

Miracles abound in both ordinary and extraordinary moments of our lives, but go mostly unacknowledged or unappreciated. While the miraculous is woven into the very fabric of our existence, it does not render us immune to adversity. The human journey is inherently filled with challenges: pain is palpable, betrayal jolts us, lies wound deeply, sadness can be engulfing, disappointment is a heavy burden, and despair can cast us into profound darkness.

In moments of confusion or suffering, we may feel abandoned, as though all hope has vanished. However, it is precisely these challenges that are most crucial. They urge us to confront our deepest fears, serving as pivotal milestones on our soul's path.

In a world defined by constant contrast and change, such trials are not just unavoidable but essential for our spiritual maturation.

Paradoxically, we often find ourselves resisting these very experiences, despite their indispensable role in our personal and spiritual evolution. In the same way shadows stretch and deepen as evening approaches, our efforts to escape from our inner demons through avoidance, denial, or distraction only serve to intensify our fears. This evasive pattern can trap us in a continuous cycle of anguish, potentially extending throughout many lives.

The true path to liberation from this dark spiral requires us to confront and transcend our fears. It's a journey deeply rooted in personal courage and self-awareness. By bravely facing the darkness within, we engage in a transformative process. This confrontation is not merely a necessary challenge; it's a pivotal moment of growth, leading us towards a more liberated and enlightened state of being.

Our life is the sum of our choices across time.

Courage and bravery are vital to overcome feelings of smallness and scarcity. It's a personal choice to focus on positivity and be a source of light. We're supported in this journey by the universe, which guides us with signs, dreams, and subtle hints, helping us navigate our spiritual path.

In just this manner, through visions, prophetic dreams, and spiritual insights, I have unveiled solutions to many of life's most enigmatic questions. In one immensely profound and transformative dream, I was plunged into absolute darkness and faced the embodiment of malevolence—*a manifestation of my most feared anxieties*.

Grotesque monsters with bloody hands and sharp claws came snarling toward me. Every instinct urged me to flee, hide, and escape their terrifying presence. I was consumed by a desperate desire to save myself. Yet, in that moment, I grasped a profound truth: if I succumbed to fear and ran or hid, I would be trapped in a perpetual cycle of evasion.

As the shadows deepened and the night grew darker, a stark realization washed over me: unless I confronted my fear directly, I would forever be trapped in this abyss. In that pivotal moment of absolute clarity, I made a courageous decision. I stopped, turned, and confronted the looming specters and nightmarish amalgamation of my deepest fears.

With unrelenting force, these ominous creatures attacked me, unleashing an overwhelming surge of torment, terror, and unbearable pain. Trembling an besieged by fear, I somehow summoned the strength to stand my ground and utter what I believed to be my final words: "*You can kill me, but I am not running.*" In a raging thunderous storm, all the malevolent forces of the night, along with grotesque, bloody monsters, surged forth in a furious onslaught of all-consuming rage.

In the tight grip of fear, I kept my gaze fixed upon the hollow center of the dark energy that had engulfed me—*an abyss of sorrow, despair, and the gnashing of teeth*. I remained motionless, resolute, and prepared to die. Amidst the chaos of both my inner and outer worlds unraveling, a profound understanding emerged: the dark energy that enveloped me symbolized pure evil, a complete void light—*utter darkness*. Yet, what was even more astonishing was the realization that these perceived forces of darkness were but illusions.

In a loving universe, everything and everyone exists on a continuum of light, from less to more radiance.

What we perceive as evil is merely the most base and vile manifestation of divine light, but it is still, fundamentally, light. Even the darkest night is a subtle hue of radiant light.

To my surprise, with this profound revelation, the darkness burst into a grand explosion of iridescent light. It was so incredibly bright I was blinded and had to shield my eyes. I found myself cradled in a shimmering pink mist that bathed the space around me with the sweet fragrance of roses. It was an ecstasy beyond compare: pure love, gentleness, grace, kindness, and absolute compassion.

I am not sure how long I remained in this ecstatic state, but it seemed eternal and unending. When I realized that my eyes were open, that this was really happening, and that it was not a dream, I was overtaken by a sudden, profound fear, and gasped out loud. In that instant, the mist, fragrance, and ecstatic bliss disappeared into a tiny pinpoint of light at the far corner of the bedroom ceiling.

I immediately understood that love and fear cannot exist in the same space. I had many other beautiful insights and takeaways from this prophetic dream. Most importantly, I understood that what we call evil, and all its fearful derivatives, is nothing more than a dark illusion. It is a nightmare that we hold as true until we stop running from it and turn to face it. Only then do we recognize it for what it is: *a dark lie*.

The truth of existence is an eternal, unending, and all-encompassing love that permeates the entire universe, bursting forth like the sun melting away dark clouds of ignorance, doubt, and fear.

This prophetic dream forever changed the course of my life, altering how I perceived myself, others, and the loving universe. Through this experience, I realized what, previously, I had only understood intellectually. Everything that exists is a manifestation of God in its most radiant unfoldment. Even those things that appear to oppose God are but shadows of the truth, and a necessary part of our evolution.

With this understanding, my secret fear and hidden darkness vanished into the radiance of boundless love. On a deeply personal, profound, and visceral level of the soul, I understood that love is the answer to everything. Even the dark and vile things, beyond my comprehension or ability to reconcile, immediately vanished into the truth and light of God's unending love.

Much more is happening in the small space of our existence than the apparent and mundane. We are forever surrounded by and bathed in absolute love and compassion. Though, the night is dark, the terrors terrifying, and the monsters frightening, they are not ultimate truth of our existence, unless we choose to believe that they are. Our thoughts and beliefs create and shape our worldview. To be truly free and alive, we must be willing to walk away from everyone and everything, including our own beliefs, and even life itself.

Freedom requires both autonomy and non-attachment.

We must have the capability to relinquish everything or be a slave to our desires, beliefs, and fears. Though the earth may quake, oceans may roar, and darkness may consume us, to be a free and liberated being, we must stay strong in our resolve to choose love above all else.

Freedom calls for courage, determination, and an unwavering resolve to let go of everything in the name of love.

Most of the time, this liberation requires making challenging decisions, confronting our deepest fears, and summoning the courage and inner strength to remain faithful to ourselves, even in the face of potential loss.

While in the short term, losing everything for the sake of freedom may be hard to imagine and even more difficult to embrace, in the long run, honoring the profound longing of the soul will prove the wisdom of our decisions. Indeed, freedom calls for a willingness to lose everything, including our very own lives. Though our physical body may be wounded, injured, and even die, our eternal soul remains pure and untouched. We are radiant beings of light, the manifestation of love as more love—*God manifest as more God.*

As children of the Divine, born of a benevolent universe, our potential is limitless.

We are so very loved that even the vast expanse of time and the boundlessness of space cannot contain such immensity. This love is the very essence of our soul.

There is, indeed, a divinity to our lives and a sacred purpose to our existence—and all is well.

Though a human life can be difficult, everything inevitably works out. It may be hard to conceive that all our problems, stress, and chaos will one day subside, but they will.

No matter what happens, you are going to be okay, I promise. After the storm, crisis, heartbreak, betrayal, or any other unexpected tragedy or loss, we may find ourselves covered in soot and drowning in the ashes of our broken dreams, but the sun will rise again. In the aftermath, when we find our footing, we will emerge from the chrysalis of our pain, wiser, stronger, more vibrant, and truly alive.

Indeed, in the wake of personal challenges and collective pain and sorrow, we will be free of the fear that once kept us chained to a lesser version of ourselves. In the light of a new day, we will find our way back to the beginning that has no end, back to the love at the unmoving center of it all, back to the loving arms of God. Like the phoenix, we will rise from the ashes of yesterday with our spirits refreshed, our eyes set on a hopeful future, and our hearts open to love. Understanding our place in the loving universe, life unfolds as a precious journey—*every moment a new adventure, each breath a rebirth, every dawn a step towards a destiny illuminated by unending love and possibility.*

As luminous beings on a journey of love, we are destined for goodness and grace. Life's oceans, mountains, and deserts challenge us into change, gifting us the experience of being alive. We exist to embody love and experience the entirety of the human condition.

Our sacred purpose is to be ourselves and find our way back to love.

Each moment, with its unique blend of shadows and light, is a precious jewel, a gift to our souls. Every courageous step we have taken through the sands of time and across many lives has brought us to this precise moment of personal autonomy, liberation, and freedom. Bearing this in mind, we should celebrate our smallest of victories, often, they have greater significance than most of us realize.

As creative beings, born of love and made of light, our power is immense and unyielding.

Our every thought and action, transforms not only our lives, but universes. Everything works together for the good. Every footstep through fields of flowers, and every courageous venture through life's muddy paths, empowers us to be our most authentic selves. Though some roads are rocky while others are smooth, all roads lead home—*back to love, back to God.* The darkest shadow and the brightest light are included in love. Nothing and no-one is excluded, or left out of God's loving embrace. Even our darkest shadow, deepest sorrow and most profound suffering contribute to the radiant light of the loving universe.

A human life, though glorious, is not always easy; sometimes, it can be quite daunting. During moments of pain and suffering, it's challenging to accept that everything is love or that the dark night of the soul will ultimately resolve itself, but I promise it will.

Every seed of light or shadow of the night is a burgeoning forest of possibilities yet to be born.

There is a divinity to all things. Everything works together for the good, even the "*so-called*" bad. There's no need to immediately solve all of our problems; a new day always dawns. Things usually fall into place when we allow ourselves time to breathe, think, recover, and rest. As morning breaks, answers that eluded us in the dark of night often become clear. And if they remain elusive, we find peace in knowing we did our best.

The unseen possibilities of an empty dark night are unveiled in the warmth and comfort of the glorious morning light.

Be patient with yourself, and take it one day at a time; very soon, the sleeping flowers of the future will blossom and bloom, as will you. Your pain, sorrow, and sadness will be a distant memory, adding to the radiance of tomorrow's sun.

You will find your purpose and joy again, I promise. Then, looking back over your shoulder, your struggles will all make sense, even if they don't right now. You will know why you are going through this trying time. In the aftermath, you will be wiser, stronger, and more alive. Have faith, my dearest, the storm will pass, but you must hold on. Give it one more minute, hour, day, week, month, or year; give it as long as you need, but don't give up hope.

You stand on the brink of a breakthrough, poised for change and ready for transformation. In your very next breath, the shattered fragments of your brokenness will assemble into a breathtaking mosaic of poignant beauty and love. Our greatest joys and deepest sorrows add to our personal growth, the enrichment of the universe, and the unfoldment of the Divine.

The fragrant flowers born of your dark night will unfold in an array of spectacular colors and sparkling morning light. You have all of eternity to figure things out. So, please don't worry, you will be okay, I promise. You can trust that the love reaching out to you in this very moment is meant for you. Let it guide you and be your pillar of strength when the world comes crashing down.

Choose to be the good you want to see in the world; choose love no matter what.

Every footstep into and out of the physical world is necessary, weighted, and important, more important we may realize. How we frame the story of our life (*as a victim or victorious*) changes our experience of it.

We are powerful beings of light on a divine mission of love.

Our every choice ripples out endlessly, changing universes. What we do or don't do, not only alters the present moment, but also impacts the past and future. This life, and the entire human experience, is a glorious, transformational opportunity of exponential growth, but it is not easy. We came to planet Earth on a fast track of evolution, knowing it would be challenging. And yes, you have taken on a lot in this life, more than most.

You are a powerful warrior of light on grand mission of love. You cannot fail: love conquers all. Even so, there will be times that despite your best efforts and earnest intent, you will be swept away by life's storms. Sometimes, there is no other choice, but to surrender to the inevitable. This surrender is not a failure, but a valuable contribution of experience and love to the whole of creation. We come to planet blindfolded, hiding from what we seek. The path home is not straight or narrow, it is a winding road and endless journey of love.

Listen to the quiet whisper of your soul and you will find your way home, I promise. The moment we lift our gaze, the vast universe is revealed. As the children of the divine, the progeny of God, we are far more powerful than is known or acknowledged. Nonetheless, being human is no easy feat, only the bravest souls venture into this temporal realm of shadow and light. The trials and tribulations of a physical existence can be tumultuous for our delicate souls. We need courage to confront our demons, audacity to stand by our values, and a willingness to stumble, fall, and rise again. Often it is through our mistakes and missteps that we find learning and growth. Life is not one dimensional, it is multifaceted, complex, and simple at the same time.

Look for the light, but allow for the darkness too.

Instead of fighting the wind of change, battling the black of night, or being crucified by your pain, let the present moment be as it is. Allow yourself to feel all your feelings without judging them as right or wrong; just feel. Feel what it feels like to be you in your life right now. Allow life to unfold as it does; feel deeply, hurt intensely, and live fully.

Allow yourself to feel life's pain, sorrow, joy, and elation, but let go of the story that defines it as good or bad. Our stories are a glorified or demonized perspective that we superimpose on life. A negative story adds to our pain, while a positive story, most certainly, will come to an end.

Either way, when we tell ourselves a story, we suffer. Instead of storytelling, become the silent witness of your existence, the spectator of your life, the observer observing itself. Experience the totality of your existence, both the joys and sorrows, with acceptance and awareness. Move through the unfolding moments of beauty and horror with the innocence, curiosity, and joy of a child. Embrace the mystery and magic of your very existence. Trust that every dark shadow and expression of light is God manifest in the splendor and glory of divine intelligence.

Good or bad, let go of the stories that add to your pain and suffering. We are much more than the small stories we tell ourselves. Indeed, we are God personified in myriad expressions of love and light. We are the necessary evolution of love as more love, light as more light, and God as more God. Please allow me to address this directly to your beauty-filled soul.

You are a being of light born of love for the purpose of love. You are the most exquisite expression of God, manifested through you, within you, and for you. This life, your beautiful life, is the most precious gift and wonderful opportunity to experience love in real-time.

Love is the answer to all our questions, even those yet to be asked.

Love is the solution to all our problems and love is why we exist. Love is all that matters. This fleeting, ephemeral world soon passes away, but love never dies. Love is a cup brimming with a luminous light that illuminates the soul. Even the darkest journey through the fiery pits of hell eventually leads us back to God's loving arms. Love always finds a way to love. The darkness will not last forever; the sun will rise again, and the skies will clear. Everything will work out, and you will be okay, I promise.

Love does indeed conquer all.

As we come to the end of this Love Letter, I promise that it will all work out—it always does and always will. Even if life doesn't work out how we thought it would or hoped it would, it will all make sense.

On that note, please allow me to remind you, yet again, that our bond of love is far greater than the short span of a human life; *it is eternal and timeless*. I will never abandon you, never forget you, and never leave you. I will forever be by your side. I will find my way back to you in every life. Look for me in the unexpected shapes and shadows of your life, and you will find me. I will linger in the morning haze that fades into the afternoon sun. I will be a bright star, forever shining in the black of your night. I will call to you like the morning sun seeping in through your bedroom window. I will hold you safely in the black of night. I will be the blossom and bloom of the fragrant flowers, sitting quietly in a vase on the corner of your desk.

Wherever you go, I will find you and remind you that God loves you, and that I love you too.

The love you seek is seeking you—it is you.

You are the blessed one, a beloved child of the universe, the progeny of God. You are the blossoming of love as more love—*and God is the bloom*. You are the rising sun, the waning moon and the flickering stars; without you, there is no light, and no reason to be. You are that important to the whole of creation, and to me. Our meeting again in this life is born of the sacred fire of our ancient bond of love. It is a divine appointment of our souls for the betterment of all.

My eternal vow and heartfelt promise to you is that I will forever find you, always love you, and never leave you. Read and reread these words as many times as you need; read them until you know that they are true and meant for you.

Everything will work out, I promise.

*I am forever with you
and will always love you.
— Chrystal Rae*

Love does indeed conquer all

Crises will come and go, change is inevitable,

but suffering is optional

Letter 18

storms
crises come and go

To stay calm and rooted through life's storms and hurricanes of change requires a level of consciousness that many have yet to attain.

We are easily overwhelmed by personal crises and the innate uncertainties of life. The slightest gust of wind can pull us into a vortex of negativity, stress, and dis-ease. Indeed, in the human condition, we are often swept away by the fluctuating currents of mass consciousness and never-ending cycles of chaos and change.

At certain evolutionary stages, this volatility is understandable and quite normal.

Staying calm during life's storms is a sign of spiritual development and not a measure of our inherent worth.

Most assuredly, because you are reading these Love Letters, you are further along than most. As a result of your heightened level of awareness, you are not so readily drawn into the negative pull of mass consciousness and collective suffering. Instead of getting lost in the mire of everyday existence, you attract experiences of higher learning, self-realization, and personal development.

This elevated level of consciousness is why you are reading these words. While you may occasionally be affected by discordant energy, you now grasp the transient nature of the universe. It's evident that even the darkest storms pass, gray clouds are temporary, the sun always rises, and fragrant flowers bloom after the storm. By taking full responsibility for your life, you acknowledge that your choices are precisely that: *yours*. Hence, you are less likely to project anger or angst onto others or get drawn into their stories of suffering and sorrow. Because you have cultivated a heightened level of inner calm and personal awareness, you are less likely to sink into the shadowy depths of fear and pain, or get pulled down by the undertow of everyday existence.

In the wake of this shift in consciousness, we become more loving, aware, compassionate, and kind. Our presence is a true blessing and guiding light for those who follow in our footsteps. In fact, many in our care would be lost if we did not pave the way or light candles in the night.

We make world a better place by becoming better people.

Like a vigilant shepherd tending to their flock, we, as conscious beings aware of our inherent unity, diligently care for those entrusted to us. We protect them from harm and guide them on their journey back home. Caring for others is a labor of love and a natural consequence of shining brighter. These shifts in consciousness and new levels of awareness are essential to our spiritual progress.

Love is our silent power and true strength.

We transform ourselves and the world when we embody our spiritual heritage and reclaim our divinity. Instead of leaping off a cliff, like one sheep following the other, we become good shepherds of our energy and more discerning of the direction of our lives. We ground ourselves in the truth of love, the goodwill of compassion, and the freedom of non-attachment.

When we step into our power, we experience the world quite differently. We lean in rather than out, walk when everyone runs, remain silent when others scream, and stand strong when those around us tumble and fall. By moving beyond the limits of the ego and its narcissistic tendencies, we leap past boundaries that once kept us trapped in smallness. This shift in consciousness requires that we step into our power as heroic spiritual beings born of love and made of light. As children of the loving universe, we are far more powerful than most realize. Our heritage is divine; we are the progeny of God. Each soul that comes into being is unique, singular, irreplaceable, and never to be replicated for all of time and space, including your beautiful soul.

These are not mere platitudes or fluffy words; they are the truth of who we are. We are radiant beings, luminous stars forever shining in the night. More directly, your presence on the planet and in the universe is necessary and meaningful.

You are God in the making, God expressed, and God manifest.

You are so vital to the whole of creation that everything would collapse in your absence. You are cherished and loved beyond words and surrounded by teachers, angels, and guides.

We are all blessed by the love and grace of our celestial family. In silence, they nudge us to turn right instead of left to avoid an accident. With a gentle touch, they urge us to be kind rather than cruel. Patiently, they remind us that we live in an abundant universe. With quiet calm, they encourage us to be tolerant, generous, kind, and forgiving. Indeed, without the gentle assistance, loud prompts, and soft whispers of these radiant beings, we could not find our way out of ignorance and darkness. Having said that, it is always a personal choice whether we listen to or disregard the wise counsel of our angelic family and teachers.

We alone choose the direction of our lives, a path that cannot be set by others, including those who lovingly watch over us from a distance.

Part of our soul mission is to overcome our primal tendencies and negative predispositions, striving to transcend the energetic constitution of this world. We each possess a distinct disposition and energetic constitution, yet at our core, we are neither inherently good nor evil. Yet, it is through our choices and the nature of our energetic constitutions that we attract life's circumstances. Each event becomes an opportunity for self-awareness, personal growth, and the expansion of our soul. Our time on planet Earth is part of our accelerated evolutionary path back to the love and light of which we were born. Each soul that comes into being is meant to exist. No one is here by mistake, accident, or default. The universe is purposeful and loving, and everything works together for the good. In an intriguing interplay of fate, we find ourselves drawn toward the precise circumstances, people, places, and conditions that catalyze our soul's expansion and personal growth.

Exploring the dynamic contrast between the shifting shadows and radiant light of the temporal world provides the soul with immense joy and opportunities for expansion.

Please allow me to elaborate without delving too deeply into the science or metaphysics of our existence. In the realm where science meets the soul, our brain orchestrates a symphony of sparks, a dance of neurons, and a vast tapestry of interconnected thoughts. Divine consciousness encapsulates into a human form for the purpose of experience and expansion. While our thoughts set the tone of our experiences, the heart writes the lyrics, sings the melody, and weaves an enchanting song. Its silent electromagnetic signal resonates out to the far corners of the universe and beyond.

When the heart and mind unite in harmony, the impossible suddenly becomes possible, and our hopes and dreams magically manifest.

When the brain, with its electrochemical wonders, entwines with the heart's electromagnetic allure, it merges into a powerful magnetic field, drawing experiences, connections, and serendipities that shape our lives. This magnetic field pulls us toward growth, joy, and fulfillment. In the coherent dialogue between heart and mind, a loving choice ripples out as more love, while the opposite is also true.

The most powerful and profound choice we can ever make is to love.

We have the opportunity to choose love in every moment and in every encounter. A simple act of kindness, a warm embrace, or a gentle word can set a chain reaction of love's transformative power in motion. In this light, to make a more loving choice, we must first align the heart with the mind. This alignment can be challenging for those more emotionally driven or intellectually oriented, but it is possible and not as complicated as it may at first seem.

To truly love, we must permit our hearts to guide us, while, at the same time, allowing the mind to accompany us on the journey. Though this may sound counterintuitive, it is really quite practical. Even if we make the "*quote, unquote*" wrong decision, leading from the heart with discernment and wisdom of the mind is always the right answer.

The heart aligns us with our higher self, the loving universe, and God.

Though this is a self-evident truth, dependent upon our evolutionary state, we may or may not fully grasp its profoundity and simplicity. We may even be aware of better choices and higher paths, yet still find ourselves unable to do the right thing. Habits are formidable adversaries, anchoring us to comfortable and familiar repetitive, and many times unhealthy patterns. It is not that we are not trying to change; most of the time, we try very hard. We may try and fail over and over again.

However, our efforts are often misguided; we keep doing the same thing and expecting a different outcome, but the universe does not work this way. For something different, we must do something different. The paradox of purposeful transformation lies in the need to align with untapped, energetic possibilities that we have yet to achieve.

This alignment requires a profound shift in consciousness and a willingness to embrace discomfort. For true transformation, we must be willing to venture into the unknown and embody a new energetic state, transcending the boundaries of the familiar and comfortable. Change requires that we change—*our thoughts, behaviors, and attitudes. In other words, we must upgrade our energy to be able to hold the space for an energetic shift to occur.* To illustrate this concept, consider the example of aspiring to a leadership role. Before we can step into a leadership role, we must first upgrade our thoughts, dress, speech, actions, and work ethic to achieve this goal. When we become an energetic match for the role, opportunities for advancement naturally unfold.

Although the formula for change may seem straightforward, it is not effortless. It requires overcoming self-imposed barriers and getting out of our own way.

The biggest obstacle to our personal growth is the habit of being ourselves and doing the same thing over and over again.

To start the process of transformation *(change)* we have to be willing to do something different. Embracing this path demands a leap of faith, finding comfort in discomfort, and an openness to failure. Indeed, on the journey to mastery, we are bound to experience many setbacks and failures.

"The master has failed more times than the beginner has even tried."

Often we are hindered from a fulfilling life by the fear of failure and a lack of motivation. Clinging to outdated beliefs or a longing for comfort, we cease to push ourselves towards change. Opting for safety, we become sedentary, trapped in familiar routines, and consequently lose the sense of wonder and excitement once abundant in childhood.

As we age, we often lose our sense of adventure, shy away from risks, and neglect the joy of fun. In pursuit of safety, adventure takes a back seat. The transition from adulthood to old age frequently sees the fading of childlike wonder and curiosity. Gradually, seriousness, stoicism, bitterness, or anger can take hold.

There's a valuable lesson to be learned from children in overcoming the fear of failure and reigniting ambition. They approach new experiences with openness and don't harshly judge themselves during the learning process.

Recently, I had an inspiring experience at the lake with my grandchildren. They invited me and other adults to join them in the water, but surprisingly, all the adults remained comfortably seated. Acting spontaneously, I decided not to overthink it and jumped in. For the next thirty minutes, I was wholly engaged in the fun, splashing and playing, feeling rejuvenated and vibrantly alive.

Following this joyful experience, I found myself reflecting deeply. I questioned when had I stopped seeking new experiences, having fun, and being joyful. Then I made a conscious decision that reshaped the subconscious narrative I held about adulthood and its potential. This joyful experience marked a significant shift in my perspective and approach to life.

The stories we tell ourselves shape our reality.

The belief that we are too old, the fear of looking foolish, or the apprehension of failure can hinder us from trying new things. These fears have a basis in reality; failure can occur, and we might feel foolish or old. However, I urge you to persevere regardless—to venture forth, embrace fun, and truly experience the vitality of being alive.

In order to succeed, we must be willing to fail.

Unfortunately, many miss the joy and thrill of vulnerability and innocence, choosing safety over the risk of failure and avoiding the brave expansion of life's possibilities. This leads to a stagnation in growth. We often measure ourselves by our successes or failures, overlooking the real essence of life's journey and adventure. Yet, it's important to remember that these external markers do not define us, as they are not accurate reflections of our soul's true worth.

Navigating the physical world of shadow and light, we are presented with many opportunities to choose between love and fear. The power to decide our path lies within us. Every soul undertakes a distinct and vital journey, yet ultimately, all paths guide us back to the loving arms of God. Indeed, in a universe that is loving and kind, even the smallest efforts to make better choices and improve our lives bring us nearer to the profound reality of God's endless love.

Every footstep into the light or the dark of night, shifts the ground underneath our feet, quaking through existence, instantly creating and destroying universes.

One direction leads us back to the radiant light and ever-expanding love of God, while the other takes us on a rough and rocky ride into dark places of fear, sorrow, and isolation. Whichever path we take, we will all eventually find our way home.

Evolution is an inevitable consequence of existence, and no one will be left behind; only the timing is not set. With our every thought and action, we determine whether our journey into and out of the three-dimensional world of form and matter is enjoyable or not. Every path, even those leading into the dark pits of hell, takes us one step closer to the truth of love and the light of God.

Every soul, including your divine soul, is destined for greatness, goodness, grace, and God.

Most of the time, and for most people, this movement toward or away from God is unconscious and automatic. However, this is not the case for you; indeed, at this point in your spiritual journey, you understand the significance of even the smallest act of kindness and love, and its opposite. Because you are awake and conscious, the habitual ways of mass consciousness no longer drag you along. Your footsteps into and out of the physical world are deliberate and purposeful.

With this heightened awareness, you are deeply connected to the loving universe and better able to embrace a more purposeful evolutionary journey. Rather than perpetually resisting life's unpredictable currents, you joyfully ride the waves of life, gracefully navigating their ebb and flow while firmly anchoring yourself in God's unconditional love.

As we evolve, suffering as a means of spiritual advancement will be the road less traveled. In our alignment with more radiant realities, our nature becomes more peaceful, kind, and benevolent. Our transformation to a more expansive version of self is a result of moving beyond the familiar and consciously shifting to higher vibrational states.

The loving universe will not allow for a vacuum, as we release one reality, another simultaneously takes its place.

Whether by intentional action or unconscious default, this transition always aligns perfectly with our soul's need for experience and learning.

Furthermore, in the realm of the Eternal Now, where all is complete, our present life is but one of many potential realities, chosen as the most beautiful possibility for our soul. Indeed, a human life is a continual and ever-evolving adventure, leading us into the enigmatic depths of the unknown and guiding us back toward the illuminating shores of knowledge. We are gifted with the opportunity to consciously explore and manipulate energy in the realm of shadows and light.

We exist for the blissful experience of being human in a material world on the path to God.

In this light, there is no need to race through levels of consciousness as we return to God's love; no one will be left behind, and there is no hurry to evolve. So please remember to have fun and enjoy the journey of being you. In addition, our personal evolution and spiritual advancement are not necessarily tied to a single lifetime. Therefore, in the loving universe of infinite possibilities, the lack of perceived spiritual progress in a particular life does not imply eternal damnation or inherent evil. The speed or timing of our transformation does not define our moral worth.

Evolution is symmetrical but not necessarily linear.

Each soul follows its unique path and timeline, and the journey toward growth and understanding may extend beyond this life. Spiritual advancement does not label us as good or bad based on our progress. Through our diverse life experiences and learning opportunities, we enrich and enliven the whole of creation.

The universe orchestrates many spectacular occurrences, filled with mystery and magic, guiding us toward our most radiant and authentic selves and corresponding realities. The speed of our evolution is not inherent in our worthiness; instead, it is intricately linked to the unique nature of our souls.

For some, evolution unfolds gradually and steadily, while others rapidly transcend time and space constraints with sudden bursts of energy. Both paths are valid, and neither is superior to the other. What is important to remember is that just as we cannot force a flower to blossom or bloom, we cannot force the process of our evolution.

Everything happens when it is supposed to happen, and not a moment before or after.

While it is essential to acknowledge our limited control and trust in a higher power, we still have to show up with "*readiness*" for life's abundant opportunities and complex challenges.

When we consciously surrender to the rhythm of the universe, we open ourselves to the beauty and growth that comes with the unfolding of our unique destiny. Through this surrender, we find true alignment with our soul's purpose and reach the heights of our most authentic selves. Then, when it best serves our soul, the loving universe unveils new possibilities and wonderful worlds of opportunity. Indeed, many mysterious and magical things happen daily, pulling us towards our evolution and the unfoldment of light.

The universe is mystical and magical, it is also logical and organized. Once we understand the laws of the universe, we can manage our lives with more conscious intent. One of the most important universal laws is the law of attraction: Like attracts like. Therefore, adopting a healthy lifestyle is the first step towards being healthier, and assuming a leadership role paves the way for opportunities to manifest. Similarly, in seeking a harmonious relationship, we must embody the energetic space to attract and support a loving partner.

As previously mentioned this transformational process of moving from lesser to more radiance, involves consciously breaking free from familiar and habitual patterns and embracing the unknown and the uncomfortable.

Energetic realignment is the first step in manifestation.

We must change our thoughts, open our hearts, foster a mindset of gratitude, and cultivate a joyful anticipation to shift from one reality into another. Even with no outward sign indicating how or when our desires will manifest, through our good intentions and affirmative action, we inevitably shift our energy, drawing the circumstances we desire into reality.

When we change ourselves, we change the world.

When we purposefully elevate our energy, we align ourselves with new circumstances, timelines, and unexpected opportunities. This awareness enables us to deliberately position ourselves within a desired energetic state, creating an entirely new reality.

In the energetic realm, we attract what we are, not what we want. Thus, it's crucial to continually grow our consciousness in love. Even as we stand still, the world moves on, with change as its constant companion. We face a choice: to be passively swept along by these changes or to navigate them with intention. Understanding that change is inevitable brings a profound realization of the importance of living with purposeful intent. To truly grasp this concept, reflect on the journey of a baby bird. It starts its life within the safe confines of its shell, a place of security and shelter. Yet, to thrive and survive, staying within this limited space isn't viable.

The baby bird must find the courage to break free from its shell and venture into the unknown. This is the only way it can learn to spread its wings, take flight, and realize its full potential. Likewise, in our quest for personal growth and empowerment, we too must be willing to step beyond the familiar boundaries of our comfort zones. Taking this brave evolutionary step involves the readiness to shed the constraints of our past and any limitations that have hindered our progress. Once we break free from the chains that bind us to yesterday's pain and energetically align with a more desirable state, our reality reshapes with remarkable ease and little resistance.

Conscious evolution requires we step into the unknown and get "comfortably uncomfortable."

This energetic shift necessitates our willingness to embark on a journey of self-exploration and growth. By doing so, we unlock the potential to reach higher levels of understanding, fulfillment, and purpose.

In terms of soul evolution, being uncomfortable can catalyze rapid change and personal transformation.

Much like a grain of sand that irritates an oyster and transforms into a pearl, embracing a state of being "*comfortably uncomfortable*" enables us to broaden our horizons in the journey of evolution, uncovering fresh avenues for personal growth.

This process is both exciting and empowering, but we must exercise caution to avoid taking on too much too quickly, which could lead to self-sabotage. As with the oyster, where a tiny grain of sand creates a pearl while a large stone may harm or destroy it, finding the right balance between challenge and overwhelm is crucial. Only we know our limits and boundaries, and it's essential to be mindful of them. Discomfort in the face of change should be invigorating and empowering rather than debilitating. Too much discomfort (*pain*) is not sustainable and may be detrimental or harm our souls. We may snap back or default to familiar but lower energetic states that do not serve our highest potential.

The conflict between the desire for change and the need for comfort can impede our personal growth and trap us in repetitive cycles. Our natural inclination is to repeat familiar actions because they're comfortable. We desire change yet cling to comfort in the familiar, but the universe does not work like that.

We must step out of our comfort zone and do something different to evolve.

We upgrade our energetic alignments by letting go of our attachment to the tangible and known and purposefully stepping into the nebulous unknown. As a result of our heightened energy, new realities are available, and change is possible. This process is commonly referred to as facing our fears, and it is a necessary step in self-development and personal growth.

The understanding of how energy works in a magnetic universe is a most essential tool of empowerment in the midst of crisis and change. The universe is dynamic and ever-changing; therefore, we must be open to change and continuous improvement in our inner and outer worlds. Again, if we want something different, we must do something different.

For change, we ourselves must change.

To live authentically and align with our truth, we must do the things we've been putting off or dreading because they make us uncomfortable or afraid. For example, to be honest with ourselves and others, we must speak our truth and have difficult conversations even when the outcomes may not always be positive. The only way to break free from complacency and stagnation is by tempering our actions with wisdom, love, and grace. This thoughtful approach ensures that we progress steadily and avoid unnecessary setbacks. The good news is that even if we experience setbacks or regress, we can still rely on the boundless grace of the loving universe.

God's grace is precisely that: grace.

This grace is freely bestowed upon us without any conditions or expectations attached. There is nothing we must do to be worthy of God's love. Our journey as humans is remarkable, characterized by free will, growth, and constant change. It is a wonderful and sometimes daunting path of evolution.

Throughout this profound adventure, our souls are enriched and enlivened. As sentient beings, we have the extraordinary opportunity to experience a human life in a physical world of shadow and light. Every breath presents us with the grand opportunity to explore our true selves and forge new connections with the Divine.

A human life is not a test; we cannot fail; our existence is our success.

In the loving universe, nothing happens by accident, and evolution is an inexorable force. Every being is destined to evolve; none will be left behind, forgotten, or forsaken. Our evolution is not a matter of *"if,"* but *"when."* Each soul progresses on its unique evolutionary journey at its own pace. As noted earlier, everything occurs in its own time, never a moment sooner. Just as we cannot hasten a flower's bloom by forcing its petals open, without risking harm to the bud, so too we cannot rush our own evolutionary process.

On the other hand, when it is time for the flower to blossom, all the forces of God and nature propel it toward its next most radiant state, and there is no stopping it. The same is true for us;

when it is our time to evolve, nothing can hold us back. We must do our part, trust God, and leave the details to the loving universe. Although "*to do our part*" sounds great in theory, it can be quite challenging. We won't always feel good, and life won't always be easy. Some days, we will feel great, and life will flow smoothly, while on other days, it definitely won't.

Regardless of the weather of our lives, behind the dark clouds, the sun is always shining.

In the loving universe, all things work together for the greater good, including life's most devastating storms.

Indeed, with the more expansive perspective of the soul, we realize that regardless of how life unfolds—*clear skies or torrential rains*— it all serves a purpose in the grand scheme of life. Everything, whether joyous or painful, is a part of the natural unfoldment of the loving universe. Recognizing the inherent good and grace in life enables us to find meaning, even in the toughest situations. While we might not always understand the reasons behind certain events, embracing this idea can provide solace, acceptance, and peace. Our continual effort to better ourselves and trust in the grace of God is essential to living a more fulfilling life.

How we show up to life is more important than how life shows up.

The adage "*don't cry over spilled milk*" is a powerful reminder to let go of the past and conserve our energy for the present and future. Dwelling on things beyond our control hinders our progress and drains our life force.

Accepting the discomfort that may arise in challenging moments while maintaining peace and acceptance frees us from unnecessary suffering, allowing us to use our energy in more positive and constructive ways. Instead of being consumed by regret or anger, we can focus on finding solutions, making a difference, and contributing positively to our lives and those around us.

This positive mindset empowers us to move beyond the limitations of dwelling on unchangeable past events and to step into a more purposeful and fulfilling existence. We become agents of change and a source of goodness, positively impacting the world. While we cannot control everything in our lives, we can control our responses and attitudes and be a force of good and grace.

Storms will come and go, change is inevitable, but suffering is optional.

Rather than reacting in the heat of the moment, we can purposefully move away from emotionality and superimposed filters of good and evil. When we choose a more loving, enlightened response from a space of non-attachment, inner peace, and calm, we re-frame our story to serve our soul better and naturally align with higher vibrational possibilities.

Rather than being a victim, we are victorious. When we change our story, we change our lives. The magnitude of this simple shift in perspective is often undervalued. As we align ourselves with heightened energetic possibilities and make more loving choices, unforeseen universes and radiant possibilities for a yet-to-be-born future unfold before us.

In the silent space between our first and last breath, we gather treasured bits of light, venture into the farthest reaches of the night, and discover who we really are.

I hope these words and this book serve your soul in ways that continually improve your life. It is my greatest joy and honor to be part of your personal development, growth, and evolution. I know how difficult a human life can be, but I also know it all works out.

We live in a benevolent, kind, and loving universe where love is the propelling force. We are spiritual beings with immense power, often unaware of our own greatness. More directly, you are a formidable spiritual being, capable of much more than you may know, realize, or acknowledge. As a child of the loving universe, and the progeny of God, you are a necessary never-to-be replicated expression of the divine—*loved beyond all concepts of love*. We willingly and joyfully signed up for the human experience with great enthusiasm and anticipation. We knew the outcome of life was not predestined, we completely understood that nothing is guaranteed or set, and we were fully aware of the great difficulties and dark nights we would endure.

A human life, with all its joys and sorrows, is a transformational adventure of the soul.

We knew all of this, and yet, we still came. We entered this wondrous world of shadows and light with the extraordinary opportunity to choose love at our own discretion and in our own time, ultimately returning to God enriched by the journey. We came knowing that the temporal world would provide our soul with glorious experiences and heartbreaking lessons.

On this sacred journey of self-empowerment and unconditional love, we have traveled through barren deserts, climbed tall mountains, and searched the deep depths of the oceans. The trials of a human life have given us deep roots and a grander reason to be—*love*.

The seeds planted today are the bloom of a magnificent tomorrow yet-to-be-born.

Thank you for confronting your fears, lighting candles in the night, and faithfully weathering the storms of your own transformation. You have made the world a better place by continually challenging yourself to improve.

Amid the crises of life, winds of change, and most devastating storms, your courage and grace have shifted the compass of eternity. Your effluent radiance leaves me in awe, and your benevolence touches my heart. The beauty and grace of your soul humbles me. From a place of admiration, I cheer you on from the sidelines. You are truly an incredible being of light, more powerful than you know, and an inspiration to all. Your transformative journey has shattered many old paradigms and given birth to new stars and distant suns of hope and inspiration. Indeed, the light of your consciousness has made a profound difference in the world—*far more than you can possibly imagine or know.*

As we conclude this Love Letter, my hope is that I've imparted wisdom, knowledge, and tools to bring you peace amidst storms, joy during sorrow, and a guiding light in your darkest moments. Life is an ever-evolving journey, filled with unanswered questions and inevitable change. Yet, one thing remains unwavering—*Love.*

Love is the timeless answer and the essence of life. Even now, as the flickering lights and heavy shadows fade back into the black of night, love's eternal light shines forth as a beacon of hope and a reason to believe. Beyond shifting shadows, dark nights, raging storms, and uncontrollable crises and the inevitability of change, love endures as the luminous thread intricately woven into the very fabric of our existence, binding us to our true purpose and the eternal embrace of the divine.

Everything works out in the end, and yes, love wins.

Remember, my dearest, though storms may rage and the unrelenting winds of change may carry you to distant lands, everything is divinely purposed for your soul, and you are never alone. Alongside your soul family, angels, and guides, I am with you—now and forever. Across our countless shared lives and to the end of time, I will stand by your side, unconditionally loving and caring for you

Your presence in my life, and this world, is a precious gift, and your positive impact reaches far beyond the limited time and space of this temporal world.

You are the brightest star in my night.
I am grateful, and I love you.
— Chrystal Rae

To truly love, we must default to the wisdom of the heart over the mind

The most powerful choice we will ever make is to love

Letter 19
choice
compass of destiny

We are always one choice away from a completely different life.

In truth, we only have two choices: *to love or fear*. Whatever we choose instantly shifts the sand beneath our feet, forever alters our direction, and profoundly affects our destiny. Even the most seemingly insignificant choice changes everything, changes entire universes. Irrespective of what occurs in the outer world, our experiences will differ significantly based on our choices. A loving choice moves us toward goodness and grace, while an unloving choice does the opposite. Not only do our choices determine the experience of our lives, they ripple into the vast universe, endlessly impacting the whole of existence.

The most powerful choice we will ever make is to love.

Love changes us, the world, and the universe. Love changes everything and everyone, including God. Love gives depth and meaning to an otherwise hollow and flat existence. Though our outer world may not change, love reinterprets it. With love, we see the old with new eyes. An ant is a tiny and wonderful expression of God. A heartache is a bleeding opportunity to forgive and to love profoundly. Joy is a reason to be grateful and to share. Tragedy is a seed of growth that makes us stronger and more resilient. Failure teaches us humility and perseverance. Success is a movement of grace and a seed of gratitude.

Through the eyes of love, everything has purpose, depth, and meaning.

When we consciously choose to love no matter what, we are no longer a victim of our circumstances. Love awakens us from the perennial, deep slumber of mass consciousness. It empowers us to be self-reliant and to stand strong when those around us tumble and fall. Love is the key that opens the heavy door of heart, setting us free to be our true selves and follow our dreams wherever they lead.

When love is our anchor and faith is our ship, joy is the wind in our sails.

Nothing can move us from our center when we consciously navigate the changing seasons and unexpected weather of our lives with love. Come what may, we are unmoved by passing clouds, frigid nights, or warm summer days. We are free, liberated beings, at peace with ourselves and the world. This is the peace *"beyond all understanding"* described in many spiritual texts, which can only come from God's unconditional love and grace.

However, even God's love is not forced upon us. As free beings, nothing is forced upon us. We freely choose everything in our lives, including to love our Creator or not. This freedom doesn't mean we get to choose all the people, places, circumstances, or conditions of our lives, but how we experience them is always our choice. Everything in life is a choice.

We can lower our eyes and see the mud or lift our gaze and see the stars; it is all available in the loving universe.

Each of us chooses, consciously or not, where we set our gaze and what we focus on. This freedom makes a human life stunningly beautiful, vibrant, and alive. No other being is gifted with such liberty and grace; we are truly blessed; our life experiences directly result from our choices and nothing else.

The power of conscious discernment is the unique gift and opportunity of being sentient. Unfortunately, we often default our decisive power to others or, out of fear and lethargy, choose not to choose, which becomes our unspoken choice. Instead of deciding for ourselves and taking full responsibility for our choices, we mindlessly follow the lead of others: parents, community, church, government, and so on. Though not ideal, deferring our birthright of autonomy, freedom, and choice is part of our personal development and evolutionary process.

To be both human and divine comes with its gifts and burdens.

The power of choice is weighted and heavy with consequences, and there is no guarantee that we will always make the right choice. Most assuredly, we won't, at least not until we evolve out of this particular realm and world. As conscious beings, we are limited by our analytical thinking and emotional volatility. Most of us will make wrong choices many times over and repeat the same negative patterns until we learn the lesson.

Bearing this in mind, it may be surprising to know that making bad choices is not a problem, at least regarding our eternal soul. The inherent limitations and frailties of being human ultimately serve the soul by providing a depth of experience that would be otherwise unavailable. So please take a deep breath and lighten up. All we can ever do at any given moment is our best, and that's enough. Acknowledging our limitations is not a call to surrender or give up hope. Instead, it suggests that we be kinder to ourselves as we find our way through the darkness and back to the light. When we criticize ourselves we suffer and our progress slows.

Everything comes in right timing, including our understanding and evolution. The right choice at seventeen may not be the best choice at seventy. The familiar saying *"hindsight is 20/20"* is absolutely true.

We don't know what we don't know until we know it in the future.

Everything works together for the good, including our missteps and mistakes. It is all a part of the divine plan and the human experience. We come into the physical world of free will and choice, purposefully veiled from the truth and shrouded in shadows, to have the visceral experience of making unencumbered choices. We knew that a human life would be a challenge and that we would make many mistakes and wrong turns, yet we were still excited for the opportunity and willing to come and explore the radiant possibilities of love. This willingness does not negate our responsibility nor does it mean we should purposefully or casually make bad choices or irresponsible decisions.

On the contrary, because our choices map out the landscape of our lives, rippling out and affecting others, the consistent effort to make better choices is paramount for our soul development. Again, there are only two choices: *to love or fear*. Even our choice not to choose is a powerful choice.

If we do not choose love, by default we choose fear.

Whatever we choose has a direct and immediate impact on our lives and the lives of others. Although there is no definitive wrong choice, there is most definitely a right choice. The right choice is always love.

However, a loving choice may not be the easiest or most convenient. Many times, the opposite is true; choosing love may be the least convenient and the most difficult choice. In the human condition, it is usually easier, perhaps even more natural, to hide, defend, or hurt. For many, lost in the chaotic noise of life or overwhelmed by fear, choosing love may feel unsafe, too vulnerable, or like weakness. Choose love anyway. Go against the grain and challenge yourself to make a better choice, even if it is difficult. The choices we make matter, and they matter a lot.

Every choice has far-reaching consequences that affect our lives and the lives of others.

Our karma is ours, and also part of a larger group karma. The people closest to us are most greatly affected by our choices, as is the wider group of humanity and the entire universe. We are creative, powerful beings of light, and our influence is immense and unending. The love that created us, and created the entire universe cannot be stopped or altered. This love, the love of God, is beyond boundaries or limits; it is an all-encompassing love. As an expression of divinity, born of love for the purpose of love, each soul is a singular and unique manifestation of the divine.

Indeed, as a vital part of this wondrous universe, you are enveloped in a love that transcends all bounds. The entire universe, from the tiniest particle to the grandest galaxies, exists in harmony to support your spiritual sojourn. In my role as a humble messenger of this loving universe, I returned to the physical world with a purpose: *to love, guide, and support you through your earthly journey.* My specific mission was to find you and create this book as a testament to you. It's a reminder that love and the divine are ever-present realities. Regardless of what you've done or not done, the constancy of divine love remains unaltered, a unwavering force in your life.

You are not a prisoner of the past nor a victim of the future.

You are beloved child of God, more powerful than you know or realize. As a self-aware, luminous, being of light, on a sacred mission of the soul, the entire universe is at your beck and call. Unlike less evolved species, you have the freedom and volition to do whatever you desire or choose. At any moment, you can change your life by making a better choice, a more loving choice.

Discernment and choice pave the way for our freedom and liberation.

As beings endowed with consciousness and awareness, we are at liberty to choose our soul's journey. We possess the freedom to pursue what brings us joy and excitement. This liberty extends to our emotions: we can choose to love or hate ourselves, others, and even our Creator.

This freedom, perhaps, is the most profound expression of love — a Creator granting creation the gift of autonomy and choice. Arguably, this might be the greatest gift bestowed upon humanity by God: the power of personal autonomy and freedom. Consider the notion of a deity demanding love or worship from its creation. What nature of deity would that be? A tyrant, a dictator, or a despot? Certainly not a kind, loving, or benevolent one. To further examine this, imagine if someone tried to coerce you into liking or loving them. Such an attempt would not only be futile but would likely breed resentment, fear, or even hatred. Even if love were to eventually develop, it would be overshadowed by the initial coercion, rendering it impure and tainted.

Now, picture the inverse scenario. Envision someone whose love for you is so profound that they grant you total freedom, allowing you to either draw closer or distance yourself from them. Picture a love that is unconditional, offering unwavering support and care regardless of your actions or inactions. This unconditionality is the truest expression of love, mirroring the love of the divine. It is unwavering and consistent, regardless of reciprocity. It endures even in the face of a broken relationship or if you decide to walk away and never return.

To be loved without conditions liberates, empowers, and heals the soul.

This unconditionality is precisely how the universe works and how God loves us. We are lovingly given absolute freedom to choose, explore, and discover the possibilities of love and fear. Irrespective of our actions, good or bad, we are unconditionally loved, supported, and cared for by our loving creator.

We are so very loved that not a single tear or expression of joy goes unnoticed or unacknowledged.

God's love is a vast sky without boundaries or borders.

We are indeed fortunate to be human, to have full autonomy, absolute freedom, and to experience unconditional love. From the quietude of nothingness, we miraculously unfold into existence, representing and personifying the infinite grace and love of the divine. Our lives, in all their intricate layers, are wonderfully complex and meaningful. We are the architects of our destiny, the ones who fulfill our own desires. With every thought and action, we bring entire universes into being, reveling in the sheer joy of experience.

Our sojourn in the physical realm, though fleeting and poignant, holds transformative significance. Each soul that emerges is a blessing, a unique gift to the universe, including your radiant soul. The entirety of creation is enriched and vitalized by every individual expression of the divine, manifesting through each one of us. Even the souls that seem lost or astray are gaining essential lessons and have their own purpose in the grand tapestry of existence.

Whatever happens to each one of us, happens to all of us.

The shepherd, sheep, grass, flowers, weeds, and everything else are all part of the grand matrix of life. We are all part of the greater good of humankind and the universe.

The human story is a divine love song, echoing out in shimmering shadows and hues of light, forever blossoming more radiant, fragrant, and alive. There is a divinity to our lives and all of existence, and all is well. More directly, without your beautiful and irreplaceable soul, nothing would exist, not even God. How could the sky exist without clouds, the grass without weeds, the flowers without the bloom, or the shepherd without his sheep? How could our loving creator exist without his beloved children, without you and me?

Everyone and everything has a grand purpose and meaning.

This grand purpose includes our every shadow and expression of light. You are God expressed as you, for you, and through you. The implications of this statement are profound and life-changing. God is pure consciousness, intelligent energy expressed in the form of sound and light, and that's what we are, too—*energy, intelligence, light, and sound expressed in multiplicity and diversity*. We are all connected in the radiant field of consciousness; we are sparkling particles of light, God expressed and manifest in all things; all opposites merged into one radiant light We are the birds soaring high in the sky, and the snakes slithering low into the dark shadows.

We are everything and nothing at the same time.

Everything is pure consciousness, love, and God manifest. Some might argue this point, and perhaps rightly so, based on their limited worldview. Nonetheless, from a higher perspective, everything and everyone is perfectly imperfect. Nothing is broken; nothing needs to be fixed, changed, or rearranged. The universe is complete in every way and every moment.

We are here to be human, not to be perfect.

Still, many argue they would not purposefully choose the life they are currently living. They believe they have been thrown to the wolves by default or by some cruel, unkind, and unfair God. Again, this sentiment is understandable and may seem true from a limited human perspective. However, our souls have a different agenda and broader scope than the human mind's narrow understanding and simple logic. Our life situation, good or bad, offers the most expansive experiences and opportunities for growth.

Sometimes, in some lives, we succeed; we overcome the shadows, make it through the night, and stand more radiant in the light of a new day. In other lives, we are conquered by the darkness and exist as a ghost of who we were meant to be. We took on too much pain, sorrow, and suffering in these darker lives.

Then, like sheep following each other off a rocky cliff, we, too, follow and fall into the black abyss of our own shadow and ignorance. Even this, in terms of our soul, is not a failure; it is all part of our heroic journey. A life of heavy burdens and missteps provides the soul with what it needs most to experience and learn. Whatever the case, we cannot, and will not, fail at being human. We may move forward, backward, up, down, or even slide sideways, but it is always a movement of love.

The seed and the source are never separate; God is pure love; therefore, you and I are love.

There is a divinity to all things and no mistakes in the loving universe. Every shadow, black night, and radiant ray of morning light provides the soul with the experience of contrast, choice, and change. It is all a necessary part of the soul's joyful exploration, inevitable evolution, and dynamic expansion. Regardless of how far we fall or how endless the dark of our night, we will all find our way back to the love and light of God. How do I know? Because God is pure love and the universe is kind and benevolent. No one will be lost, left behind, or abandoned. The love that created the entire universe, and all that IS, also created us.

We are so very loved that the whole of creation is service to our soul.

Understanding that the challenges, pain, and sorrow we face are integral to our human journey can be profoundly difficult. Accepting that a universe filled with love also encompasses evil, pain, sorrow, and suffering is a complex and often painful realization.

The difficulty intensifies when we or our loved ones are plunged into the depths of fear, pain, suffering, or loss. In these moments of profound darkness, where despair seems all-encompassing, it can feel as though the forces of nature and even the divine have forsaken us.

It is during these times that we may find ourselves feeling like broken fragments of our true potential. Indeed, when the sun retreats, and we are left in opaque darkness and despair, it can be terrifying and even painful to continue on. Such experiences, while harrowing, are part of the intricate tapestry of life, challenging us to seek resilience, understanding, and growth even in the face of our deepest trials. Even in moments of great joy, the stark contrast between those who have much and those who have little can cast a shadow over our happiness, leading us to perceive the world as harsh and question the presence of a benevolent deity.

This dichotomy often prompts a deep and difficult question: How and why would a loving God allow for a world filled with such apparent cruelty and suffering? The answer to this profound question may elude the confines of human comprehension. Nonetheless, just as we understand the concept of light by pointing to the sun, we can begin to bridge the gap in our understanding of the divine by broadening our perspective. This expanded view helps us see that the world's challenges, much like the night's shadows, do not represent the ultimate truth.

The truth, like the sun, is always shining, even behind the darkest clouds of ignorance.

With this broader perspective, we can begin to comprehend that the universe, in its vast complexity, operates under principles that extend beyond our immediate understanding. Every facet of existence, whether it be joy or sorrow, abundance or scarcity, contributes to the grand design, where everything ultimately converges in an expression of love, further expanding into even greater love.

This expanded perspective invites us to dive deeper into the events and circumstances of life, recognizing that experiences, even those perceived as harsh or painful, may hold deeper meaning and purpose. They are integral to the universe's complex and overarching design, each moment playing a crucial role in the unfolding of divinity and the perpetual movement of love.

Even the darkest night surrenders to the truth of love and the wisdom of light.

The very instant we light a candle, the night recedes into the darkness of which it was born. After the storm subsides, the sun and the soul rise again in all their glory and splendor, brighter and lighter. In the light of a new day, the flowers blossom, the skies open, the air freshens, and the snow melts away.

Love conquers all.

Goodness and grace are the seeds of a majestic forest of possibilities, bursting forth out of dark nothingness into the light and fullness of being. All our unanswered questions are instantly resolved in the light of love and the presence of God. All judgment of self, others, and even of God fade back into the beauty of being with all its complexity and splendor.

When seen through the eyes of love, the world makes sense, even the seemingly broken parts. Just as the seed must first be planted in the dark earth to take root, grow, and finally find the sun's nourishing light, we are rooted in the darkness of the human experience to once again recognize and remember our inherent light and divine heritage.

The nutrient-rich, dark soil of planet Earth nurtures the tender soul.

Bearing this in mind, we can see that even darkness can be a path to light. In the prime of our lives, filled with vigor and joy, it's easy to believe that we will never experience such moments of darkness and despair. However, no one is immune to the vulnerabilities of human existence—*not you, me, or anyone else*. With this understanding, self-righteousness and judgment give way to compassion, patience, tolerance, and forgiveness.

How can we judge another when we ourselves have made less than radiant choices? We have all been predator and prey; no one is an innocent little lamb. Who hasn't mindlessly or purposefully stepped on an ant, said an unkind word, stolen, lied, or lashed out in anger? When we move from fear, we categorize, judge, and act according to our biases and beliefs. With this grandiose, inflated sense of self or out of entitlement, ignorance, and arrogance, we consciously or unconsciously believe ourselves superior to others. Nevertheless, life invariably humbles us all. Even the greatest among us will suffer the effects of age, illness, and loss. These conditions come as teachers; they are not the unkind act or punishment of an abstract, angry God. We purposefully choose our paths, our demons, our delights, our darkness, and our light.

This world of contrast, change, and choice is the true garden of Eden. Duality is the root of change. Everything works together for the good of all. The homeostasis of the soul is stirred, aroused, and forever changed by the human condition. The terms of a human life include the extremes of joy and sorrow. No one is perfect in a human state, nor imperfect from the more expansive perspective of the soul.

Our very imperfection is our perfection.

The gift and challenge of a human life is to be flawed and beautiful at the same time. Other realms do not allow experiencing such extremes. We are the fortunate and brave ones planted in the rich soil of Mother Earth.

The divine plan, as we know it in this realm, includes the innate complexities of a human life. Each soul that finds its way to this realm is a beloved child of the universe, including your precious soul. You are so loved that your darkest shadow is framed in the imperfect perfection of life. You are loved without judgment, without exception, without reason or conditions. You are eternally and unconditionally loved just as you are.

The asymmetry within the symmetry of a human life is divinely orchestrated for the betterment of the soul and the good of all.

No one is exempt from the weakness of the flesh; not you, not me, not anyone. *"To err is human, and to forgive is divine."* Irrespective of our frailties, strengths, good, or bad actions, God is benevolent, kind, and loving. Our every footstep leads us to the radiant light of heaven or into the dark, fiery pits of hell. It is not God that sends us to heaven or hell; we make that choice each time we choose love or fear.

However, even in our darkest moments of despair and fear, we are not doomed; the very moment we call out for help, all the forces of heaven and earth come rushing to our aid.

The opportunity to discover what is true and good of our own accord in a physical world is proof of God's benevolence and love.

Nothing is forced upon us. No retribution is required. No amendment need be made or could be made to our loving creator. God's love encompasses all possibilities, outcomes, and opposites without differentiation.

In other words, we are loved no matter what. The proof is that we are free to choose the roads we travel, the pace of our journey, and our preferred path back to God. We are free beings, free to be, free to choose, free to love, and yes, we are free to hate, too. From a less evolved state, even the choice to hate is an expression of love. Please allow me to explain. The most beautiful expression of self possible, within our current life circumstances, is continually unfolding. In this sense, we are all equal. Some are given more and some less, but it is always exactly what the soul needs to experience. In a loving universe, it could not be otherwise.

All souls are equally cherished and loved.

Just as a loving mother equally loves all her children, our loving creator loves us without any conditions or differentiation. Our good or bad behavior does not limit God's love for us. The love expressed for one child is the same love given to another but bestowed differently. With loving kindness, a thoughtful mother responds to each child in the way that most befits their character. Some children need tough love, while others need soft nurturing. Regardless of how a mother expresses her love, gentle or stern, it is always the same love. Similarly, we are uniquely and profoundly loved by our creator. God's love is not measured in degrees of virtue or vice. God's love is unconditional, eternal, unchanging, and paradoxically, ever-expanding.

In the intricate balance of life, every occurrence, whether perceived as tragic or joyous, contributes to individual growth and collective well-being. Seen through a broader lens, even great tragedies can unfold as acts of grace, hidden blessings, essential for soulful evolution. In the same way, experiences of happiness, comfort, and beauty act as potent agents of change and development.

No path, be it shadowed or illuminated, holds inherent supremacy; they are simply diverse journeys all leading to the ultimate embrace of divine love. In this universe orchestrated by love, each event is purposefully woven into the fabric of existence, leaving nothing to chance.

Everything is divinely purposed for our soul to not only rise, but to also shine.

Even the most minor everyday occurrences benefit our souls. The cool ocean breeze is God's breath on the wind. The quiet thunder, rumbling in the distance, is a song of hope. The endless collapse of crashing waves is sweet music for our soul. Every drop of rain that finds its way to the earth does so to quench our thirst. All of this, and more, is divinely purposed to bring us joy, edification, and, yes, for the expansion of our soul and the enrichment of the universe.

Every moment is yet another blossoming opportunity to bloom.

Life is the fertile soil and rugged terrain of growth. Each challenge we encounter plants a seed of opportunity and transformation. The condition of our life's garden, whether it's lush and fragrant or barren and neglected, is determined by our choices and actions. While it's tempting to attribute our hardships, sorrows, and setbacks to external influences like friends, teachers, partners, or parents, the ultimate responsibility for our lives rests solely with us. It's true that certain circumstances are outside our control, but how we choose to respond to life's challenges and the narratives we construct around them ultimately shape our future.

Though the past may weigh heavy on us, it does not dictate who we are, or what we can become.

Despite what we've experienced in the past, it's up to us to carve our own paths and plant the seeds for a hopeful future. With this in perspective, I invite you to take a moment of stillness, to contemplate the garden of your life. Acknowledge the flourishing plants and flowers, and also those that need more care. Notice the insects and weeds that might disrupt your growth, but see them through the eyes of compassion and understanding.

This moment of introspection is not meant for self-judgment, but for self-empowerment. Recognizing how our past shapes our present thoughts and actions can enlighten us about our emotional and instinctive responses. Such awareness is a powerful tool, guiding us to make decisions that are more deliberate, conscious, and founded in love.".

The seeds we plant today will be the blossom and bloom of a more radiant tomorrow.

Please remember, the life you aspire to is within your power to create. Achieving this often means transforming our thoughts and actions, shifting from fear-based reactions to more loving responses. However, this may be a daunting task if we have suffered trauma, especially in our formative years. Overcoming childhood conditioning, traumas, and life's various trials is undoubtedly a difficult path. If you find yourself confronting such challenges, seeking professional help is not only wise but a profound act of self-care.

While science and therapy offer vital support, it's love that truly heals the soul. In your journey of healing, it's important to treat yourself with compassion and kindness. Understand that every challenge, regardless of its intensity, is a crucial part of your personal growth and discovery. As you navigate through life, remember that each choice has its significance. Some choices may lead you directly to love, while others take a more serpentine path.

Choices that appear less than ideal still have their place, fitting perfectly into the specific moments and contexts of your life. Every decision you make is an important step on your journey, each one contributing to your personal development and the enrichment of all.

We are always doing our best, even when it seems like our worst—until we learn and are able to do better.

The evidence lies in the fact that we didn't choose differently. Allow yourself the grace and freedom to stumble multiple times, recognizing these as steps towards success. Our true purpose in life isn't to succeed in a conventional sense, but rather to flourish as spiritual beings, learning to love more deeply and profoundly.

Our journey of spiritual growth is not measured by worldly achievements, but by the expansion of our hearts and souls. Furthermore, the unconditional love of God does not depend on our actions or words, nor does it fluctuate with our successes or failures.

God's love is like the sun, graciously casting its radiant light upon the earth, bringing warmth and illumination to every dark place and cold surface.

Nothing we do or say will change or alter God's unending love. We are the unfoldment of that which is most beautiful, necessary, and true in every moment. The seeds we plant and the crops we cultivate, however beautiful or unattended, are not our fullest expression of self. We are much more than the ever-changing seasons of our lives: we are children of the loving universe, the progeny of God.

Please allow me to say this more directly to your brave, beautiful soul. You are a child of God, incarnate and reborn in every possible expression of love and light. You are the glorious morning sun rising over the dark line of the horizon and the deep longing of the soft velvet night, embracing the sudden arrival of a new day.

Nothing is left out of God's all-encompassing love.

Even on our darkest day, when the night seems endless, we are unconditionally and eternally loved and cared for. Each soul is the magnificent unfoldment of God's grace, goodness, and love, including your precious soul. You are the love of all love and the perfection of imperfection.

You are God in the making, God realized, God expressed, and God manifest.

If this does not astound you, please reread the above statement until it does. To know the truth opens the door to living the truth. Again, what we do with our precious time on this planet and in our lives is always our choice. We are free to live in the truth of love and the radiance of light or to hide in the darkness of shadows, fear, and deception. One path will be painful and hard, while the other will be brighter and lighter, yet both eventually lead us back to God.

In life's sacred journey, though we tread our individual paths, we are never truly alone. Each step we take, both into and out of the realm of form and structure, is guided and supported by angels, teachers, and guides, with the divine's all-embracing love enveloping us. This love warmly accepts every aspect of our being, from the darkest shadows to the most radiant light, offering boundless compassion and understanding.

This ever-present, nurturing presence is more than just comfort; it is a testament to the sacred gift granted to us: *the power of personal will and choice.* With this invaluable freedom comes a path filled with uncertainty, coupled with the profound responsibility to use our will wisely, channeling it as a force of love and light in both our lives and the wider world. Life, in its splendor, is also marked by unpredictability and shadows. Like wandering sheep, we sometimes lose our way, feeling isolated and adrift. We may stray into the darkness of our desires or be ensnared by the allure of our attachments, burdening us and hindering our spiritual progress.

Yet, nothing is eternal; a time will come for each of us when we will overcome the deepest shadows of the night and find our way back home—to a realm of boundless light and love. There, no soul is eternally lost, forsaken, forgotten, or left behind. In this journey, every being ultimately finds their way back to the embrace of the divine, where all are welcomed and loved unconditionally.

Every soul is essential and deeply loved—including yours.

Your presence is valued and necessary to the whole of creation—*more than you may know.* Though it is easy to judge ourselves or others harshly, many times it is our failure that is the root of our success. No matter how old or young we are, it is always possible to begin again. At any moment, we have the power to reinvent ourselves and create a life that is truly fulfilling.

With every breath a world of possibilities opens, but what we do with it is always our choice.

As we conclude this Love Letter, remember that your choices hold immense significance. A single thought can create and destroy universes in an instant, so choose with care, dear one. Above all, remember that when we make different choices—*more loving choices*—we immediately shift the compass of our lives, altering the direction of our footsteps in the sand, and realigning with the purpose of our life and the divinity of our soul.

A human life is like a garden rich with potential and excitement. We have the power to transform not just our own lives, but also to impact the universe. Our actions, choices, and the love we share create ripples of change, touching lives and shifting universes.

As we step away from the entanglements of the past and shed the less radiant versions of ourselves, we undergo a glorious rebirth into our own lives. With every choice, we stand at the crossroads between love and fear—*and only we can decide which way to go.*

My heartfelt wish for you is that you find strength, courage and wisdom to always choose love.

My choice is always you.
I love you now and forever.
— Chrystal Rae

You are a masterpiece: magnum opus

Letter 20
reality
it's not what you think

Now, let's talk about the reality of your life.

Your life is an absolute miracle, more astounding than you may realize or know.

A single moment of conscious awareness is a treasure beyond all treasures, and yet, most of us take our lives for granted. We act as though being alive is a given, but life isn't guaranteed for any of us. It is an absolute marvel and mystery to exist, to be you, and to be alive. To be aware that we are aware is evidence of God and gives rise to joyous celebration. When set against the backdrop of empty space, being alive, aware, and conscious is truly spectacular.

Nevertheless, we tend to see life as ordinary rather than extraordinary. In our everyday busyness, we overlook that to exist and to be alive in whatever condition is beyond astounding. We are oblivious to the miracle of life. To recognize one's existence within the context of all existence stuns the thinking man.

The convergence of love, light, and Divinity within each of us is an undeniable miracle.

If your existence doesn't shock you into gratitude, it most definitely should. The odds of you, me, or anyone being born are an astronomical one in four hundred trillion, yet here we are. From within the complex system of chaotic possibilities, we burst forth as a unique, necessary, and never-to-be-replicated manifestation of the Divine. Each soul adds to the radiance of the loving universe and the glorious realization of God.

Indeed, everything in the known and unknown universe would collapse if a single soul were missing. Still, most find it difficult to believe or fully comprehend the stunning reality of their own life, or the critical part they play in the loving universe. The idea that the microcosm is a replica of the macrocosm is not only startling, it is mind-boggling. On a subatomic level, everything that exists, including you and me, is created from the same basic building blocks: atoms and molecules. By analogy, the tiniest pebble and the largest mountain are born of the same stardust.

We are children of the loving universe, the progeny of God.

If God is pure love, then it follows that we, too, are a profound embodiment of love. That which springs from love can only be love itself. For the sheer delight of existence and as the natural unfoldment of beauty, love perpetually unfolds as more love.

Indeed, the center point of all that exists is born of this unfathomable radiance, beauty, and love—*including you and me*. We are the natural unfoldment and wondrous outpouring of God manifest, emanating out in all directions as an infinite array of radiant light. From this jubilant eruption, the entirety of existence took form. Each element is a unique, essential, and beauty-laden expression and manifestation of the Divine.

In essence, as integral components of the microcosm within the macrocosm, we are God manifest in an evolving kaleidoscope of radiant hues of light.

Everything that exists is God, including God.

You are God. I am God. We are all manifestations of the Divine. Each one of us is a unique expression of the same radiant light, a microcosm of divine essence at a subatomic level. Just as a pebble reflects a part of a vast mountain, we mirror the Divine in our existence. We are, like God, embodiments of light, continually expanding through love. In every shadow and light, the divine shines endlessly as love and more love. This eternal, unchanging truth is rediscovered in each life through new perspectives and an open heart, bringing immense joy to our souls and opening pathways for learning and growth.

Our incarnation into the physical world of form and structure serves this very purpose—to *explore and reveal the essence of love in countless, ever-evolving ways.*

A human life is rich with complexity and excitement, marked by both moments of exquisite joy and profound sorrow.

The material world, with its structure and form, serves as a catalyst for our soul's growth and evolution. It provides an array of experiences and opportunities for development, expansion, and transformation that no other realm can offer. As a result, our life experiences may span the spectrum from blissful and beautiful to challenging and transformative.

Every life experience contributes to our personal and collective evolution.

As a result of our unique perspective and innate predispositions, these experiences can be as vast and varied as clouds in the sky. The following summary eloquently captures the profound and poetic essence of our most universally shared human embodiments and life experiences.

For a mathematician, life is a delicious and unsolvable equation. The philosopher experiences life as highbrowed thoughts and elevated thinking. For those who are depressed, sad, or angry, life is a constant, uphill battle. It is a locked door for those suffering and heavy with abuse or loss. For the scholar, stuck inside her head, life is accumulated wisdom and knowledge garnered from books and ancient texts. The more science-minded understands life as the frigid result of a highly improbable and random coincidence. For the musically inclined, life is a collection of musical notes linked together to make a beautiful or discordant song. A religious person views life as a sacred, unfolding prayer or an ominous, threatening storm of stringent rules and oppressive rituals. The poet and the artist experience life as a magnificent collection of shadow and light. And, on and on it goes.

None of the above scenarios is the absolute truth. Life is far more exhilarating and intricate than the tales of heroes and villains we create in our mind and entertain in our imagination. Even in the depths of great sorrow and despair, life is an astounding, sacred gift to the soul.

"To be" rather than "not to be" is a most radiant unfoldment of the divine.

Nothing compares to a single breath of life. Without the foundation of life and self-awareness to recognize it, even the empty void of time and space would be nonexistent. Indeed, to be conscious, have volition, free will, and choice is beyond all concepts of beauty and splendor; it is a treasure beyond all treasures. Nothing can accurately describe the gift and grace of life. It is like pointing to the moon and trying to explain the vast universe; nothing said is the absolute truth.

To this point, every soul is revered, singular, and indispensable in the grand matrix of life and a necessary part of the whole of creation, including your precious soul. The ripple of your thoughts, words, and actions can move mountains, create tsunamis, reverse rivers, and flood deserts.

You are far more powerful than you know or could possibly imagine.

The concept that our actions have far-reaching effects is supported by many spiritual teachings and even by scientific principles. The Butterfly Effect Theory, introduced by Edward Lorenz in the 1960s, illustrates this well. This theory suggests that in complex systems, a tiny change at one point can lead to significant differences in a later state. Essentially, even the smallest alteration in the beginning can drastically change the outcome. The implications of this idea are vast, particularly when considering the impact of our choices. What we do, think, or say holds immense power;

a single thought, word, or action can have monumental consequences, capable of both destruction and creation on a grand scale.

Our every choice pulls us towards or away from love, and is a catalyst of change.

The rippling effect of our choices impact and transform everything and everyone, even the Divine. If we did not exist, the universe, at least as we know it, would be forever altered or nonexistent. Out of the dark nothingness, we arise as a radiant light. We are born of the silence to make a sound for the absolute joy of it.

The sound of you and me manifesting into being is the echoing sound of creation—*the sound of God*. Indeed on a subatomic level, we are a frequency, vibrancy, color, light, and yes, we are a sound. The stunning sound of God is alive, expressed through us, endlessly echoing out to the furtherest reaches of the loving universe. The whole of creation, including you and me, is the unfathomable outpouring of God as more God. Please allow me to express this directly to your beautiful soul.

You are a masterpiece: magnum opus.

Words are too small and limited to fully describe the value of your beautiful soul or the grand purpose of your life. Most assuredly, you don't realize your true value, worth, and purpose, but I do. One of the principal reasons I wrote these Love Letters is to remind you of your intrinsic worth and value; you are a beloved and cherished child of God.

Even these words are simply pointers to this truth, and not the absolute truth. Each of us must see the beauty, truth, and grace of our existence for ourselves, and no one can do it for us. Just as we must choose to see the endless blue sky, the blossoming, fragrant flowers, and the shimmering rays of light slicing through heavy clouds on a dark, rainy day, we must also choose to see our soul's beauty, grace, and goodness.

A poignant and profound quote by Frederik Langbridge highlights this point. *"Two men look out between the same prison bars; one sees the mud, the other sees the stars."*

Our perspective defines our life experience.

Where we set our gaze determines what we see and manifest. Everything is available in the magnetic universe; we can live in lack or embrace our innate abundance. Whatever we choose will be our reality; either way, life is a magnificent gift to our soul. Through our earthly sojourns, we realize our eternal connection with each other, the loving universe, and God.

The good news is that regardless of the direction of our footsteps in the sands of our many lives, we will all eventually find our way home. Just as the waves inevitably find their way back to the seashore, only to return to the ocean, we inevitably find our way back to our loving Creator.

Our lives are a continuous, unfolding love story with the Divine, written in real time.

Each soul that comes into existence is a shimmering spark of light. We are all part of the natural unfoldment of the loving universe and a radiant expression of God's love. Our existence is most definitely not an accident or the random working of fate. Everything that exists is meant to exist, including you and me. We do not live in a cold and unloving universe; the exact opposite is true.

In an effusion of bliss, God manifests into every possible expression of love and shimmering light. One particle is you; another is me; joined together, as an expression of Oneness, they are us. We are one light, one love, and one God. We are not separate or alone. We are part of a greater good experiencing itself in the singularity of multiplicity. For precisely this reason, we came to planet Earth to experience ourselves in individuation, enhance the fullness of Unity, and find our way back to God: brighter and lighter. When we meet each other in the context of a human life, we experience the truth, grace, and goodness of the loving universe alive within us.

Through the looking glass of life, we meet and know ourselves, others, and God in every possible way and hue of light. To witness the beauty of a blossoming flower, taste falling rain on our tongue, savor the scent of freshly baked cookies, and feel the soft touch of a hand is the profound richness of being alive. The myriad of life experiences add to our personal development, expand the experiential knowledge garnered by the soul, and contribute to the evolution of all.

Each time we return to this world of form, matter, and structure, we add another golden thread of love and a shimmering spark of light to the glorious tapestry of the universe.

Free will and choice make us uniquely human.

We have the autonomy to choose the direction we walk in life, each step shaping our reality. Yet, our path is not rigidly fixed; it is in a state of constant change and flow. While we have the power to choose our life's journey, the final destination of our soul is not ours to select. Securely cradled in the divine embrace, our souls find their ultimate rest and safety in the loving arms of God.

Both our individual paths and our collective experiences contribute to the broader narrative of the loving universe. Our journey, woven through eons of joy and sorrow, has brought us to this moment. This life presents as a significant opportunity for transformation and change, serving as a portal to a more luminous version of ourselves and marking a period of rapid spiritual growth. However, this spiritual journey through the three-dimensional realm of choice, change, and contrast isn't bound by linear constraints of time or space. While it might seem we traverse a path from point A to point Z, the reality is far more complex; in truth, all experiences unfold simultaneously in both time and space, revealing the multidimensional nature of our existence.

Time is not linear; it is stacked upon itself in the "Eternal Now."

This topic invites a longer discussion, which extends beyond the scope of these writings.

Nevertheless, it's worth noting that the time and space of our current reality are aspects of what can be called the *"Eternal Now"*. In this realm, everything exists in a state of completion, lovingly awaiting our arrival. The experiences we encounter in the present moment are intricately aligned with the choices we make and the corresponding energetic field we create. This interplay between our decisions and the universe's response is a dance within the Eternal Now, where each moment is both a creation and a destination in itself.

Regardless of the paths we choose or how we navigate through the time and space of our existence, love is an unwavering constant, and vital animating force. This life, your precious life, is a beautiful masterpiece being painted in real time. Every stroke on the canvas of your existence is necessary and cannot be left out; all souls are cherished and forever loved. Wherever we find ourselves in the grand matrix of our life is precisely where we should be.

There are no mistakes in the universe.

On another level, we have already found our way back to God in every possible expression of love and variation of light. Because everything is already in completion, we have limitless roads leading back to the same place, back to love: *God.*

In other words, in this particular sphere of existence, within the freewill paradigm, we choose the roads we travel but not the destination.

Where we find ourselves in every moment matches our energetic state, resonance, and vibrational alignments.

We are not stuck on a particular path; nothing is set in stone. At any moment, we can make a different choice and shift the compass of our current and future lives. These subtle shifts in consciousness can significantly alter the course of our destiny. They can lead us down roads that result in entirely different, and perhaps unexpected and glorious outcomes. On the other extreme, traveling down the darker avenues of life can be difficult for the soul, slowing our evolutionary process, and sometimes even moving us backward.

Whatever road we choose, the human experience is enriching for the soul. When seen with a broader, more expansive lens, everything works together for the good, even the bad. Bearing this in mind, though we may still have regrets and need to make amends, even our worst mistakes provide wisdom and knowledge that promote our spiritual evolution.

Our most horrible and beautiful expressions of self are equally loved and cherished by our loving Creator. Every grain of sand, stone on the ground, leaf on a tree, cloud in the sky, star in the night, and soul that exists is essential to the whole of creation.

Nothing is left out of love; all shadows and light are included.

Nevertheless, many of us have regrets as we get older. We wish that we had done this, that, or the other differently. To repent and make amends is beneficial for the soul, but regret doesn't serve anyone. To wallow in the past, with no possibility of changing it, is a waste of our precious life force and a heavy burden that shackles us to our pain. Focusing on the negative, we attract it to us. It would be wiser to learn from our mistakes, make amends when possible, and then use our energy to make the world a better place. This not only changes our reality, it changes the world.

We make the world a better place by being better people.

A powerful story illustrating this point comes from a great Buddhist monk, Thic Nahn Hanh. An American soldier went to this great spiritual teacher, tormented by a recurring dream. He explained that a crowd of Vietnamese children came running toward him during his duty, possibly concealing explosives or bombs. He shouted for the children to stop, but they didn't; instead, they charged forward. The soldier retells the horror of shooting a small boy as he leaped toward him and the recurring dream that replayed the event nightly, over and over again.

The great master, with compassion and kindness, reminded the soldier that he could not bring the boy back to life, telling him that instead of needlessly suffering or tormenting himself, it would be a better use of his life force and soul energy to be in service, and to do good. He suggested the soldier find an orphaned Vietnamese child and raise him as his own. The soldier followed the master's directive and his nightmares immediately stopped.

This story serves as a poignant reminder of how dwelling in bitterness and regret depletes our life force, diminishes our vibrational frequency, and keeps us stuck in the repetitive patterns of the past, perpetuating a low vibrational energy field. The uplifting truth is that it's never too late for a new beginning. Instead of succumbing to regret, we can gratefully seize the opportunity for change and embrace the unyielding freedom to start anew.

As liberated beings, we hold the power to amend our past and shape our future.

And when the past is irreversible, as in a soldier's regret over a young boy's fate, our best response is to glean wisdom from these moments, offer ourselves forgiveness, and pledge to be catalysts for positive change. This gracious approach transforms our regrets into meaningful lessons, guiding us away from the futility of dwelling on past failures and towards a path of growth and healing.

Within our shared humanity lies a collective depth that profoundly molds the vast and varied experience of mankind.

Please give your self permission to be both human and divine. No one is perfect; we all have our challenges and strengths. Though there is no single right way to live our lives, a good rule to follow is to always try to do our best and continually improve. To this point, we are always doing our best, for if we could have done better, we would have. Even when we're conscious of better alternatives, the truth is that in those specific moments, different choices weren't within our reach—*the evidence being that we didn't make them*. Falling into self-judgment can be easy, yet it often achieves the opposite of our goals, dragging us down instead of lifting us up.

Rather than engaging in self-judgment or criticism, it's wiser to hold firm to the belief that, even in our failures, we are all continuously striving to do our best.

Each setback presents an opportunity to take responsibility, not by dwelling on the past but by reflecting on what can be learned and how we can grow and improve moving forward.

We never step into the same river twice; change is not only a constant, it is unceasing.

Each moment offers us a new beginning. Along with the universe, and everything it encompasses, we are continually changing and evolving at the speed of grace. And again, no matter which path we take or how long it takes to reconnect with our source, no one is ever permanently lost, abandoned, or forsaken.

To this point, life offers a spectrum of paths, some winding through shadows and challenges, others illuminated by peaceful serenity. Yet, each path, in its own unique ways, guides us back to the origin of divine love. It is our individual journey to choose and explore the path that aligns most deeply with the essence of our soul.

The human experience is enriched by our decisive power, the freedom to choose, and the ever-present potential for change, making our journey both exhilarating and challenging. Opting for a different road can profoundly transform the course and results of our lives. In any given moment, we are either progressing or regressing on the paths of our life's journey and soul evolution. In the vast array of choices available in a human life, it can sometimes be difficult to know which way to go, but the truth is that whatever road we travel is the right way for the soul, even if it is the long way home. And remember, no one will be lost forever, forsaken, or abandoned. We will all eventually and inevitably find our way back home to God.

Life is not static; it perpetually moves forward, even if we move backward.

In essence, progress is essential, as standing still means falling behind in the relentless march of life. The diverse paths and adventures life offers are fertile ground for our souls. We mirror our Source through our choices and journeys, shaping our experiences and evolution. Yet, we often face indecision and shifting desires, which scatter our energy and slow our progress.

In addition, we are born with inherent limitations that contribute to our soul's growth. For instance, specific physical traits may determine our suitability for certain professions, such as height influencing a career in basketball or gymnastics.

Rather than viewing these limitations as setbacks, they are pre-birth soul choices meant to shape our life's opportunities and enhance our evolution. Each time we enter life, we carry precisely the resources necessary for particular lessons, providing us with a unique chance to share our light and love. With this perspective in mind, take a moment to reflect: *"What am I doing with my precious life? Is it filled with meaning and purpose? Do I find joy in it? Am I serving both my soul and others? Is this truly the best life I can live?"* These questions may seem critical, but they are not meant for judgment or criticism; instead, they are intended to encourage reflection and personal growth.

Judgments point to opposites, love has no opposite.

The purpose of this self-inquiry is to gently remind us that even subtle shifts and small choices can take us to entirely new and, perhaps, unimagined destinations. Indeed, the tiniest decisions and the slightest adjustments in the course of our lives hold more significance than we might initially realize. They steer us in a particular direction, ultimately leading to specific crossroads rather than others. Our lives are shaped by countless dynamic alignments that are not fixed but constantly change in response to our choices.

The continuous, dynamic flow of the universe underscores the reality that we always possess the power to select a new direction and completely reshape and reinvent our lives and ourselves. While this understanding might make us nervous or anxious about making the right choices, the truth is that sometimes we will, and sometimes we won't.

In the end, when our intentions are rooted in love, everything tends to find its way.

Regardless of the outcome of our choices, good or bad in worldly terms, aligning with our higher values enlivens our soul, paving the path to the Divine. So, dear one, please be a little gentler with your precious soul. Take a deep breath and trust that all is well, even in moments of doubt. Life is a continuous journey of growth, personal development, and soul expansion. To live a peaceful and fulfilling life, we must have patience, extend kindness, and offer forgiveness to ourselves and others.

When life demands adjustments or significant course corrections, instead of being swept away by a sudden flood of emotions or fear, hold onto your loving intentions, stay true to your authentic self, and keep moving forward.

Courage, determination, and strength of character are essential for success, whether in the material world or on a spiritual journey.

By persevering through life's challenges and refusing to give in, we establish a strong foundation for our well-being, ongoing growth, and the evolution of our soul. Consistent effort is crucial for achieving personal goals and worldly success. Having said that, please understand that material success alone will not bring genuine fulfillment.

To the contrary, many times, worldly success, fame, and all the other accolades of life, can leave us feeling empty. For a meaningful and fulfilling life, we must use our success as a tool for personal growth and contribute to making the world a better place through selfless service to others.

As we come to the end of this Love Letter, let me once again remind you that, from a broader perspective, all paths are already complete in the *Eternal Now*. Success, evolution, and the return to the loving embrace of God have already occurred in every possible iteration. What we currently experience as our life is the inevitable unfolding of our choices and their energetic alignment with certain experiences—all for the benefit of our soul and the enrichment of the entire universe.

Thus, whether we journey through darkness or find our way to the light in this specific life is not the ultimate concern; it is a given. What holds the utmost importance is our unique journey of self-discovery and authentic expression of love as we make our way back to God.

Love is all that matters.

Because we are experientially aware of this particular point on the map of our existence, it is a beautiful and necessary opportunity for transformational and spiritual growth. The roads we travel and experiences we have are necessary lessons of self-referential knowledge that contribute a unique hue of light to the radiant universe and the inevitable unfoldment of God.

This life, and all lives, add to our soul's ever-expanding bliss.

Bliss is inherent in our very being and not a consequence of our life circumstances. However, we have to choose to see the good, grace, and God at the center of all things. Life is a glorious gift we get to unwrap and experience in real-time. We are not here by accident; we chose to be here.

In fact, we were excited to come and explore the possibilities of free will, dive into the depths of sorrow, and climb to the heights of joy. We took on the heavy weight of a physical embodiment and willingly came to this world to experience all aspects of life—*to laugh all of our laughter, cry all of our tears, and to know ourselves, others, and God more fully: to evolve.*

The reality of human life is that there is no wrong way to go—all roads lead back to God.

Contrary to popular belief, there is no rush to evolve, and there's no possibility of failure in terms of the soul. Enjoy the experience of being alive and being you; it's a wonderful existence. We are children of the light, and our heritage is Divine. With every thought and action, we create and influence the world in profound ways.

We are far more powerful than most realize. Our unique expression of love and the specific hue of our light have the profound ability to make a difference in this sometimes dark and turbulent world. Reclaiming our inner wisdom, innate goodness, and grace empowers us to become a force of positive change.

Love is our power, grace is our guide, and God is our Source.

Choose wisely, dear one; remember that what you do matters, and it matters a great deal. You are the center point of all existence and the blossoming of the loving universe.

All my love, light,
and blessings now and forever.
— Chrystal Rae

*We must love and respect ourselves
before we can gift this to others*

Letter 21

relationships
lessons of love

All relationships mirror the relationship with ourselves and the Divine.

When we acknowledge the divinity within us, it naturally reveals itself in those around us. Every individual transforms from mere acquaintances or strangers into soul companions on a shared journey of discovery and love. The formidable barriers of ego, judgment, and prejudice dissolve in the profound truth of love and the radiance of divinity.

Every encounter is a sacred dance and communion with the Divine—*a profound, authentic, and deeply sacred experience*. Conflicts, while inevitable in any relationship, are approached with a mindset of resolution rather than retaliation. We actively seek common ground, mutual respect, and deep understanding.

As we tap into the deep reservoir of God's love, our capacity to love expands and extends to encompass the universe and everyone within it. We celebrate the successes of others as our own and offer support during challenging times without expecting anything in return.

Freed from conditions and expectations, love blossoms into selflessness and generosity.

Instead of asking, "*What can you do for me?*" the question shifts to, "*Is this alignment beneficial for both of us?*" Relationships are the foundation of self-discovery, spiritual growth, and the evolution of the soul. Among all human experiences, none holds greater value than relationships. And, the most important relationship we will ever have is the one with ourselves—*though frequently the most neglected*. The kindness we extend to ourselves reflects how we will interact with others.

Self-love and self-respect are essential for nurturing deep and empathetic connections.

When we prioritize self-care, we set a higher standard not only for ourselves, but also for those around us. This act of prioritizing our well-being leads to a transformative effect in our lives, reshaping our relationships in the process.

As we evolve, some relationships naturally come to an end, while others become stronger and more united. Cultivating healthier relationships is much like exploring unknown territories— *it can be demanding, often entailing periods of solitude and uncertainty*. Indeed, the realignment of our relationships may resemble a storm, tumultuous and unsettling. Yet, many relationships, despite their challenges, serve as powerful catalysts for rejuvenation and fresh beginnings that emerge in their wake.

After the storm, the sun reclaims the sky, hope blossoms into endless shades of blue, and flowers bloom in a vibrant celebration of life.

This rebirth brings vitality and strength, yet embracing our true selves and staying authentic doesn't mean imposing our will or wishes onto others, coercing them to change according to what we want or expecting them to behave differently. Each of us is entitled to be ourselves. Our personal growth does not mandate that others follow suit. Whether others change or not remains their prerogative, a choice they make independently.

The path of our individual lives is always ours to determine. Irrespective of the actions or inactions of others, our well-being remains solely our responsibility. Nevertheless, if we have energetically outgrown a relationship, it will come to its natural end. Often, both parties sense the dissatisfaction, even if unspoken. While disharmony in a relationship may appear one-sided, it is energetically implausible. The magnetic universe operates on the law of attraction, where "*like attracts like*." Thus, if one person in the relationship is unhappy, it suggests that the other person may share similar feelings, whether consciously acknowledged or not.

Because our lives are our responsibility, how, and with whom we invest our energy and time is of the utmost importance.

Deciding to stay in or leave a relationship is always within our power. It's unrealistic to expect someone else to change to meet our needs and preferences. Instead, we should focus on our own inner growth and personal improvement. As we improve ourselves, we naturally uplift those around us. This positive influence promotes a culture of integrity, respect, and love, rejecting substandard behaviors. Setting new boundaries and exploring new possibilities, we establish higher standards for ourselves and those we interact with. Tolerating disrespect or being taken for granted is no longer an option. We fiercely guard our energy and choose carefully where and with whom we share it.

It is a common misconception that a loving person is merely a "*lovey-dovey*" pushover or easily swayed. This is far from accurate, the opposite is true. It is much easier and more natural to succumb to unkindness, cruelty, or react with negativity. This fear-based behavior is a natural alignment with our more primal and predatory instincts, and is to be expected at certain levels of consciousness.

On the other hand, staying aligned with higher values and choosing a path of love over fear requires a concerted effort and a conscious departure from automatic, fear-driven human behavior.

To break free from the heavy chains of fear, we must, first and foremost, honor ourselves.

When we stand up for ourselves, recognize our inherent value, and establish healthier boundaries regarding how we are treated, we experience a transformative rebirth in our lives. This transformation leads to a heightened sense of self-worth and personal value.

As we reveal our inner light and allow it to shine brighter, its warmth and radiance naturally reach and affect those around us. Just as the sun breaks through heavy winter clouds, warming and enlivening the cold Earth's surface, our brighter presence transforms and revitalizes all our relationships.

Our conversations and even simple gestures become infused with kindness, patience, and genuine concern, creating a positive impact on those we interact with.

As we purify our inner world of thought and emotion, the outer world of relationship undergoes radical transformation and realignment to meet our heighten state of consciousness.

Indeed, with this heightened awareness and the expanded capacity to love, we reshape the landscape of our relationships with ourselves and others. What was once barren and cold transforms into a warm sun of boundless possibility. This is a conscious movement from the inner world to the outer world, one of self-reliance and grace. Instead of desperately searching for love outside ourselves, we move inward, accessing the eternal wellspring of love continuously emerging within each of us.

As part of our radiant transformation, we naturally move beyond feelings of smallness, unworthiness, and fear.

Much like the caterpillar destined to become a butterfly, we emerge from the dark cocoon of fear and discover our soul's burgeoning capacity for flight.

This transformation not only elevates our energy and aligns us with radiant possibilities for our life, but also contributes positively to the universe we inhabit. In this expanded state, love and kindness become our spiritual wings, lifting us above the mundane cacophony of daily life into a realm of limitless possibility and boundless potential.

This shift in consciousness ripples through all of our relationships, prompting energetic realignment and personal transformation. As we traverse the ever-changing terrain of personal connection and disconnection, the universe broadens, collides, and occasionally collapses. Consequently, our relationships may either naturally grow closer and strengthen, or diverge and dissolve.

In the name of love and for the sake of love, we must be willing to walk away and lose everything.

Yet, this doesn't mean we should quickly end a relationship because of a sudden storm or an unforeseen setback that temporarily clouds our world. Instead, we need to decide carefully and with compassion and discernment whether the relationship serves our greater good. If it does, and if there's enough love and mutual respect, then it's worth every effort to strengthen and maintain the connection, even amidst challenges.

On the other hand, when a relationship no longer contributes to our soul's well-being, it is advisable to conclude it with grace and swiftness. Lingering in unhealthy relationships may be harmful to both our inner and outer selves.

That said, there is no right answer or universal solution as to whether we stay or leave a relationship, but the one constant is always love.

Love is the bond that keeps us connected when the waves of change are crushing and cruel or the seas of life are rough and raging.

However, what many refer to as love is nothing more than a union of convenience. The true expression of divine love cannot be compared to the utilitarian expression of personal needs and ambitions, sometimes cloaked as love. True love is independent of a transactional union based on convenience, propagation of family, economic resources, personal security, or social benefit.

Though everything is included in the broader scope of love, the aforementioned superficial unions are not its fullest expression. They are divergent paths of convenience or advantage that resemble a business deal rather than a loving union. When the binding force of a relationship is negotiable and the terms become unsatisfactory, one or the other will likely terminate the contract. Though not ideal, even these divergent paths will eventually lead back to the truth of love. The simplest expression of love is a doorway to the Divine and a passage to something greater than the transient, temporal world.

All relationships gift the soul with treasured bits of light and necessary pieces of the night.

Everything in the loving universe is born of the unmoving foundation of love and the whole of creation. In addition, everyone in our sphere of influence, particularly those nearest to our hearts, serve a profound purpose. They either fortify our strength or catalyze transformative growth.

True love is a raging, savage bonfire of the soul, burning wildly in the heart.

Love is both the fuel and the fiery flames consuming the past and clearing the way for a brighter tomorrow; it cannot be dampened, altered, or stopped. Love is an invincible force of goodness, grace, and God, showing up in many unexpected ways. To this point, even the most loving acts of benevolence and kindness can at times seem cruel or unkind.

For example, a rebellious teenager might perceive his parents' disciplinary actions as unwarranted and unjust. Yet, in such instances, these sanctions might indeed represent the most profound form of love and concern from his parents.

Without such boundaries and repercussions, he might struggle to navigate the tumultuous waters of adolescence, let alone thrive into mature adulthood. Furthermore, whether someone stays or leaves does not necessarily reflect their love or lack thereof.

In fact, certain people enter our lives to agitate or make us uncomfortable, at times even miserable. Though it may be unpleasant, their presence ignites change that otherwise would be unavailable. Indeed, some of our most transformational relationships will be highly complicated or complex. Challenging relationships can be like a roller coaster ride—thrilling at times and overwhelming at others. If a relationship flows effortlessly, or is difficult yet still brings joy, it is worth nurturing and improving.

On the other hand, if a relationship consistently depletes our energy or diminishes our life force, its long-term sustainability comes into question. Either way, it's important to remember that every relationship, regardless of its nature, has value.

Even our most difficult relationships contribute to our personal growth and empowerment.

Bearing this in mind, a complex or challenging relationship doesn't automatically warrant an end. Deciding whether to stay or leave is a deeply personal choice and should not be influenced solely by the good or bad opinion of others.

Relationships are unique and varied; often, it's the struggles we encounter in them that provide the necessary lessons for our personal growth and development.

In some instances, enduring challenges can foster a more profound commitment, unity, and affection. Nevertheless, if a relationship consistently depletes our energy or hinders our spiritual progress, choosing to separate, amicably or otherwise, becomes a means to further our soul's journey and honor the self.

On the flip side, some relationships may appear fine on the surface, with nothing overtly wrong, but also lacking any substantial positivity. Despite their outward appearance of harmony, these connections offer limited opportunities for personal growth or spiritual progress.

Often, relationships marked by apathy can leave us feeling empty and without purpose. Moving away from these unfulfilling or stagnant connections is essential for our spiritual growth. Having said that, ending a relationship can be quite daunting. This is especially true when we are comfortable with our own discomfort. However, it is a necessary step to open our hearts to deeper, more meaningful connections that truly contribute to the evolution of our soul.

All relationships, whether pleasant or not-so-pleasant, provide unique opportunities for personal growth and spiritual advancement.

The decision to leave or to stay in a relationship is not subject to moral judgment; we must do what most benefits and nurtures our soul. Even if we perceive our choice as *"wrong"* by societal standards or religious doctrine, there is no condemnation on a soul level. Our decision to leave or stay is a deeply personal one, guided by our own understanding and needs.

In the complex landscape of human existence, compassion abounds. We are forever loved and supported by a loving universe.

When we honor the deep longing of our soul, even the ending of a relationship can unfold with serenity and grace.

Whether we draw closer or step away from a individual or a relationship, our intentions of love and kindness turn each step into a silent prayer, a heartfelt offering, and a genuine wish for our shared well-being, safety, joy, and abundance.

Having said that, for the vast majority, untangling the intricate web of emotional bonds and bringing a relationship to its conclusion can be a profoundly intense experience of much pain and heartache. With this in mind, deciding to stay or step away from a relationship should never be approached lightly. The profound and sacred connections we forge with others have a lasting impact on the journey of our souls. Rather than succumbing to impulsive reactions amidst emotional turmoil, it is much wiser to find our equilibrium before making substantial changes to our relationships.

Some conflicts or problems make our relationship stronger and more loving. They unite us in ways that otherwise would not be possible. Just as the roots of a tree become stronger when tested by the wind, our relationships can also deepen and strengthen through the process of overcoming adversity.

In the wake of today's storm, flowers of tomorrow blossom.

Weathering storms together can strengthen our bond an deepen our connection. On the other hand, some storms sweep into our lives with such intensity, pain, havoc, and ruin, that there is no other choice but to end the relationship. This process can be intricate and difficult, especially for those who fear change or are entrenched in unhealthy co-dependent patterns.

However, if a relationship blackens the light of our soul, it becomes crucial to gather courage, embrace bravery, and be willing to do what's necessary to reclaim our independence and self-identity. True liberation requires stepping out of our comfort zone and venturing into the daunting realm of uncertainty. This is important not only for our psychological well-being but also for the evolution of our soul.

We must hold ourselves in the highest regard or no one else will.

Bearing this in mind, some people come into our lives as stern teachers, pushing us towards transformation. While others serve as mirrors, gently reflecting our intrinsic worth and inner beauty. On a soul level, whether a relationship serves as a mirror or stern educator, the love that binds us remains unaltered. Given this perspective, it's crucial to exercise discernment in selecting a life partner. Merely experiencing attraction or love for someone doesn't necessarily equate to compatibility or a healthy match. Profound affection can exist even when it's not reciprocated. Moreover, we might be captivated by someone who exhibits cruelty and unkindness. Opting to enter or persist in such a relationship implies settling for less than we deserve. By permitting mistreatment, we generate an unhealthy energetic imbalance that reverberates across various dimensions.

While love must be our foundation, it is not the sole factor in partner selection.

Recognizing our worth and embracing relationships that nurture rather than diminish our well-being is essential for maintaining emotional, mental, and spiritual equilibrium. Equally important is choosing someone who respects us, esteems our worth, and extends kindness toward us. When we meet someone who not only sparks mutual attraction but also loves us unconditionally, enabling us to flourish authentically, it paves the way for profound transformation and growth. Nonetheless, a thriving and harmonious relationship necessitates more than love; it requires a connection on multiple levels: physical, mental, emotional, intellectual, and spiritual. These levels collectively contribute to a more profound and enriching bond between partners. Let's delve into each dimension:

Physical Connection: Establishing physical intimacy and attraction forms a pivotal aspect of a romantic relationship. This attraction encompasses not only sexual intimacy but also non-sexual physical gestures such as tender touches, embraces, hand-holding, and other forms of affection. Feeling secure and at ease in each other's physical presence can reinforce the emotional connection.

Mental Connection: Nurturing shared interests, values, and life aspirations cultivates a robust mental connection between partners. Engaging in activities that stimulate mental acuity that both enjoy or indulging in intellectual conversations can create a unique bond based on shared experiences and ideas.

Emotional Connection: Building emotional intimacy involves openly exchanging feelings, vulnerabilities, and life experiences. The ability to communicate candidly and empathize with each other's emotions serves as the bedrock of this connection. Trust and emotional support are pivotal elements that underpin this dimension.

Intellectual Connection: Participating in stimulating discussions and dialogues about diverse subjects contributes to an intellectual connection. This entails respecting one another's viewpoints and being receptive to learning from each other. Intellectual compatibility can lead to continual personal development and mutual admiration.

Spiritual Connection: In some partnerships, a shared spiritual or philosophical belief system serves as a source of connection and purpose. This might encompass engaging in spiritual practices, attending religious ceremonies, or having conversations about the essence of life and existence.

Every individual and relationship is distinct; a complete alignment on all levels is not realistic, and such diversity is entirely normal. What truly matters is that both partners feel acknowledged, valued, supported, fulfilled, and connected within the relationship.

We started this conversation by saying that for a strong and lasting partnership, first and foremost we need love. In addition, we also need to have shared values, be able to communicate, respect each other, and keep our agreed upon commitments within the union. While not all categories of connection may be fully shared, having common ground enhances the potential for personal growth and a lasting, meaningful union. An additional aspect to take into account is the possibility of having lived multiple lifetimes with the same individual, encountering similar situations for the purpose of soul growth and the resolution of ongoing lessons. This repetitive cycle can be why we might experience an instant sense of familiarity or aversion with someone, rooted in past lives and karmic connections.

Though it may be true that "opposites attract," when our dissimilarities are too pronounced or our commonalities too sparse, the odds of the relationship enduring over time are low.

After the initial butterfly stage of a relationship, most default back to their true likes and dislikes. Once we re-embrace our authentic *"likes and dislikes,"* we might find ourselves moving in divergent directions or gradually growing apart. Consequently, before formally committing to a relationship, it is crucial to make an objective assessment regarding the presence of shared interests substantial enough to uphold a meaningful connection over the long term.

For a relationship to thrive, evolve, and persevere, a shared space of connection and common ground is essential.

Alongside the essential prerequisites of love, mutual respect, and aligned values, the greater the number of shared areas of common interest, the higher the likelihood of the relationship's endurance. Nevertheless, the weather of life is unpredictable; even the best relationships will endure stormy days and dark nights. However, navigating challenging relationships requires careful consideration due to their potential impact on our physical, emotional, and mental well-being.

If a relationship consistently brings about stress, dissatisfaction, or unhappiness over time, it's essential to recognize the toll it can take on our overall health—*body, mind, and spirit*. When faced with such situations, we have two viable options, each with its complexities:

Collaborative Rebuilding: When a relationship has hit a rough patch, proactively working together to rebuild friendship, love, and mutual respect can be a transformative approach. The process involves respecting differences, identifying areas of commonality, and fostering a sense of connection. Although challenging, this path can lead to growth and healing if both individuals are dedicated to making meaningful changes.

Compassionate Closure: When it becomes evident that the relationship lacks shared ground, potential for growth, or essential respect, it may be more beneficial to end it peacefully. Though we intellectually grasp that this step is necessary for our own well-being, the emotional aspect remains delicate. Letting go of any relationship, particularly one with a shared history, is laden with emotional challenges. Ultimately, acknowledging when a relationship no longer enhances our well-being and then to find the courage to make the difficult choice of either staying or leaving is a necessary act of self-care, signifying an investment in our personal growth and happiness. Nonetheless, fear and apathy often keep us trapped in unhealthy or outgrown relationships.

Embracing a bit of discomfort now is preferable to facing greater challenges later.

As previously mentioned, many people choose to stay in negative relationships due to their familiarity and convenience. However, this approach is neither advisable nor beneficial for our souls. Staying in a stagnant or outgrown relationship adversely affects our health, stifles personal growth, and blocks spiritual advancement.

When a partnership becomes a joyless, barren desert, offering neither hope nor happiness, it is a definite sign that the journey together has ended. If we remain, driven by fear or apathy, our lives become empty and void. On the other extreme, in a protective stance or through unconscious self-sabotage, some of us may inadvertently avoid or disrupt the chance for lasting connections and intimacy. This pattern, often stemming from underlying fears or past wounds, can unintentionally impede our journey towards happiness and deep, meaningful bonds. Either way, our ability to create and sustain harmonious relationships is a key indicator of our overall well-being and happiness. While a partner can bring immense joy and love, or the opposite, it is ultimately up to us to ensure our own well-being. With this broader perspective on the soul's journey, it's important to note that happiness is not the sole objective of a human life.

A truly fulfilling existence is born of a purpose-driven life that embraces a wide spectrum of experiences, emotions, and feelings—from sheer bliss and happiness to the depths of sorrow and despair.

This rich tapestry of experiences contributes to our personal development and soul advancement, whether our relationships are pleasant or not. In this context, some relationships act as catalysts for change, offer comfort, and provide genuine support that enhances and enriches our lives. Indeed, when a relationship brings joy, stimulates growth, and enriches our spiritual journey, it's worth every effort to reinforce our bonds of love.

Continuing our soul's journey with a beloved, growing together, is an experience of unparalleled beauty and sacredness. The seeds of such a union create universes of blossoming flowers and warm sunny days.

To be held in the arms of the beloved for lifetimes is a joy beyond joy.

On the other hand, when a relationship no longer nurtures the soul or is detrimental to our well-being, it is prudent to go our separate ways. The most challenging scenario is when there is nothing wrong with the relationship but also nothing right. Then, the relationship will feel dull, apathetic, and empty.

To paraphrase Khalil Gibran, we will "*cry half of our tears and laugh half of our laughter*" and live a mundane and ordinary life of little or no personal growth. This mundane, apathetic state often spirals into "*the dark night of the soul*" or "*hits rock bottom.*"

Allow me to elaborate. When we reach the nadir or hit rock bottom, we must acknowledge our vulnerability and seek divine guidance and aid. Essentially, we are forced to get out of our own way, move out of stagnation, and step into the unknown. While this transformational process can be painful, it fundamentally nourishes our soul and promotes our evolution.

On the upside, as we spiritually progress, suffering, pain, and dark nights of the soul cease to be the automatic markers of our transformation and change. Instead, we are naturally drawn to make more conscious choices, reclaim our decisive power to direct our future, and lovingly explore our relationships.

To truly love, we must be willing to fight for love, die for love, and live for love.

Indeed, it takes great courage to stay for love, not leave, or to go in love and not stay. It requires immense inner calm to walk when everyone runs, to remain silent when everyone screams, and to choose love and light in a world of fear and darkness. When we realize that no one is coming to save us, and that we get to save ourselves, we take our power back and are empowered to do our soul work. We have to be willing to go it alone and able to lose everything, or be a slave to our desires or a prisoner of our fears.

We are spiritual beings having a spiritual experience in a world of form and matter for the absolute joy of the experience.

Being unshackled from the past and moving past our fear is the great blessing of being human and the gift of free will. Only when we willingly step into the fire of our transformation are we truly free to be who we are meant to be.

This realization liberates us from those things and people that keep us in smallness and shame. Then, all our relationships are instantly transformed, including the most important relationship with ourselves. It is essential to mention that regardless of our spiritual attainment or lack thereof, not all of our relationships will turn out well.

On the contrary, as previously mentioned, many outgrown relationships will fade away in light of our transformation. This progressive change and downward spiral will be most notable in a marital union. Although it may seem better to remain bonded to one another for life, *which is ideal*, this is not always true.

Marriage is a sacred commitment that expresses love and merits both respect and preservation.

Yet, when it has fulfilled its course, it may be best to conclude the relationship—*for your well-being and the betterment of those who draw from your light*. Disengaging from relationships that no longer nurture us not only liberates us to pursue soul growth and personal progress but invariably extends the same liberation to others. Dissolving a marital bond might seem contradictory to the notion of indissoluble matrimony, yet the core of love is unequivocal freedom. True love is the opposite of being held hostage to preserve an outgrown vow.

When genuine love exists, our primary concern is the well-being of each other, regardless of whether it entails staying together or parting ways.

Within a marital bond, it's commonly assumed that preserving the union is synonymous with pursuing the greater good for both parties. However, this assumption doesn't always hold. When it becomes evident that separation or dissolution is in the best interest of one or both individuals, the most compassionate choice is to set each other free.

As a point of reflection, we should ask ourselves if our presence in another's life serves the betterment of both. If the answer is no, then it is necessary and crucial for the well-being of our soul to release ourselves and others from the relationship. On the other hand, if the answer is yes, then regardless of how complicated the relationship may be, we should commit to making it better and better every day.

Many underestimate the value of small, meaningful gestures of love that collectively weigh heavier on a relationship than a one-time grand act.

The foundation of a happy partnership is the consistent practice of kindness, consideration, grace, tolerance, and forgiveness towards each other, in both grand and simple gestures.

Sadly, the initial thrill of a relationship often gives way to the routine of daily life, leading us to take our partners for granted. Such neglect is detrimental both in the short and long term. Over time, this complacency is often the main culprit behind the breakdown of many relationships. Though it may take years, neglect and entitlement are typically at the heart of these endings.

For a healthy relationship, it's essential to continually reflect, asking, "*Is this the most loving response I can offer to this person or situation?*"

Please include your well-being when you ask and answer this question. If it aligns with genuine love and kindness, proceed; if not, make a different, more loving choice for yourself and others. This one exercise, to pause and consider whether our thoughts, words, and actions are loving and kind, will significantly improve all our relationships. Love holds the power to transform everything and everyone, including us.

When our relationships are grounded in love, everything works out, even if it does not. Opting for love, no matter the circumstances, might seem simple but requires deep personal honesty. Many of us simply skim the surface of our lives, avoiding the depths of our feelings. This superficiality limits our compassion for ourselves and others.

Every relationship is a gift to the soul, even those that challenge us.

Whether we are talking about a marriage, a friendship, a co-worker, a boss, or a random stranger on the street, it is always a personal choice to lovingly engage or disengage. Still, it can be difficult to know if we should stay or go, especially with intimate relationships. The feeling body always knows the answer, but we have to quiet down to hear its soft whisperings.

A powerful exercise to access your inner knowing is to imagine yourself in one experience and then the other. For example, imagine staying in a relationship. As you do, fully experience all the feelings, emotions, and sensations that arise in the body, both good and not-so-good. Then, do the same exercise, but this time, imagine leaving the relationship. Again, experience the feelings, emotions, and sensations in your body. Notice how one experience feels more truthful and abundant while the other does not.

This exercise offers crucial insights, guiding us towards more heartfelt, soul-aligned decisions. No matter the direction we take, we are always journeying towards the divine. Even if we stray or choose a less direct route, we will eventually return to the truth. The path we choose, whether meandering and long or short and direct, doesn't define our value or worth on a soul level.

Every soul, including your precious soul, is a unique manifestation of the Divine.

So please be a little kinder and more gentle in regard to your relationships, including the most important relationship with yourself.

Allow yourself and others the space and grace to embody both human and divine aspects. Remember in a benevolent universe, all paths lead home, and every life experience and relationship, even those that challenge us, serve the soul's evolutionary process and the greater good of all.

As we conclude this Love Letter on relationships, remember that despite our differences and challenges, we are all bound by love. Our relationships are threads of light linking us to each other and to the Divine. In this light, all our experiences and relationships are essential to our spiritual journey, enlightening and enriching our souls.

With this more expansive perspective, a heartache becomes a seed for growth, and a joyful union a gateway to the Divine. Indeed, every interaction, even those that challenge our capacity to love, is sacred, holy, and treasured by the soul.

    I hope these words find a safe and comforting place in your heart and that our footsteps again meet in the sands of our many lives yet to come.

My most important relationship has always been, and will always be—you.

— Chrystal Rae

A human life unfolds as a thrilling adventure of the soul

Letter 22

adventure
the epic journey

Life is a grand and glorious adventure of the soul.

It is an unfolding journey filled with joy, laughter, tears, pain, and sorrow. The physical embodiment afforded on planet Earth is much sought-after in soul realms. The human experience is a fast track of personal growth and evolution. Life is a grand adventure of the soul. Each breath is a wonderful gift we should unwrap with great care and appreciation. Every beat of the heart brings us closer to the truth of love and the "*why*" of our existence. It is a magical opportunity to know the fullness of being, the beauty of existence, and the grandeur of God.

The journey of the soul into and out of the temporal world is a radiant adventure of deep contrast, limitless choices, and constant change. Our very existence, within the context of all existence, is as spectacular and nuanced as the sun breaking through the heavy curtain of clouds, announcing the arrival of a new day. We get to unwrap these shining moments of love and expansion in real time.

Experience teaches us what cannot be taught through words or any other way; it is the greatest of teachers. The *"experience of experience"* is the most crucial teaching of a human life.

A single breath holds an entire universe of possibility in its open hand.

Just as a wave inevitably makes its way to the seashore and then returns to the ocean enriched by the journey, we, too, during the tides of our lives, collect hidden treasures, radiant bits of light, and dark remnants of the night. As we fall into the endless sky of a new day, there are no limits or boundaries except those we bring upon ourselves.

Every breath is a lifetime unto itself.

Though the ever-changing weather of life is beyond our control, we alone decide the direction of our footsteps in the sand. The ordinary and the extraordinary may dull and amaze us, but only love is real. Everything else is a dark illusion, mere shadows dancing on the walls. This truth is unveiled in the silence of morning stars, before the lingering shadows of yesterday darken the bottom of our shoes. Together with the rising sun, we rise, lighter, brighter, and more alive. With the seamless arrival of golden light that slowly spreads across the earth in a warm blanket of renewal and life, even the blackest of nights is absorbed into the sun of a new day.

Though a loss is forever a loss, the past cannot be altered, and yesterday's tragedy cannot be changed, each new day is yet another opportunity to start over. In the soft light of this awakening, before the busy unveilment of the rising sun, hidden truths are unveiled, and God is revealed. The morning knows why the songbird sings and the church bells ring. Every musical note is a song of hope just waiting to be sung. Even a sad, painful song is a happy moment gone wrong. Every beat of the heart is Nature's way of welcoming what may be. Each soul is a tall, towering tree, born of divinity and the root of God. Life is reborn, again and again, in the fragrant glory of a new day.

Nature serves the soul, as shadows serve the light.

A walk along the ocean's edge teaches us as much or more than anything spoken or said. All knowledge is incomplete without the muddy dirt of Mother Earth under our feet.

The human experience of love and fear fills the hollow void of the known and bravely dives into the dark depths of the unknown. To this end, we come together with certain souls to have specific experiences and learn about ourselves, life, and God. Every moment is a priceless jewel. It is a timeless treasure and a fortunate turn of fate to be conscious and aware.

The moments we share are necessary and divine. However, our time together quickly fades into the horizon along with the setting sun.

To be alive, to exist, and to be you is the most miraculous expression of the Divine.

To be you, the perfectly imperfect you with all that encompasses, both the beautiful and the broken, is a blessing beyond all blessings, and a gift of unparalleled magnitude. From within the elegant complexity of eternity and a place of absolute completeness, we shrink ourselves into the smallness of a human life.

The inherent constraints of a physical world are our temporary home and the hollow seashell of our personal transformation and soul expansion.

Gathered bits of light and broken pieces of the night add to the heroic journey of humanity.

The wisdom and knowledge acquired in a single human life is greater than many lives in any other realm or world. Nevertheless, the sacred sojourn of the soul, from the relative perspective of the infinite, comes to its completion almost as soon as it begins.

After we take our last breath, at the very moment of death, we are once again wrapped in the warm embrace and loving arms of the Divine. Our awareness quickly expands as we escape the harsh confines of the body and Earth's density. We fade back into the warm blanket of the night and re-emerge on the other side as shimmering light.

The stories we bring, and songs we sing, add to the larger context of humanity and the absoluteness of God. The love that created us also expands with us.

We are born of love and shall return to love as more love.

From this broader context, it all makes sense. When we see ourselves and the world through the eyes of love and compassion, everything works together for the greater good of all.

Despite all the beauty and horror, when life in the physical realm comes to its inevitable end, there is a great sadness, shock, and deep longing for one more breath. We long for one more experience of life and love in a visceral embodiment. We long to do something we didn't do, go somewhere we didn't go, and say something we didn't say. We long for one more heartfelt embrace and to walk along the seashore of life one more time.

Even the sad, suffering souls, who take their own lives, hunger to rewind time and start over again. The surprise for many will be that, even as the looming shadow of death darkens the halls of our home, love does not die. After we leave our body, the radiant truth of love is revealed in a spectacular burst of light, more glorious than a thousand suns. Though we often take our existence for granted and overlook the miracle of life, when our sky suddenly turns dark, the heart stops beating, and the clock stops ticking, none are without regret. Indeed, every breath, even our very last breath has a lesson to impart.

When there is more time behind us than before us, each breath becomes a priceless treasure.

Every moment of life has something to teach us if we listen and learn. Everything, and everyone, is both our student and our teacher. If we are aware, watch, and listen, a random dust particle, suspended in the heavy afternoon haze, has a secret message of hope and an untold truth to unveil.

Everything works together for the good, even the *"so-called"* bad; this includes our unexpected arrival and sudden departure from this world. When we have completed our learning in a particular life, we are drawn back to our source, leaving our earthly body and cares behind. Then, like the foamy bubbles that quickly dissolve back into the seashore and are reborn in another wave on another day, we, too, re-emerge from our radiant source and find our way back to the ocean of life.

After a time of rest and recuperation, we have in-depth consultations with our beloved guides and caring teachers who lovingly assist us in reviewing the lessons of our lives. We see what we have done and what we still need to do.

We are shown, in great detail, our accomplishments and failures. We see the most important moments of our lives from every perspective and point of view. In this way, we understand the truth of who we are, what we have done, where we are going, and why we exist.

Without the heavy veil of the physical body, we see everything and everyone from the more expansive perspective of infinite connection, radiant light, and unending love.

After an honest review of the life that we just completed, we willingly, happily, and gratefully continue our earth-bound exploration of shadow and light. With much excitement, joy, and enthusiasm, we incarnate into the exact circumstances and conditions that best promote our individuated soul expansion and benefit all. However, contrary to what many believe, we don't necessarily return to planet Earth or into another physical embodiment. There are many universes, multiverses, and species of life.

Like a shooting star swallowed back into the dark of night, we, too, return to our source in a radiant burst of light.

Either way, the love that created us and is us (*God manifest*) dives back into the ocean of life for the glorious adventure of being. For many, the sorrow of leaving the earthly realm behind is realizing they forgot to enjoy the journey. They focused on the forest and overlooked the trees.

They cursed the bumps on the road instead of enjoying the wild and wonderful ride. They hid in the shadows, wallowed in their pain, and locked the doors of their heart. Like a caterpillar, unaware of the possibility of flight, they never spread their wings or stepped out of the night.

Many do not recognize the beauty of their existence until the door of life closes behind them. Then, with the clarity born of much sorrow and regret at the moment of death, they long for another chance to do it differently. Soon, they are reborn in similar circumstances to complete life lessons they neglected or left undone.

Others, further along the evolutionary path, live with their eyes and hearts wide open. They watch the leaves change, along with the seasons, and understand life's grandeur, beauty, and majesty. At the end of their time on Earth, they return to God's loving arms, content and prepared to continue to the next most radiant expression of self.

These more advanced beings rarely choose to reincarnate on Earth. Instead, they gravitate towards an alternate dimension that reflects our world but exists in a state of greater compassion and consciousness, far removed from the physical density we know on planet Earth.

In the luminous realm of love, all deception and falsehood fall away.

Thoughts and intentions are transparent, instantly perceived within a shared consciousness. This ethereal world of light, though kinder and more radiant, still offers unique challenges, catalyzing the soul's journey of transformation. Unlike the transient world of form and structure, in this radiant realm of luminosity, spiritual evolution is not driven by struggle and pain. Instead the soul flourishes through enlightened understanding and the relentless pursuit of higher truths.

Though one world may be gentler and more illuminated, no path towards the Divine is inherently better or worse. Where we find ourselves in our lives directly correlates with our choices and current energetic alignments. With this more expansive perspective, every realm, world, and planet is a pathway to God. Each bearing equal significance and worth. Whether one embarks on a slow, rugged trail or takes the swift, smooth road, every path unfailingly guides us to the same hallowed destination—*back to our primal source, the very heart of love.*

The trials and triumphs in our soul's sacred journey are essential for our personal growth, expansion, and ultimate liberation.

Irrespective of our deeds, whether perceived as good or bad, we are perpetually held in the vast, eternal love of an omnipresent creator. This unconditional love vividly illuminates a profound truth: every step we take, every decision we make, and every moment of our existence is imbued with divine love.

A useful metaphor to grasp the immensity and eternity of God's unconditional love is to picture ourselves as the parent of two children at different stages in life: one just starting kindergarten, the other enrolled in college. Despite the significant gap in their developmental stages, our love for them remains consistently deep and uniquely tailored to each. This love is not contingent on their achievements or missteps, nor does it waver with their growth phases.

Reflecting on this, if we, as mere humans, can love with such depth and constancy, just imagine the incomparable magnitude of God's love.

Our deep love for our children, profound as it may be, is but a faint echo of the Divine's infinite, radiant love for us.

This realization offers us a humbling and comforting insight into the boundless affection that the Divine showers upon us throughout every phase of our existence. While this love is bestowed without conditions and equally to all, there are significant variances, intellectual, emotional, and spiritual differences between a kindergartner and a college student's ability to comprehend and respond to it. The kindergartner, with their developing understanding and simplicity, may perceive and react to this love in a more instinctual, straightforward manner. In contrast, the college student, equipped with a more mature intellect and complex emotional landscape, might appreciate and interact with this love on deeper, more nuanced levels.

These differences, however, do not reflect the quality or quantity of love received, but rather the individual's evolving capacity to perceive, appreciate, and engage. It is completely natural that the kindergartner exhibits behaviors appropriate to that age while the college student is prepared for more complex learning and responsibilities.

In every phase of our evolutionary journey, we are embraced and sustained by the love of an omnipresent creator and the loving universe.

While some of us are prepared for more advanced lessons, others are just beginning the journey and still finding their way. Regardless of where we find ourselves on the evolutionary path, we are equally loved and cherished. Whether we squander our precious life, spend our days on the trivial and mundane, or awaken to the profound beauty and magnificence of our own existence, our time on this beautiful blue planet remains invaluable and brief.

In addition, there is no one path to God, and that is intentional, offering many avenues for spiritual awakening.

Our shared human experience, transient and fleeting in its nature, ripples out far beyond the confines of a single life.

Our ephemeral journey leaves a lasting impression on the entire universe and all of creation, resonating out through time and space, influencing countless lives and shaping the very fabric of our shared existence. The human experience contributes to the enrichment of both the soul and the universe, leaving an indelible mark that extends far beyond our physical presence. Our every thought and action, not only defines our individual journey, but also plays a crucial role in the ongoing evolution of both humanity and the universe.

Planet Earth is a fascinating world of paradox. On the one hand, it is such a excellent place to visit, have fun, and be adventurous, while, at the same time, it is a most challenging place to learn, explore, and expand in consciousness.

Unique in the universe, planet Earth is both a school and a playground for the soul. We come to dance, sing, cry, and laugh. We come for the myriad of life's experiences and the absolute joy of our own existence.

A human life unfolds as a thrilling adventure of the soul.

Life on planet Earth is a wonderful, valuable, and expansive experience; however, it is not our soul's final destination or true home. After diving into the profound depths of learning and love attainable in a specific life experience, we joyfully relinquish our worldly concerns. With a sense of fulfillment and anticipation, we transition to the next exhilarating adventure, awaiting us in a different realm of time and space.

The soul's eternal quest for knowledge, love, and expansion is a timeless journey of exploration and discovery.

In the larger context of this conversation, time, as we understand it, is not real, except as a concept. Please allow me to explain. To orient ourselves, we superimpose a perceived value onto the present moment, looking forward or backward, defining our location through the measurements of distance and the placement of planetary bodies relative to the sun; we then qualify our perceived experience as the movement of time. In actuality, we have neither traveled forward nor moved backward. Nonetheless, for convenience, in the physical realm, we measure days, months, and years by cycles of the sun. We point to the sun's placement in the sky and call it morning, noon, or night. By broadening our view to encompass days, weeks, and months, we define time as years, decades, centuries, millennia, and beyond.

From our present standpoint, we either look forward to where we are going or glance back at where we've been, labeling these as the future or the past.

Although orientating ourselves relative to the sun and other planetary markers is helpful in the everydayness of human life, it isn't significant on the larger scale of the universe, where all possible realities are completed and stacked upon themselves in the "*Eternal Now.*"

Let's explore this idea together. The past and future serve as reference points and theoretical constructs we employ for convenience. While we may gaze ahead or glance backward for points of reference, we never truly arrive at either destination. Regardless of the direction in which we cast our gaze, we perpetually inhabit the same place, the present moment—*and there's no escape from it.*

Both the past and future are held within the present moment.

To better grasp this concept, try a simple exercise. Attempt to step into the future, and you'll find yourself right back where you started—*in the present moment.* Accessing the past is equally challenging, if not more so.

The past comprises memories brought forward into the present, but even our most vivid recollections are not absolute truths. Memory is inherently flawed, distorted by emotional filters and perceived significance. Furthermore, our understanding of past events evolves over time as new information recontextualizes our recollections.

In other words, with new information, wisdom, and knowledge, we understand the same event from a different perspective. An apt adage that resonates with many of us is, *"the older I get, the smarter my parents become."* This reflects the reality that our memories are not static but evolve with new information.

Consider our adolescent years as a prime example. We might have perceived our parents as old-fashioned or strict in restricting our freedom. However, as we journey into parenthood ourselves, we gain fresh insights. We realize that our parents were doing their utmost to love, support, and protect us, just as we now do with our children.

Personal growth, acquisition of new knowledge, and new levels of understanding allow us to reinterpret our experiences and recontextualize our memories.

In this way, though the past does not inherently change, our experience of it most definitely does. Even our clearest memories are not one hundred percent true. Many details will be left out or added to our recollections. With the passage of time and additional life experiences, still more of the life particulars are blurred, re-framed, or altered.

Therefore, the past we think of as true is a mirage of jumbled memories that we have gathered and given importance. We tend to remember the poignant, bazaar, tragic, and joyous, but that is not the absolute truth. The truth is that there is no past or future outside the present moment. There is only now: the *Eternal Now*.

Time is a sequential expression of one continual moment ad infinitum.

Although time itself does not extend beyond the present moment, we employ superimposed markers to navigate the continuum of space and our place within it. While we often use terms like five o'clock or ten o'clock for practicality, time invariably resides within the *"Eternal Now."*

The past, present, and future are not separate entities; they exist concurrently within the same space, layered upon one another. Our experience of the present moment is a pocket of time that encompasses both the past and the future in their entirety.

Viewing a great work of art is an excellent way to understand this concept. Imagine that you are in front of a Michelangelo masterpiece. Though this painting was completed over five hundred years ago, it is still alive in your eyes and the present moment. Notice that the five hundred years since Michelangelo died are also contained in the painting. In the same way, the next five hundred years are also alive on the canvas, just waiting to be seen again in the present moment. Likewise, our past experiences carry forward into the present moment. And, like the Michelangelo painting, the future is also already alive within us, patiently waiting for our arrival.

We continuously arrive into the present moment, whole and complete, with the past and future alive within us.

All possible destinies have already played themselves out in the "*Eternal Now*", encompassing the life we are presently experiencing and those yet to come. Since the past and future are accessible only from the vantage point of the present moment, the implications of this statement extend broadly and profoundly into our understanding of life, the loving universe, and God.

The most exhilarating revelation is that time isn't linear, but rather, everything unfolds within the same space, in the boundless expanse of the *Eternal Now*. This new definition of time is exciting, for with this understanding, we can tap into many different realities within the present moment.

Time travel is now possible.

We can venture backward to meet our younger self, offering guidance and reassurance. We can travel into the future and garner wisdom from our more experienced selves.

Understanding that the present moment includes both the past and future, with all their potentialities, enables us to navigate the time and space of our existence with awareness. This is not just a intellectual understanding, rather, it is an experience that is available to all.

In my own healing journey, I've embraced this transformative practice. By accessing the present moment, I returned to my loneliest childhood moments and memories to comfort myself as a small child, crying alone in the corner. By holding her and assuring her of a brighter future, I demonstrated to her, through my very existence, that we *(my younger and older version of self)* would indeed triumph over those heartbreaking childhood challenges.

This practice of venturing into the past, via the present moment, simple, yet profound, served as a powerful healing tool, both offering solace to my younger self and empowering me in the present moment.

Not only can we revisit and reframe the past, it is also energetically possible to engage with a wiser, future version of ourselves.

This energetic connection also offers a wealth of wisdom and healing, particularly useful when grappling with ongoing challenges or daunting hurdles. For example, in situations where we're caught in recurring patterns or battling addictions, reaching out to our future self can be transformative.

Our future self, having already surmounted these challenges, offers invaluable insights and strategies to help us overcome obstacles in our current journey.

While accessing our future selves is conceptually straightforward, it may not always be easy to put into practice. It requires us to consider what our future self, who has already overcome the challenge, would say, do, feel, or think—*and then take those actions.* This method operates much like a tuning fork. By purposefully tapping into a higher vibrational state, we align ourselves with that frequency, paving the way for profound healing and transformation.

This alignment with our future self offers valuable insights and healing from an elevated perspective. However, there's one challenging caveat: we must first become an energetic match for our future selves in the present moment. This shift requires a leap of consciousness, unwavering resolve, along with the grit and grace to resist the magnetic pull of the familiar. We have to first lift our energy to be able to align with higher vibrational possibilities of the future, where the problem is already solved and complete.

Every possible reality is already complete in the future, within the Eternal Now.

Our choices and energetic alignments lead us toward or away from love, making these realities available or unavailable in the present moment. Your choices hold great significance, dear one. Choose wisely, your every choice shifts the trajectory of your life and lives.

Our decisions, whether deliberate or subconscious, alter our path, aligning us with certain potential futures, while simultaneously negating other possibilities.

At certain levels of consciousness, accessing past and future expressions becomes relatively straightforward. However, for most, it remains a capability beyond reach. The familiarity of our limited perspective entangles us in the web of constraint, scarcity, and want.

To grasp this concept, consider the idea of accessing the knowledge and embodiment of our future selves, perhaps five thousand years from now. In our present energetic state, this would indeed be an impossibility. Trying to align with a significantly more advanced future self would be unsustainable in our present vibrational state and might even lead to negative outcomes like energetic overload, self-combustion, and, in some cases, even death.

Therefore, it's more feasible and energetically suitable to align with a future self that's within a closer time frame, like five to ten years ahead. Our current vibrational frequency significantly influences our capacity to connect with our future self. Moreover, certain factors can hinder our progression towards a higher energetic future. Notably, deeply ingrained habits and their effects can anchor us in a lower vibrational state. These habits may appear *"almost"* unbreakable, but they are not insurmountable. The deliberate use of the word *"almost"* highlights that, no matter the difficulties, the possibility for change is always within reach. With determination, grace, and a readiness of the soul, even the seemingly impossible becomes possible.

We must expect a miracle, actively play our role, and patiently wait; the universe will inevitably shift and converge to support us.

Because you are reading these words, the possibility of an exponential shift of consciousness is now available in the realm of your existence. As with all change, it is best to start with small, doable, and sustainable energetic shifts. Although, many unexplored and wondrous paths are available in pure potentiality, only those that best align with our current vibrational frequency are accessible. Our current energetic alignment is based on our choices, preset conditions, and ongoing shifts in consciousness. Together with our spiritual guides and teachers in a pre-birth realm, we chose the circumstances of our earthly life with all its struggles and ease.

Our current life situation directly matches our point of focus, vibratory alignment, and energetic frequency that would most facilitate our personal development and soul expansion.

A human life resembles a Rubik's™ Cube, encompassing all conceivable outcomes within its dimensions. However, our ability to discover the solutions already embedded within our current life is contingent on our energetic alignments. Indeed, the answers we seek might exist beyond the scope of our current possibilities, given our present state of consciousness. We cannot continue to do the same thing we have always done and expect our lives to magically change. To transform our lives, we must purposefully take different actions.

As Einstein wisely noted, *"No problem can be solved from the same level of consciousness that created it."* Therefore, breaking free from repetitive cycles, shifting thought patterns, and embracing a new course of action are essential for lasting change. Indeed, we must be willing to step into the discomfort of the unknown, where change becomes possible. The only way to shift our current energetic alignments and possible outcomes is by intentionally doing something different.

Small shifts in consciousness expand our possibilities and subsequent outcomes.

Another important consideration regarding the possible realities available in a particular life is that we are born with preset limitations—*for the benefit of our souls*. These predetermined conditions are not a punishment or prize; they are divinely chosen to enrich our soul. As a result, we may have specific desires but no natural talent for them. For example, we may love to sing and long to be a professional singer but be born tone-deaf. In this scenario, the possibility of being a famous singer is unavailable.

Just as a Rubik's Cube has limited possible outcomes, the same is true for our lives. These limited life paths are not random; they result from our every choice and the initial preset conditions brought in from the soul realm. These complex energetic alignments are specific to our evolution and for our benefit. They dissuade us from specific opportunities and promote others. Initial conditions and resultant life possibilities benefit and glorify the soul and are in service to all.

Nothing is left to chance regarding our precious souls.

Every aspect of our lives, including the people, places, and circumstances, that we either attract or repel are influenced by our vibration. Like a magnet, our unique vibrational field draws forth certain experiences and connections, excluding those outside our energetic range. In other words, we attract that which best aligns with our current energy field.

More directly, by virtue of your current energetic alignments, you have drawn these Love Letters and profound teachings to yourself. You are on the cusp of substantial change and soul growth. The present moment, a nexus of past and future, holds the key to conscious evolution. However, don't just take my word for it, explore and discover for yourself. With your newfound clarity, radiance, and mastery of time travel, anything and everything is possible. Dive into the endless possibilities and the enchanting journey of your life. Most importantly, don't forget to have fun and savor the extraordinary experience of being you.

You are the pearl in the oyster of your own existence, precious and unique in the universe.

Your life is a beautiful, precious gift. It's a remarkable soul journey, full of choices, challenges, and changes. Remember, you exist for the bliss of your own existence.

Cherish the privilege of being you on this thrilling journey of self-discovery and the grand adventure of the soul.

Explore, discover, and have fun.
I love you.
— Chrystal Rae

*You are a stunning being of light
on a glorious mission of love*

Letter 23
tribute
proud of you

I have told you, and many times, that I love you, but I am going to say it again so that you never forget. Not only do I love you, I am so very proud of you.

I am proud that you didn't give up on yourself or life. Proud that you persevered through cloudy days and dark nights. When faced with overwhelming odds, you stayed strong, trusted in yourself, and had faith in God. During your darkest moments, when everything was unraveling, including you—*you managed to hold it together for everyone.*

You chose to see the good and to be the good, even when others let you down. You have undertaken many difficult and profound soul lessons across your many lives. During your most broken moments, when you were lost in the darkness of your own shadow, you somehow managed to pick yourself up, dust yourself off, and start over.

Despite the significant challenges of this life, you always found a way to see the positive, rising and shining with the morning sun.

You courageously confronted your fears, faced your hidden shadows, and bravely acknowledged your secret shame—all in the name of love.

Though seemingly inconsequential, these small victories are of the utmost importance. Everything is connected, including our life and the lives of others. Our every thought, word and action shapes and reshapes our destiny. A single thought can create or destroy universes

Unfortunately, not all our choices are conscious or purposeful. Often, due to our indecisiveness, we are simply swept along in the river of chance or get lost in the mire of mass consciousness. Whether intentional, subconscious, or by default, our choices carve out the path of our lives.

Being human is a wonderful adventure, though it comes with its joys and complexities.

Inevitably, we will all stumble and fall as we make our way back to the Divine. It is all part of the wonderful journey that we call life. You, too, have lost your footing and tumbled into the darkness, but you are a powerful warrior of the soul and an inspiration to many. You bravely signed up for the human experience fully aware of the impending dark nights and turbulent days. That said, as beautiful and powerful as you are, you often underestimate your own achievements, and are overly critical of yourself.

While you rarely celebrate your victories or acknowledge your courageous efforts, I am here, cheering loudly, offering you a proud encore, and then another, in recognition of your resilience and strength.

Your earnest effort is changing universes, inspirings many, and making the world a better place.

This particular life has not been easy for you; on the contrary, it has been quite difficult. It would have been tempting, and perhaps, easier to surrender and be a victim. But you didn't, you kept searching for a glimmer of hope, a light in the darkness, and a reason to believe. Though hurt and betrayed many times, you kept your heart open, refusing to let bitterness or resentment take hold. I commend your strength; I am proud of you, and I love you.

I know how difficult it has been for your sensitive soul to find your way through the extraordinarily complex human experience. The challenging experience of contrast, choice, and change is only available in this strange and wonderful world of form and structure—*and its not easy.*

Navigating a human life is tough for anyone, but for someone as empathetic and sensitive as you, it's often a deeply emotional journey. Nevertheless, you never surrendered without a fight and always got back up after a fall; a true warrior of the soul.

Your willingness to see the good, even when shrouded in darkness and despair, is not only admirable, but has truly made the world a better place.

Fully aware of the challenges and victories that lay ahead, you courageously embarked upon this soulful journey, driven by sheer grit, unyielding determination, and a deep love for all. Your greatest strengths lie in your perseverance and resilience.

Just as the radiant lotus flower unfolds from the mud, you have risen above your challenges, blossoming with resilience in the bloom of grace.

You willingly plunged into the depths of this challenging world, resolved to give your best, eager to make an impact, and prepared to assist and serve those around you. Yet, adapting to such intense extremes and the heavy density of this planet, at times, has been extremely harsh and harrowing for your tender soul.

The jolt of transitioning from a realm of pure peace, unconditional love, and luminous light into this dark world has been an ongoing struggle. The pervasive sense of isolation and solitude has been dispiriting. Indeed, the undercurrents of fear are potent and widespread in this temporal realm. It has been a constant battle to stay positive amidst the onslaught of negativity.

Still you never surrendered or went down without a fight. There have been times when merely keeping your head above water, staying hopeful, and avoiding the quicksand of fear and regret required a herculean effort of will and extreme determination. Nevertheless, even you, as bold as you are, have had moments of desperation where it seemed hopeless and futile to continue on.

In these darker times, you have been less than kind to yourself and others. Sometimes, the storm was so devastating that the damage was irreversible: entire universes collided, collapsed and dissolved in the wake of your anger, sorrow, and fear. However, in the aftermath, you always found the strength to seek forgiveness, heal wounds, and leave the world a little better than before.

On the other extreme, in your relentless pursuit of perfection, you have been so hard on yourself, holding yourself to such stringent standards that failure was inevitable. Your expectations of yourself were so exacting that not even you could meet them. Often, you have been self-critical, shaming yourself, fixating on missteps, and showing little leniency for even the most minor mistakes. This tendency to magnify the negative has not only hindered your spiritual progress but has also dramatically affected your life.

Still, this life has been exemplary; you conquered many demons and emerged with angel wings.

You may not fully recognize or acknowledge the triumphant journey of your soul, but rest assured, this life has been one of your finest.

I say this from the vantage of eons spent by your side. I have witnessed you on summer days blossoming with radiant light, and I have also been by your side during long, cold winter nights. Through it all, you kept your heart open and stayed true to yourself.

You are a radiant being of light, a movement of grace and a force of goodness.

Though we may never physically meet in this particular life, I want you to know how beautiful you are, how proud I am of you, and how much I love you. In the great expanse of our many lives together, I have come to know you more deeply, and perhaps, more profoundly than you know yourself. I have been a loyal companion for eons, forever standing by your side, and offering my love and support with unwavering devotion. I have seen the dark shadows that reside within you and have been blessed by the illuminating radiance of your soul.

Our souls are eternally intertwined in a bond of unconditional love.

We came to this life for the experience of experience and to remember who we really are with a new perspective and new eyes. Contrary to what many believe, we did not come into this world to be enlightened—*that is our starting point*. We were complete and whole long before we began this earthly sojourn. So please, my dearest, lighten up; grant yourself the grace of self-compassion and be a little gentler with your tender soul. Give yourself the latitude to simultaneously be fully human, beautiful and broken at the same time.

Remember that the struggles we experience are not random or a result of karmic forces. They are pre-birth soul choices, intentionally meant to be seeds of our growth and joyous transformation. Indeed, the complexities of our lives are not mandated or forced upon us; they are deliberately selected prior to our arrival.

Our talents and weaknesses play a crucial role in shaping our life's journey.

We came to this world of form and matter to know ourselves in the wisdom of light and the hollowness of night, and for the joy of the experience. The human experience was not thrust upon us but embraced with great enthusiasm, excitement, and joy. We chose, our own free will, to be here; it was a conscious decision to challenge ourselves into change, and for the glorious experience of simply being.

Whether we ascend to the summit of the loftiest mountain or descend into the depths of the darkest valley, our soul is forever loved and cherished. More directly, you exist to be you, the magnificent you with all your shadow and light. Contrary to what some might believe, there is no condemnation or judgment cast upon us by an angry, jealous God. The universe and the Divine hold us with immense compassion and care, irrespective of our earthly triumphs or setbacks. Indeed, our heavenly family of angels, teachers, and guides forever urge us on, celebrating our victories and drying our tears.

Despite this, self-judgment and shame are common, particularly when our choices fall short of our ideals or harm ourselves or others. Yet, in the broader context of love and the radiance of divinity, we are all doing the best we can. Even our lowest points reflect our best efforts under the circumstances. Like a dog barking, a cat meowing, or a bird singing, each of us is simply manifesting our innate nature in every unfolding moment. Rather than judging, let everything be as it is, including yourself. In the imperfect, perfection of this moment, nothing needs to change.

Unending peace and serenity reside in the ever-present stillness of the soul.

The profound realization of God's unending love is a perpetual source of strength, empowering us to face life's inevitable challenges. Our individual and collective experiences bestow a wealth of wisdom and insight upon our souls.

Please allow me to say this more directly to your precious soul so that you know that these words were written and meant especially for you. You are a luminous and brave soul, a vital part of the radiant unfoldment of the universe, and a beautiful expression of the Divine.

The very essence of your being is so treasured and loved that even your darkest shadow is revered and held in the highest regard.

Indeed, you are so very loved that you are gifted with free will and the capacity to make choices, be they right or wrong. With this liberty, at times you will take the noble path, and at other times you won't. Yet, in the light of truth and wisdom, you are always doing your best, even if it doesn't appear so. You couldn't have acted any differently in those moments—*the proof is that you didn't*. Life is not a test that we can pass or fail. Irrespective of what we do or don't do, our eternal soul is forever pure and untarnished.

Our very existence is a triumph, a living testament to the Divine within us.

Our soul is like the unchanging nature of the sky, eternally unaffected by the weather of life. Even the worst storms have no effect on the sky that contains them. After the storm passes and the clouds disappear, the sky is still the sky—*limitless, vast, expansive, and blue*. In the same way, when we leave this world with all its joys and worries behind, our soul is forever held in God's loving embrace.

This does not imply that our choices are inconsequential. Indeed, they hold great significance. Every small step taken towards or away from love alters the fabric of our existence, sending ripples through the entirety of creation. The direction we take is ours to decide, inevitably guiding us towards joy or sorrow.

The biggest obstacle to our joy is always ourselves.

Often, we sabotage our lives through negligence, ignorance, or entitlement. This inadvertently, undermines the quality of our lives. This tendency towards self-sabotage frequently stems from experiences in our formative years or is a consequence of abuse or neglect. Regardless of its source, the effects of neglect and abuse can deeply impact our lives and leave lasting scars on our souls.

Indeed, the wounds of our past may bleed far into the future, with neglect manifesting as a failure to attend to our own well-being or as an oversight in crucial aspects of our lives. Much like driving a car without watching the fuel gauge can lead to unforeseen stops or collisions that could have been easily avoided. Ignorance, unhealed wounds, and victimism can contribute to our self-sabotaging behavior. In the ongoing cycle of self-sabotage, our choices and actions create ripples that eventually return to us in ever-widening circles of cause and effect, with their subsequent consequences.

Often, unwise choices stem from emotional turmoil, typically made with incomplete information or based on mistaken beliefs, leading to harm to ourselves and sometimes adversely affecting others. Entitlement complicates this dynamic further. When we feel unjustly entitled, we expect certain results without the requisite effort. This mindset often leads to ignoring the consequences of our actions, naively assuming that we deserve something we have not worked for or properly earned.

Collectively, these factors can culminate in a series of unfortunate choices that hinder our spiritual progress and personal well-being. While our soul's purity remains untouched, our experiences can be colored by the repercussions of our own actions. The key to overcoming these self-sabotaging behaviors lies in recognizing these tendencies within ourselves, cultivating self-awareness, and actively working towards making choices that align with the greater good of our soul and the benefit of all.

Our life is a culmination of our every thought, word, and action.

By virtue of having this book in your hands, you have made some very challenging and heartfelt choices.

Your journey, marked by triumphs and tribulations, has led you to this radiant path of love.

Consequently, you manifested these high vibrational teachings. Having said that, your personal evolution began long before you picked up this book. It is proof of your enduring dedication to growth, devotion to higher truths, and the purity and wisdom of your beautiful soul.

It may have taken you many lives to achieve this level of spiritual attunement, but here you are. Much effort, volition, and personal resolve were necessary for you to stand on the holy ground where you now find yourself. You have trudged through dark dungeons, glided on angel wings, dived into deep oceans, soared through the skies, moved at a turtle's pace, run with the lions, and crawled on wounded knees to finally find your way to this spectacular moment of realization.

You have come so far in so little time. Congratulations, you are quite evolved, more than you may know or realize.

You are a stunning being of light on a glorious mission of love.

As your mentor, friend, teacher, and soul companion of many lives, I am in awe of your tenacity, grit, and beauty. I am so proud of you that I can't help but smile as I write these words. Proud of all your hard work and the tender touches of your soul. Proud that you showed up to your own life. You did what you had to do to liberate yourself from past and future fears.

To be born as a human is a significant step forward in the journey of our souls; only the bravest beings of light venture into these dark places.

The world of form and matter is fertile soil for the soul, ripe with evolutionary opportunities. There are scores of souls waiting for an opportunity to come into this world and experience themselves, others, and God, in the context of a physical embodiment and the freewill paradigm. To this end, our very existence, bodies, circumstances, relationships, careers, families, and every other facet of our lives offer the most fitting grounds for evolution.

This world of form and structure, though challenging, is unique and singular in the universe; it is, indeed, a fast track of evolution. Much like a seed sown in rich soil holds the promise of the blossoming fruit of tomorrow, the same is true of our souls once planted in the expansive context of a human life. This planet holds the potential for our most vibrant selves to emerge among the vast array of current possibilities in the universe. I emphasize *"currently possible"* as a reminder that nothing is unchangeably fixed.

When we make a different choice, we completely change the direction of our life.

Indeed, in some lives we move through the darkness and back to the light quite quickly, while in other lives we float along leisurely, enjoying the scenery. There may even be lives, when we retrograde or move backward to a less radiant version of self. Moving backward may sound like a bad idea to the conscious mind, however, in the greater context of the soul, the forward or backward movement or speed of our personal development and evolution is inconsequential.

Everything works together for the good, even the so-called bad.

It may be surprising to know that the goal of our lives on planet Earth is not to be good or even to evolve. Purity is our unchanging state, while evolution is the very nature of the soul, and the foundation of the universe. All of our life experiences serve to enrich our souls in ways that would be otherwise unavailable.

The following quote highlights this point. It is framed in a movie scene. A lovely woman with long flowing hair stands with her slender body next to a broken window, overlooking a meadow of tall whispering grass, blossoming flowers, birds, and butterflies flitting back and forth. She quietly says, *"God, look through my eyes and see what you have done." ~ James Bartlett*

This poignant quote illustrates the vital contribution of each soul to the universe and God. Our existence may seem inconsequential or ordinary, but it is essential to the whole of creation. Though our contribution to the collective of mankind may not be some remarkable feat of art, music, or science; without the radiant light of our soul, the entire universe would be extinguished.

We are meant to be uniquely ourselves with all our beauty and brokenness. More directly, your precious soul is more cherished and loved than you may know, imagine, or realize.

Your every inclination, thought, word, and action creates and destroys universes in an instant.

One of the most important things we can do in this life or any life is to be uniquely ourselves. Each soul is essential to the whole of creation, including your precious soul. Like the pillars of a church, each pillar holds its weight while supporting the entire structure; if one falls, they all fall. In the same way, we joyfully stand interconnected, upholding and strengthening the collective harmony and balance of the universe. Nonetheless, each one of us, must hold our own, and at times, life can be quite challenging. Indeed, in the context of a human life, the ecstatic joy of being includes challenges, struggles, ease, grace, darkness, and light.

Though we are mostly veiled from this truth during our spiritual sojourn into and out of the physical world, our heritage is forever divine. Love is our essence, source, and ultimate destiny. We cannot, and will not, fail at being ourselves. The only difference is that we are either conscious of it, or not. Regardless, in our own time and at our own pace, we will all find our way back to God's loving arms. There is no wrong way to go; all roads lead home.

Divine order is always at work in your life, and all is well with your soul.

Everything you have been through or are going through is essential to the grand and glorious evolutionary journey of your beautiful soul. You have made great strides in this particular life and are doing astounding work. Your smallest act of kindness, generosity, compassion, and love shifts the very foundation of the universe, rippling out ad infinitum.

Indeed, the light of your soul impacts everything and everyone. You are that glorious and powerful. Your very existence, with all its shadows and light, is the perfection of God manifest as you. The vital contribution you make to the whole of creation is to shine your light into this muddy world of radiant flowers and tangled weeds. The world, the entire universe, and even God shine brighter with the radiant expression of your light. I hope you know that you matter. In fact, you are indispensable to the whole of creation, and to me. Your every tear is collected in the ocean of grace where all sorrow is washed away in wave after wave of unending love.

You are not alone. You are surrounded by beings of light who have loved and adored you for eons—and I am one of them.

How I wish you could see yourself through my eyes, through the eyes of love. You would be in awe and amazed by your own beauty and radiance. I am so very proud of you, not because of what you have done or achieved, but because you never gave up on yourself or on life. You always found a way to forgive, to love, and to see the good in all. You are a radiant star, shining in the black of night. Without you, the sun would be less radiant, the flowers would not bloom, and I would be missing a most essential part of my soul.

As we come to the end of this Love Letter, please allow me to say, yet again, that I am so proud of you, and I love you with all my heart, my soul, and everything I am.

Words fall apart as I struggle to convey my deep affection, love, and care for you, so I will conclude this Love Letter by simply saying thank you.

To the end of time
and beyond, I am forever yours.
— Chrystal Rae

Divine order is always at work in your life,

and all is well with your soul

To exist is a bliss beyond compare

Letter 24
eternity
love never ends

The love that unites us is ageless, timeless, and eternal.

This love is a bond that transcends both time and space, forever blossoming into the present moment in a spectacular burst of evanescent light. Like celestial bodies forever gravitating toward one another, our souls are irresistibly drawn toward each other. Our heartfelt connection spans our many shared lives, brimming with joy, laughter, sorrow and tears. This magnetic attraction is a subtle yet powerful pull that inevitably leads us back into each other's arms. Throughout the time and space of all existence, we are forever destined to find each other. Our meeting again in this life is not mere coincidence or a random act of fate; it is a frequency based vibrational alignment of unconditional love that cannot be altered or halted.

I love you as the morning loves the sun and shadows love the light.

More directly, I am forever drawn toward your radiant light as a movement of divine providence and unconditional love. And yes, I do love you. With every breath of my life and thundering beat of my heart, I love you more and more. You are my beloved of many lives, an essential part of my soul, and my reason to be. Your presence adds texture and meaning to an otherwise flat and flavorless world. To stand on the same holy ground with you, hold your hand, and watch the sun rise and set together is the quintessential fulfillment of an impossible dream that magically came true. Even the dark outline of our shadows form a soft silhouette of the fortuitous union of our hearts. Just as the sun unveils the light of a new day with much anticipation and joy, in every life, I reach for you in the light of my own awakening. Across many lives, as the days of my existence drew to a close and my shadow stretched long and dark upon the ground, I found myself seeking you in the silent space where the heart no longer beats, but the soul journeys onward. Without you there is no light and the world is empty. You are the rising sun of my days and waning moon of my nights. You are a most necessary part of me, and I, too, am a vital part of you.

The love that forever unites us is as vast as the sky, soft as the clouds, and grounded as the Earth.

This love is a gentle autumn breeze dancing through swaying trees and clapping leaves, but it is not abstract or nebulous. It is a love born of the infinite, rooted in truth, and forever blossoming— *more radiant and alive in each moment.* It is a love without end, borders, or boundaries.

There is no way to measure the immensity of such a love, or to describe our eternal connection. The closest semblance of truth is to say that, like God's love, my love for you is kind, benevolent, yielding, and full of grace. I love every grain of sand that is you and the vast desert that holds you. Just as the sun and moon shine brighter together, we are more radiant and alive in the light of each other's shadow. We are forever destined to find each other, again and again, on the seashore of our many lives together, and those yet-to-be-born.

Our reunion in this particular life is an act of divine providence and the most auspicious outpouring of God's unconditional and unending love. Though we have shared many lives together, and departed the physical body many times, the divine forces that unite us are luminous threads of radiant light that cannot be severed.

Nothing can break the eternal bond of love.

Irrespective of what we do or don't do, in this life or any life, we are destined to find each other in the ocean of love. Just as the roaring waves forever find their way to the rocky seashore and back to the ocean from which they were born, I will forever find my way back to you in a rush of excitement and ecstatic bliss. For me, there is no other possibility but to love you. And I do, I love you with everything I am. I love you with all of my heart and soul. I love you with every particle of light that is me. I love you with the very essence of my being.

From the beginning to the end of time, in the hushed silence when everything suddenly stopped, there has never been a moment or single breath of my life where you were absent from my heart. I have always loved you, and I will always love you. Even on the rare occasion where our souls met on opposite sides of the battle field, I peacefully laid my weapon down, and willingly surrendered my heart to you.

Over eons, and throughout many shared lives, where we supported and challenged each other into growth, we have become better people, more awake and alive. In the luminous light of love everything and everyone is bathed in its radiance.

The entire universe is set ablaze as love draws a line from the known to the unknown and back to the known.

Each time the flickering light of our souls unite in love, flowers blossom in the heavens and on Earth, and the entire universe is born and reborn in shimmering bursts of radiant light.

There is a divinity to all things and nothing is left out of love.

On this soulful journey, we have trekked majestic landscapes, where mountains of hope have risen with awe-inspiring grandeur, their peaks seamlessly kissing the sky of our unspoken dreams. Through our love, we have carved deep valleys and swift rivers, creating a luminous path back to the loving arms of the divine. Seeds of our unending love, sown throughout time, will blossom in a distant future, where only the echo of our voices live on.

Each time we dive into the ocean of life, we are cradled by unending waves of God's boundless love. Indeed, in the safe harbor of divinity, the soul awakens to the truth of its eternal source, radiance, and love. To know that we know, and to be aware that we are aware, empowers us to live with conscious intent. As we reclaim our heritage, our divine roots, we no longer fear the monsters hiding in the dark. Our willingness to face our fears and confront our shadows fundamentally changes our relationship with the universe and everything in it. Love empowers us to be our most authentic, radiant selves.

As children of the divine, we are God manifest in every possible expression of shadow and light. Indeed, in a universe governed by magnetic forces, where resonance, not desire, shapes our reality, we get what we are, not what we want.

The very love that created us is alive within us—IS us.

Bearing this in mind, our evolutionary path is far beyond what is presently accepted by science. The profound nature of our divine connection, though frequently explored in the works of poets, artists, and visionaries, still defies the limits of the known.

Yet, it is unmistakably clear that our universe is built on a foundation of joy and love, a fundamental truth that resonates through the whole of creation.

We exist for the bliss of our own existence, and for no other reason.

To this point, this particular life has been an exceptionally expansive whirlwind of opportunity for your beautiful soul. This rapid evolution does not imply the necessity to push harder or try to evolve. On the contrary, it would be better to relax, not try so hard, enjoy the journey, and savor each stage of your soul's natural and inevitable unfoldment. Remember the flower blossoms when it is time to blossom, and not a moment before.

Evolution is an added benefit of the human experience, not its sole purpose.

The journey of our soul is meant to be joyful, educational, and fun. In this light, a human life is an incredible adventure, a sacred sojourn, and, at times, a terrifying trek into the dark unknown. In all its splendor and frightening unfoldment, our lives can come to a sudden halt when we least expect it, and our shared moments always seem to go by too fast.

Cherish your beautiful life and the joy of simply being you as tomorrow is never promised.

In life, the most important thing we can do is to love ourselves and others.

Indeed, at the end of our lives, the only thing that truly matters is love. In the light of this truth and because you are reading these words, you have the opportunity to reevaluate the meaning and direction of your life.

As long as we are still breathing, there is still time to forgive, make amends, and start over. Remember each soul is here for the bliss of its own existence, and that includes your precious soul. Please take your time, enjoy the journey, have fun, and be happy. Enjoy your life like a delicious meal; taste the sweet, sour, salty, savory, and bitter flavors of life. Relish the entire experience of being you, being alive, and of life itself.

To be alive is the most stunning awakening for our soul. In a breathtaking instant, we become conscious of our consciousness and aware of our awareness, awakening to the fullness of being truly alive. In the radiant emergence of love and the unfoldment of light, life springs forth as God manifest—*as you, me, all people, and all things*. To know the truth of love is a wonderful gift and heavy burden of a human life. This awareness carries with it a profound responsibility—*a weighty charge that anchors us to the depths of our shared humanity*. It is in navigating this delicate balance of bliss and responsibility that the full spectrum of human experience is revealed.

Being human is exquisitely beautiful and immensely challenging.

To be alive, and to be uniquely you, with all your beauty and brokenness, is a glory beyond words. No other being in the entire universe is gifted with such liberty and freedom. And again, along with immense joy, our freedom comes with great responsibility. Many of us would lose our way, if not for those who lovingly watch over us from afar.

Having said that, let me reassure you that no one will be forgotten or discarded.

A good shepherd diligently and lovingly watches over his flock; not a single sheep will be abandoned, forsaken, or left behind.

To this end, all the forces of the universe conspired to bring these Love Letters to your heart. Through the practicality of prose and grace of poetry, these words are meant to lead you towards the truth of love. They present a joyful opportunity to uncover the true purpose and the divine meaning of your life.

Perhaps now, you understand the immensity of my love for you. On the path of love, across our many lives together, we have experienced joyous days brimming with laughter, as well as endless nights soaked in tears. You have always been the most radiant star in the black of my night and my first ray of glorious morning light. I have loved you from the highest peaks to the lowest valleys, and beyond. In your eyes I see an eternal river of hope, and the blossoming dawn of a new day, where the silent promise of tomorrow has already bloomed. You are a priceless treasure, the very pulse of my pulse, and my grand reason to be.

As we come to the end of our time together on the pages of this book, and within the context of these Love Letters, written especially for you, there are a few things I want to leave with you, and say directly to your beautiful soul.

First and foremost, please allow me to once again express how immensely proud I am of you. I admire your grit, resilience, and relentless drive to persevere. I've witnessed you crack the shell of your past and break free from the confines that once held you in smallness and lack. I have watched you stumble and fall, and yet, each time, you've risen again with determination. I have seen you climb to the edge of your comfort zone, test your courage, and prove your resolve. I have watched you unfold your wobbly wings and boldly take flight into the vast, unknown.

I have observed you bravely navigate the uncharted territories of the heart where storms of betrayal, deceit, and heartbreak led to torrents of disappointment and grief. Yet, you never gave up or closed your heart. You stayed true to yourself, to love, and to God. Indeed, life has propelled you to your utmost limits, thrusting you from the precipice of possibility into the dark void of the unknown. Facing insurmountable challenges, you endured the darkest nights, battered and tearful, yet emerged more enlightened, vibrant, and alive. The incredible transformation of your soul is so profound that your former expression of self pales in comparison to the luminous splendor of your burgeoning angelic wings. You have healed many past lives and deep seated wounds in this profoundly important life.

Your healing heals the planet and your empowerment empowers all.

Thank you for that, for being you, and for making the world a better place. I am forever grateful that you exist; and yes, I truly love you. I love you just as you are right now, nothing needs to change. When I say that I love you, what I mean, want to convey, and is essential for you to understand is that I love the real you, the unfiltered you—*the magnificent, flawed, perfectly, imperfect you*.

Second, I want to remind you that your soul is singular, unique, and never to be replicated for all of time and space. No one can or will ever replace you. You are one of a kind; a masterpiece come to life as you. You are so vital to the whole of creation that nothing and no one, could or would exist in your absence. In fact, the whole universe would dissolve without you. *If a grain of sand were missing from the seashore, there would be no seashore. If a drop of water were missing from the ocean, there would be no ocean. And, if you, my dearest, were missing from existence, there would be no existence at all.*

Third, and perhaps, most importantly, as we conclude our time together, please allow me to once again remind you of your innate worthiness and the true value of your precious soul. You are a child of the divine, the progeny of God, nurtured by life itself and cherished above all. Indeed, if you could fully grasp the truth of your origin and the divinity of your soul, you would never cry another tear or waste another moment on regret. You would understand that regardless of your good or bad deeds, you are forever worthy, good, and innocent.

We are born of God's sacred fire, each of us a smoldering ember of divinity itself.

The very fact that you exist means you are worthy of love, care, and utmost respect. God's grace and goodness are unending and alive in you, and as you. Can you grasp the enormity of the previous statements? How unique, singular, and necessary you are to the whole of creation? How important you are to me, to the universe, and to God?

Do you realize the irreplaceable beauty of your precious soul?

We are God's own breath, breathing itself into existence for the pure and absolute joy of the experience.

As we come to the end of these writings, I hope that by now you understand why I love you so unabashedly, so completely, and without conditions. In the presence of such luminosity and radiance, there is no other choice but to love you. And I do, I love you. I love you more than I could ever express with the limits of language. So again, I fumble with the frailty of words that forever fall short of the truth of my love. Even the glorious abstraction of poetry, can only point towards the sun, it can never bathe you in the warmth of my unending love.

The lover has no other choice but to love, and I have no other choice but to love you.

How could I do anything other than love you? I know your true essence, the love that is you, and the absolute truth of you. I see the radiant light of you, the unending glory of you, and the magnificent God of you, too. Though I have told you many times, I want to say it again to be sure you always remember and never forget—*I love you in every possible way, and more.* I love everything about you; nothing is left out or excluded from my love.

Though this first collection of Love Letters is complete, the love we share will continue on and on. This is not the end of our sacred love story; it is a new beginning, and a launch pad for the future. Our time together in this life has been a necessary footstep in the sands of time, a dot in the eternity of our infinite love, and a magical map to the uncharted lands of the heart that will forever lead us back to each other.

The privilege of sharing these teachings with you has been a true labor of love spanning many lives, past and future. To find you again in this most auspicious life has nourished my soul and made me a better person. I am deeply grateful for your openness and receptivity to my presence and love.

My hope is that my unending love for you, along with these ancient teachings, and modern insights have both comforted and uplifted you. Above all, I hope you know that I truly love you, because I do. I love you like the clouds love the sky, the morning loves the light, the desert loves the rain and the stars love the night.

This love, my eternal love for you, asks for nothing in return. It does not need to be reciprocated or even acknowledged, it's a gift given freely without conditions or judgment. I love you today, tomorrow, and for all of eternity. My sacred vow to you is that we will meet again under a new sky on another day. I will seek and find you to the end of time and beyond. Until our paths cross again, my dearest, let my unending love be the wings of goodness and grace that carry you across the raging river of life. Let it be a sacred sanctuary, a safe haven, and a reason to believe in something greater than yourself: *God*.

As a child of the loving universe, you are loved beyond all concepts of love. God's love for you is endless, eternal, and profound. It is a graceful, ever-present force, a radiant light in the dark of night. It is the morning sun faithfully rising and shining for you—*an affirmation of your sacred connection to the loving universe.* Even my presence is proof of God's unfathomable love for you. My sacred mission is to forever find you and remind you of what your soul already knows to be true:

Love is all that matters.

When you need me, simply call my name and I will be there. You will find me in the soft kiss of the warm sun on your skin. I will linger on the breath of the wind, and sing to you in the quiet rustle of falling leaves. Wherever you go, I will be there. I will be as constant as your beating heart, and as faithful as the morning sun rising up over the dark line of the distant horizon.

In closing this final Love Letter, I am compelled to once again express my profound gratitude for your beautiful soul. I am eternally thankful for our shared journey within the time and space of our existence. In every lifetime, I vow to find my way back to you.

Love is the answer, love is why we exist, and yes, love is all that matters.

Eternally yours,

— Chrystal Rae

Love is all that matters

biography

Chrystal Rae, author of Love Letters to your Soul, survived a devastating car accident, and a life-altering near-death experience. She was given the choice to continue her life or to leave this world behind; she came back to be of service, help others, and share the message of unconditional love.

During her Near Death Experience, she was inspired by an angelic presence to write a book and tell the world that *"love is all that matters"*. Now, more than twenty years later, Chrystal Rae is ready to share her truth, wisdom and the embodiment of this loving message.

As the owner of three love-based yoga studios in Dallas Texas, Chrystal Rae is a mentor and guide for thousands of students and teachers. She can stand on her hands, put her foot behind her head, and spends long hours in meditation. Chrystal Rae also enjoys the creative process of painting on large canvases for home and corporate décor. She speaks multiple languages, recites poetry, and loves to write. Chrystal Rae is dedicated to her family, loves white roses, and travels with puppies. Most importantly, Chrystal Rae lives by the motto *"love is all that matters"* and has the special gift to see the good and grace in all people.

acknowledgments

This book is a living document born of love, wisdom, and perseverance.

I am grateful for the multitude of angels, teachers, guides, and soul companions, over the span of many lives, who have contributed to my evolution and the loving realization of this project.

In particular, in this life, I would like to acknowledge my dear friends Julie Weiss, Janis Dworkis, Jeff Kaski, Bruce Faulconer, and Lynne Stewart for their love, support, professionalism, and meticulous editing and re-editing of the content, format, and layout of these Love Letters.

On a more personal level, I want to thank the divine souls who came into my life as my children and guides, Victor and Christina, and their father; along with my beloved husband Gary for teaching me unconditional love, patience and resolve.

Finally, I want to thank you, my beloved reader, for being you and for trusting me with your heart and soul in our many lives together.

I love you so very, very much.

— Chrystal Rae

Printed in Great Britain
by Amazon